T0214897

Communications
in Computer and Information Science   908

Commenced Publication in 2007
Founding and Former Series Editors:
Phoebe Chen, Alfredo Cuzzocrea, Xiaoyong Du, Orhun Kara, Ting Liu,
Dominik Ślęzak, and Xiaokang Yang

More information about this series at http://www.springer.com/series/7899

Chao Li · Junjie Wu (Eds.)

Advanced Computer Architecture

12th Conference, ACA 2018
Yingkou, China, August 10–11, 2018
Proceedings

 Springer

Editors
Chao Li
Shanghai Jiao Tong University
Shanghai
China

Junjie Wu
National University of Defense Technology
Changsha
China

ISSN 1865-0929 ISSN 1865-0937 (electronic)
Communications in Computer and Information Science
ISBN 978-981-13-2422-2 ISBN 978-981-13-2423-9 (eBook)
https://doi.org/10.1007/978-981-13-2423-9

Library of Congress Control Number: 2018954068

This Springer imprint is published by the registered company Springer Nature Singapore Pte Ltd.
The registered company address is: 152 Beach Road, #21-01/04 Gateway East, Singapore 189721, Singapore

Preface

It is a great pleasure and honor to present the proceedings of ACA 2018, the 12th Conference on Advanced Computer Architecture. ACA is sponsored by the China Computer Federation (CCF) and it is the flagship conference of the CCF Technical Committee on Computer Architecture (TCArch). It has been one of the most important academic conferences in the field of computer architecture in China since 1995.

The 2018 edition of ACA was held in the scenic area of Yingkou, a port city of the Bohai Sea. The theme this year was "Intelligent Architecture: From the Cloud to the Edge." ACA 2018 created a forum for academic researchers and industry practitioners in China to share their insights on the next-generation computing systems. We continued the trend of making ACA an inclusive and interactive event that features invited keynotes, top paper presentation, poster showcase, and design competition, etc.

This year, we received over 120 paper registrations. Finally, there were 80 successful submissions. Each submission was reviewed by three Program Committee (PC) members on average. In all, 13 papers were rejected immediately in the first round of review and 67 papers were sent out for a second round of review. Only the papers with an average score of ≥ 3 (borderline) were considered for final inclusion, and almost all accepted papers had positive reviews or at least one review with a score of 5 (accept) or higher. Finally, the PC decided to accept 47 submissions, including 17 papers in English and 30 in Chinese. We asked the authors of all the accepted papers to submit a revised version based on the review reports.

This program would have not been possible without the efforts of the PC, the external reviewers, and the authors. We would like to express our gratitude to all the authors who submitted their papers. We would like to convey our deepest and sincerest appreciation for all the hard work and dedication of our PC members and external reviewers. We also gratefully acknowledge the kind support from our general chair, Prof. Yong Dou, organization chair, Prof. Kuanjiu Zhou, and our Steering Committee. Our thanks also go to the China Computer Federation (CCF), Technical Committee on Computer Architecture of CCF, Dalian University of Technology, the City of Yinkou, Xilinx, Baidu, and all the other institutes that kindly helped us. Finally, we greatly appreciate the steady support provided by Springer.

August 2018

Chao Li
Junjie Wu

Organization

General Chair

Yong Dou   National University of Defense Technology, China

Organization Chair

Kuanjiu Zhou   Dalian University of Technology, China

Program Chair

Chao Li   Shanghai Jiao Tong University, China

Steering Committee

Zhenzhou Ji	Harbin Institute of Technology, China
Chenggang Wu	Institute of Computing Technology, CAS, China
Dongsheng Wang	Tsinghua University, China
Junjie Wu	National University of Defense Technology, China
Xingwei Wang	Northeastern University, China
Gongxuan Zhang	Nanjing University of Science and Technology, China

Program Committee

Quan Chen	Shanghai Jiao Tong University, China
Zidong Du	Institute of Computing Technology, CAS, China
Binzhang Fu	Huawei
Yu Hua	Huazhong University of Science and Technology, China
Weixing Ji	Beijing Institute of Technology, China
Jingwen Leng	Shanghai Jiao Tong University, China
Dongsheng Li	National University of Defense Technology, China
Duo Liu	Chongqing University, China
Yuhang Liu	Institute of Computing Technology, CAS, China
Youyou Lu	Tsinghua University, China
Guojie Luo	Beijing University, China
Bo Mao	Xiamen University, China
Songwen Pei	University of Shanghai for Science and Technology, China
Minghua Shen	Sun Yat-sen University, China
Wei Song	Institute of Information Engineering, CAS, China
Guangyu Sun	Beijing University, China
Jing Wang	Capital Normal University, China
Lei Wang	National University of Defense Technology, China

Ying Wang	Institute of Computing Technology, CAS, China
Junjie Wu	National University of Defense Technology, China
Yubing Xia	Shanghai Jiao Tong University, China
Zichen Xu	Nanchang University, China
Fengyuan Xu	Nanjing University, China
Hailong Yang	Beihang University, China
Zhibin Yu	Shenzhen Institute of Advanced Technology, China
Jingling Yuan	Wuhan University of Technology, China
Fengkai Yuan	Institute of Information Technology, CAS, China
Jidong Zhai	Tsinghua University, China
Weihua Zhang	Fudan University, China
Long Zheng	Huazhong University of Technology, China
Wenli Zheng	Shanghai Jiao Tong University, China
Junlong Zhou	Nanjing University of Science and Technology, China
Bo Wu	Colorado School of Mines, USA
Hongwen Dai	Apple Inc., USA
Lizhong Chen	Oregon State University, USA
Ruijin Zhou	VMware, USA
Shaolei Ren	University of California, Riverside, USA
Yakun Shao	NVIDIA Research, USA
Xiaoyi Lu	Ohio State University, USA
Xuehai Qian	University of Southern California, USA
Yang Hu	University of Texas at Dallas, USA
Yanqi Zhou	Baidu Silicon Valley AI Lab, USA

Additional Reviewers

Qiang Cao	Huazhong University of Technology, China
Li Jiang	Shanghai Jiao Tong University, China
Naifeng Jing	Shanghai Jiao Tong University, China
Cheng Li	University of Science and Technology of China
Tao Li	Nankai University, China
Yao Shen	Shanghai Jiao Tong University, China
Shuang Song	University of Texas at Austin, USA
Rui Wang	Beihang University, China
Chentao Wu	Shanghai Jiao Tong University, China
Qiaosha Zhou	Zhejiang Sci-Tech University, China

Contents

Parallel Computing System

Accelerators

A Scalable FPGA Accelerator for Convolutional Neural Networks

Ke Xu[1,2], Xiaoyun Wang[1,2], Shihang Fu[1,2], and Dong Wang[1,2(✉)]

[1] Institute of Information Science, Beijing Jiaotong University, Beijing 100044, China
[2] Beijing Key Laboratory of Advanced Information Science and Network Technology, Beijing 100044, China
{17112071,16120304,17125155,wangdong}@bjtu.edu.cn

Abstract. Convolution Neural Networks (CNN) have achieved undisputed success in many practical applications, such as image classification, face detection, and speech recognition. As we all know, FPGA-based CNN prediction is more efficient than GPU-based schemes, especially in terms of power consumption. In addition, OpenCL-based high-level synthesis tools in FPGA is widely utilized due to the fast verification and implementation flows. In this paper, we propose an FPGA accelerator with a scalable architecture of deeply pipelined OpenCL kernels. The design is verified by implementing three representative large-scale CNNs, AlexNet, VGG-16 and ResNet-50 on Altera OpenCL DE5-Net FPGA board. Our design has achieved a peak performance of 141 GOPS for convolution operation, and 103 GOPS for the entire VGG-16 network that performs ImageNet classification on DE5-Net board.

Keywords: FPGA · OpenCL · Convolution Neural Networks
Optimization

1 Introduction

Convolutional Neural Network (CNN) is a widely-regarded algorithm in the field of artificial intelligence. It has achieved great success in image classification [1], object detection [2], and speech recognition [3]. In the past decade, CNN has significantly improved the accuracy and performance of image classification. This is mainly due to the continuous improvement of data sets and the successive enhancement of the neural network structure. Being compute-intensive, GPUs are now widely used to train CNN. However, the GPUs with high power dissipations at the deployment level of the CNNs is not the best choice. FPGA based hardware accelerators with provide massive processing elements, reconfigurable interconnections and lower power dissipation are naturally suitable to implement neural network circuits.

The traditional FPGA development method uses hardware description language (HDL). The work of [7,8] propose efficient CNN accelerators on embedded FPGA platforms. However, traditional register-transfer-level (RTL) design

© Springer Nature Singapore Pte Ltd. 2018
C. Li and J. Wu (Eds.): ACA 2018, CCIS 908, pp. 3–14, 2018.
https://doi.org/10.1007/978-981-13-2423-9_1

flows takes a lot of time to simulate and compile before actually running hardware accelerators. With the development of FPGA high-level synthesis tool (HLS), high-level programming language (C/C++) is used to replace low-level HDL, which improves the speed of FPGA implementation and verification flows. Greatly reducing the development cycle, to design FPGA has brought great convenience. In recent yeas, the use of HLS to design CNN architecture has continued to emerge. The work of [9] using the Vivado-HLS tool on a Xilinx VC707 FPGA board. However, only convolution layers are implemented on AlexNet [1]. In [10], author present a systematic methodology for maximizing the throughput of an FPGA-based accelerator. In this work, an entire CNN model is proposed consisting of all CNN layers: convolution, normalization, pooling and classification layers. The scalable of accelerator architecture only use like AlexNet and VGG [4]. The feedforward neural networks with shortcut connections like ResNet [5] dose not work. The main contribution of this work are:

(1) Propose a FPGA accelerator with a scalable architecture of deeply pipelined OpenCL kernels;
(2) The design is verified by implementing three representative large-scale CNNs, AlexNet, VGG-16 and ResNet-50;
(3) The design space of the proposed architecture was fully explored on Stratix-V A7 FPGA.

2 Background

2.1 Classic Convolution Neural Network

AlexNet. AlexNet was able to achieve record breaking object recognition results on the ImageNet challenge in 2012. It consisted of eight layers in total, 5 convolutional and 3 fully connected, as depicted in Fig. 1. The 3-dimensional (3-D) convolution operation can be defined by

$$D_o(f_o, y, x) = \sum_{f_i=1}^{C_l} \sum_{k_y=0}^{K-1} \sum_{k_x=0}^{K-1} W_l(f_o, f_i, k_y, k_x) \cdot D_i(f_i, y + k_y, x + k_x) \quad (1)$$

where $D_i(f_i, y, x)$ and $D_o(f_o, y, x)$ denote the neurons at position (x, y) in the input feature map f_i and output feature map f_o, respectively. $W_l(f_o, f_i, y, x)$ represents the corresponding weights in the l-th layer that gets convolved with f_i. The size of the convolution filters is $K \times K$, while the total number of input feature maps is C_l. In addition to this, AlexNet considered the use of the ReLU nonlinearity instead of the saturating nonlinearites, such as sigmoids; Using dropout in training and Local Response Normalization (LRN) to reduce the problem of overfitting.

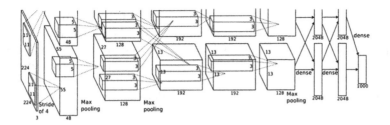

Fig. 1. AlexNet architecture. Figure reproduced from [1]

VGG. VGG achieves its depth by simply stacking more layers while following the standard practices introduced with AlexNet. The size of the convolution kernel is more regular. AlexNet use 11×11, 5×5 and 3×3 filters, but VGG only use 3×3 filters in the entire network. Notably, while using smaller filters, VGG required far more filters per layer. The amount of calculations and parameters of VGG is much larger than AlexNet.

ResNet. Deeper neural networks are more difficult to train, so in [5], author proposed residual learning framework reducing the vanishing gradient problem to ease the training of networks. This residual learning is mainly use of shortcut connections, illustrated in Fig. 2, that connect components of different layers with an identity mapping [6]. In particular, ResNet is built such that each layer learns an incremental transformation, $F(x)$, on top of the input, x, according to

$$H(x) = F(x) - x \tag{2}$$

instead of learning the transformation $H(x)$ directly as done in other standard CNN architectures.

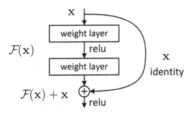

Fig. 2. Schematic of residual learning. Figure reproduced from [5]

2.2 OpenCL Framework on FPGA

OpenCL is an open, cross-platform parallel programming language that can be used in both CPU, DSP, GPU and FPGA developments. Recently, FPGA vendors such as Xilinx and Intel have released OpenCL SDK for programming FPGAs. The Intel OpenCL environment which can be a mixture of C, C++, and OpenCL, provides a complete CPU/GPU-like development experience and run-time experience on a CPU/FPGA platform, including a complete software workflow spanning multiple target devices and x86 emulation with cycle-accurate FPGA hardware models and cycle-accurate FPGA hardware.

3   Architecture Design and Optimization

3.1   Accelerator Architecture

As shown in Fig. 3, our FPGA design based OpenCL framework consists of a group of OpenCL kernels that are cascaded by using Altera's OpenCL extension Channels. Two data mover kernels, namely MemRD and MemWR, transfer feature map and weight data from/to the global memory feeding other kernel with high throughput data streams. The cascaded kernels form a deep computation pipeline that can implement a serial of basic CNNs operations without the need of storing interlayer data back to global memory. It significantly reduces the bandwidth requirement compared to the work of [10]. The Convolution kernel is designed to implement both the convolution layer and the fully connected layer which are the most compute-intensive operations in CNNs. The Pooling kernel is controlled by the synchronization signal of the MemWR kernel. When the synchronization signal set one, the Pooling kernel operation is performed. This technique is mainly used to achieve overlap between two kernels. The Batch-Norm kernel using in [5] loads mean, variance, α and β from global memory and performs the normalization directly on the output data streams of the Convolution kernel. The Local Response Normalization(LRN) kernel using in [1] fetches data from global memory and performs normalization on the feature map of neighboring neurons in deep direction. The Eltwise kernel mapping Eltwise Layer using in [5] loads data from global momory and adds each elements mainly using shortcut connections.

This architecture has the following advances:

(1) The cascaded and overlaped kernels form a deep pipeline architecture.
(2) Using a single hardware kernel to implement both the convolution and fully connected layers.
(3) Scalable hardware structure which implementation many classic CNNs operations, such as LRN kernel to AlexNet, BatchNorm kernel and Eltwise kernel to ResNet.

Convolution Kernel. A single work-item kernel with parallel convolution data paths is designed to implement both the function of the convolution and FC layers. In this paper, we propose to flatten the 3-D convolution operation into

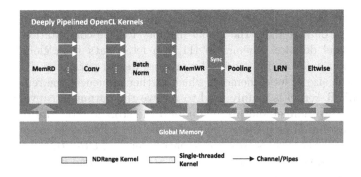

Fig. 3. The top-level architecture of CNN accelerator.

a 1-D convolution operation and integrate it with the full-connect operation as follow:

$$D_o(f_o) = \sum_{f'_i=1}^{C_l \times K \times K} W_l(f_o, f'_i) \cdot D_i(f'_i) \qquad (3)$$

In this way, data vectorization and parallel CU structure are both explored in the design. Vectorized input features D_i and weights W_l are streamed by multiple Channels. A design parameter VEC_SIZE determines the degree of data vectorization and controls the input throughput. Another design variable parameter to accelerator the convolution operation CU_NUM, represents the parallel factor of weight and reuse factor of data. Due to efficient pipelined by the OpenCL compiler, We propose an efficient convolution pipeline structure consisted of a multiplier-adder tree with a delayed buffer as in Fig. 4.

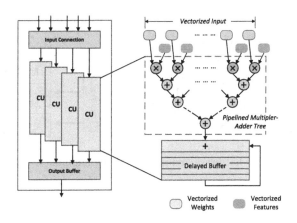

Fig. 4. The hardware architecture of the convolution kernel.

Data Mover Kernel. Two multi-model single work-item kernels are designed to fetch/store data from/to the global memory for the computation pipelines. MemRD kernel detailed schemes in [11] can fetch data from global memory to convolution mode or FC mode. We propose design parameter FT_NUM to determine the size of local memory, which further influences the reuse of input data. MemWR kernel is mainly used to receive the output of convolution kernel through the channel and arrange it into the storage structure required for the next convolution or pooling operation. For the convolution mode, the data received from the channel is arranged to have a depth of CU_NUM, and MemWR kernel need to divide the depth into VEC_SIZE copies and return it to global memory. The pooling mode simply transfer the data received from the channel and directly put back to global memory. In the pooling mode, the MemWR kernel also needs to pipe the synchronization signal to the pooling kernel at the right time for them can overlap work. Note all memory operations should be committed before sending token to the pooling kernel. Detailed MemWR schemes are illustrated in Fig. 5.

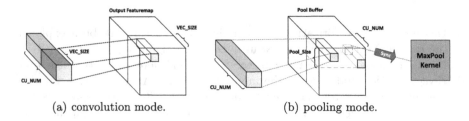

(a) convolution mode.   (b) pooling mode.

Fig. 5. The hardware architecture of the memWR kernel.

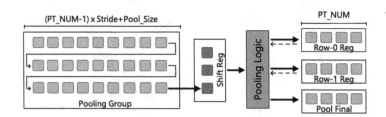

Fig. 6. The hardware architecture of the maxpool kernel.

Pooling Kernel. A shift-register-based hardware structure is proposed for the pooling kernel as shown in Fig. 6. The kernel first fetch the synchronization signal from the blocked channel, only waiting for the synchronization signal from blocked channel to come, the pooling kernel can start working. When the synchronization signal comes, the pooling kernel read data from global memory to shift register. In the process of data transfer, if the time point of pooling is reached, data will be extracted from the shift register to the pooling logic. Similarly, we designed a parameter *PT_NUM* for adjusting the size of the local memory in pooling kernel to exploiting input data reuse. In the pooling strategy, the first line is processed first, then the second line is compared with the first line, and so on. The final result of the pooling calculation is stored in the ping-pong buffer. During the pooling calculation, the result of the last calculation is also divided into *VEC_SIZE* and returned to global memory for the next convolution calculation. This process is similar to MemWR.

Other Kernel. Besides the most compute-intensive convolution and fully connected kernel, we also designed some common opencl kernels, such as LRN, BatchNorm, Eltwise for the scalability and integrity of the CNN accelerator's overall design. In this architecture, you can choose the basic units used in the network to piece together to implement different network structures. For example, implementation AlexNet just choose convolution kernel, pooling kernel and LRN kernel. Therefore, this scalable architecture can process the complete CNN forword computation flow with little involvement of host CPU.

Table 1. Operations in AlexNet model

Index	Layer	d_x	d_y	d_z	w_x	w_y	w_n	w_m	GOPS
1	Conv1	227	227	3	11	11	3	96	0.281
2	Conv2	55	55	96	5	5	48	256	0.448
3	Conv3	27	27	256	3	3	256	384	0.299
4	Conv4	13	13	384	3	3	192	384	0.224
5	Conv5	13	13	384	3	3	192	256	0.032
6	FC1	6	6	256	6	6	256	4096	0.075
7	FC2	1	1	4096	1	1	4096	4096	0.034
8	FC3	1	1	4096	1	1	4096	1024	0.008
	Output	1	1	1024				Total Ops	1.40

4 Design Space Exploration

In this section, we present an analytical performance model and resource utilization model to choose the best combination of the design parameters (*VEC_SIZE*, *CU_NUM*, *FT_NUM*, *PT_NUM*) that maximizes the performance of the CNN accelerator, while still being able to fit in the limited FPGA resources.

4.1   Performance Model

Convolution and Fully Connected Time. The execution time of convolution and fully connected layer-i is modeled as follow:

$$Convolution \ or \ FC \ Runtime_i = \frac{No.of \ Convolution \ or \ FC \ Ops_i}{VEC\_SIZE \times CU\_NUM \times Frequency} \quad (4)$$

Table 1 gives a operations summary of each layer in AlexNet model. Note that d_x, d_y and d_z represents the size of the output feature map from the previous layer, not the input size of the current layer. In 3.1 the convolution and fully connected operation have parallelism of two levels, one is the degree of parallelism VEC_SIZE based on the depth dimension of the input feature map, and the other is the degree of parallelism CU_NUM based on the number of convolution filters. So the speedup ratio for the convolution kernel is $VEC\_SIZE \times CU\_NUM$. The execution times of AlexNet, VGG-16 and ResNet-50 on CU_NUM are shown in Fig. 7.

Other Layers Time. Due to the idea of pipeline and overlap in the overall hardware design, the execution time of other kernels can be basically ignored relative to convolution and fully connected operations.

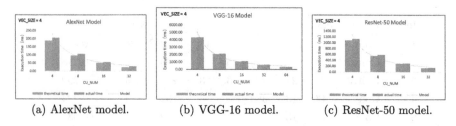

(a) AlexNet model.   (b) VGG-16 model.   (c) ResNet-50 model.

Fig. 7. Execution time empirical models for CU_NUM.

Memory Bandwidth. In order to reduce the pressure of external memory bandwidth, we use 8-bit fixed point calculations and propose a sliding-window-based data buffering scheme. Using fixed-point instead of floating-point calculations can reduce hardware synthesis costs and memory bandwidth requirements. Fortunately, research shows that using 8-bit fixed-point numbers instead of full-precision floating-point numbers is less than 1% loss in top 1/5 accuratacy for AlexNet/VGG predictions. As shown in Fig. 8, this sliding-window-based data buffering scheme use in MemRD kernel and maxpool kernel to cache data that was fetched from global memory. The filter stride S of this filter window is usually smaller than the filter size K. Therefore, a large portion of data can be reused during the convolution and maxpool computation. To exploiting data reuse, the MemRD kernel design a *FT_NUM* parameter and maxpool kernel design a *PT_NUM* parameter. These kernel fetches a window of data that covers the area of *FT_NUM* or *PT_NUM* of filters each time, and caches the data in the on-chip buffers or shift register.

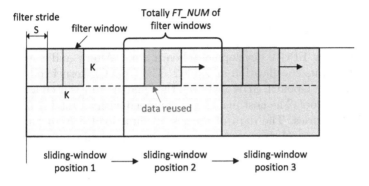

Fig. 8. The hardware architecture of the convolution kernel.

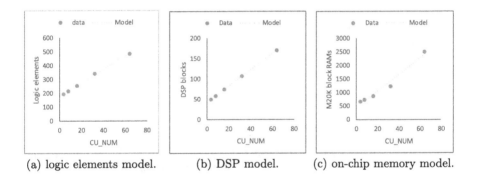

(a) logic elements model.   (b) DSP model.   (c) on-chip memory model.

Fig. 9. Resource utilization empirical models for *CU_NUM* on VGG-16.

4.2   Resource Utilization Model

In this subsection, we analyze resource utilization model on DE5-Net board. As discussed in 3.1, two design parameters *VEC_SIZE*, *CU_NUM* are used to control the hardware cost of the CNN accelerator. Therefore, we mainly consider the impact of the following two parameters in resource utilization model. Figure 9 shows the model with parameter *CU_NUM* on VGG-16. As the parameter *CU_NUM* gradually increases, both logic elements model and DSP utilization model present a trend of linear increase. However, the on-chip memory utilization model shows small discrepancy due to the complexity of load/store units.

5   Experimental Results

In this section, we present the experimental results to validate the scalable of this CNN accelerator by implementation three large-scale CNN models: AlexNet, VGG-16 and ResNet-50 on DE5-Net platform.

5.1   Experimental Setup

We use DE5-Net FPGA development board from Altera and compare with DE5a-Net listed its specification in Table 2. The OpenCL kernel codes are compiled using Altera OpenCL SDK 16.1, and the Quartus 16.1 is used as the FPGA implementation tool. The host machine is equipped with an Intel i7-5930K CPU and 64 GB memories. The data of images are first loaded from hard disks to the host programs, and then sended to the FPGA accelerators to perform CNN forword computations.

Table 2. Comparision of FPGA accelerator boards.

Specification	DE5-Net	DE5a-Net
FPGA	Stratix-V GXA7	Arria-10 GX1150
Logic elements	622 k	1150 k
DSP blocks	256	1518
M20K RAMs	2560	2560

5.2   Results and Discussion

In this subsection, we first list the best parameter configuration on different networks. Then, we show the benchmark of our CNN accelerator. Finally, we discuss the scalability of this hardware architecture. As discussed in 4, four design parameters VEC_SIZE, CU_NUM, FT_NUM, PT_NUM are used to control the hardware cost and throughput of the FPGA accelerator. Therefore, design space exploration can be quantitatively performed by implementing the accelerator with different parameter configuration. The final design variables for three networks optimized on the DE5-Net board are shown in Table 3.

In Table 4, we summarize the resource utilization, execution time and performance of different networks on the best parameters. We can see that different networks have different parameters and achieve different performance on same FPGA board. To prove how fast this accelerator can accelerate CNN computations, we also compare with CPU by using the Caffe deep learning framework. The execution time for AlexNet, VGG-16 and ResNet-50 is 189 ms, 1547 ms and 1238 ms, respectively. We can see that using FPGA-based accelerator can achieve more than 10 times faster on average in implementation CNN-based

Table 3. Optimized parameters.

	AlexNet	VGG-16	ResNet-50
VEC_SIZE	8	8	16
CU_NUM	48	32	16
FT_NUM	7	7	7
PT_NUM	2	4	4

Table 4. Summary of the resource utilization, execution time and throughput on different networks.

	AlexNet	VGG-16	ResNet-50
Logic elements	491.3 k	368.5 k	532.6 K
DSP blocks	236	170	256
M20K RAM	2252	1133	1537 .
Frequency	197.9 MHz	219.7 MHz	223.6 MHz
Execution time	18.08 ms	355.92 ms	102.97 ms
Throughput	77.5 GOPS	103 GOPS	75.7 GOPS

image classification applications. In future works, we will explore sparse convolution algorithms and using Winograd transformations to reduce the number of computations and to improve the performance of this accelerator.

6   Conclusion

In this work, we implemented a scalable FPGA accelerator for convolutional neural networks using OpenCL framework. An efficient and scalable hardware architecture with deep pipelined kernels was presented. We proposed and explored four design parameters for hardware costs and bandwidth limited, and implemented three large-scale CNNs, AlexNet, VGG-16 and ResNet-50 on DE5-Net FPGA board.

Acknowledgment. This work was supported by NNSF of China Grants NO. 61574013, 61532005.

References

1. Krizhevsky, A., Sutskever, I., Hinton, G.E., et al.: Imagenet classification with deep convolutional neural networks. In: Advances in Neural Information Processing Systems, pp. 1097–1105 (2012)
2. Ren, S., et al.: Faster R-CNN: towards real-time object detection with region proposal networks. In: Advances in Neural Information Processing Systems, pp. 91–99 (2015)

3. Abdel-Hamid, O., et al.: Applying convolutional neural networks concepts to hybrid NN-HMM model for speech recognition. In: Acoustics, Speech and Signal Processing, pp. 4277–4280 (2012)
4. Simonyan, K., Zisserman, A.: Very deep convolutional networks for large-scale image recognition. arXiv preprint arXiv:1409.1556 (2014)
5. He, K., Zhang, X., Ren, S., Sun, J.: Deep residual learning for image recognition. In: Proceedings of the IEEE Conference on Computer Vision and Pattern Recognition, pp. 770–778 (2016)
6. Hadji, I., Wildes, R.P.: What Do We Understand About Convolutional Networks? arXiv preprint arXiv:1803.08834 (2018)
7. Qiu, J., Wang, J., Yao, S., et al.: Going deeper with embedded FPGA platform for convolutional neural network. In: Proceedings of the 2016 ACM/SIGDA International Symposium on Field-Programmable Gate Arrays, pp. 26–35 (2016)
8. Wang, C., Gong, L., Yu, Q., Li, X., Xie, Y., Zhou, X.: DLAU: a scalable deep learning accelerator unit on FPGA. IEEE Trans. Comput.-Aided Des. Integr. Circuits Syst. **36**(3), 513–517 (2017)
9. Zhang, C., et al.: Optimizing FPGA-based accelerator design for deep convolutional neural networks. In: Proceedings of the IEEE Conference on Computer Vision and Pattern Recognition, pp. 161–170 (2015)
10. Suda, N., et al.: Throughput-optimized OpenCL-based FPGA accelerator for large-scale convolutional neural networks. In: Proceedings of the 2016 ACM/SIGDA International Symposium on Field-Programmable Gate Arrays, pp. 16–25 (2016)
11. Wang, D., Xu, K., Jiang, D.: PipeCNN: an OpenCL-based open-source FPGA accelerator for convolution neural networks. In: Field Programmable Technology (ICFPT), pp. 279–282 (2017)

Memory Bandwidth and Energy Efficiency Optimization of Deep Convolutional Neural Network Accelerators

Zikai Nie, Zhisheng Li, Lei Wang$^{(\boxtimes)}$, Shasha Guo, and Qiang Dou

National University of Defense Technology, Changsha, China
zikai93@163.com, leiwang@nudt.edu.cn

Abstract. Deep convolutional neural networks (DNNs) achieve state-of-the-art accuracy but at the cost of massive computation and memory operations. Although highly-parallel devices effectively meet the requirements of computation, energy efficiency is still a tough nut.

In this paper, we present two novel computation sequences, $NHWC_{fine}$ and $NHWC_{coarse}$, for the DNN accelerators. Then we combine two computation sequences with appropriate data layouts. The proposed modes enable continuous memory access patterns and reduce the number of memory accesses, which is achieved by leveraging and transforming the local data reuse of weights and feature maps in high-dimensional convolutions.

Experiments with various convolutional layers show that the proposed modes made up of computing sequences and data layouts are more energy efficient than the baseline mode on various networks. The reduction for total energy consumption is up to 4.10×. The reduction for the off-chip memory access latency is up to 5.11×.

Keywords: Deep learning · Convolutional neural network
Acceleration · Memory efficiency · Data layout

1 Introduction

Deep Neural Networks ($DNNs$) are Machine Learning (ML) methods that can learn a generic but effective representation of an input space from large amount of data. They extract high level features using previous learned models from raw data to infer the final data distribution.

Over the past decade, DNNs, especially deep convolutional neural networks, have gained a huge development due to the outstanding experimental achievements of multiple related fields including computer vision [14], speech recognition [9], and natural language processing [8]. In many specific situations, DNNs used in some domains are now able to beyond human in both accuracy and speed.

The success of DNNs can be attributed to three main reasons: the availability of large-scale data sets, the developments of deep structures and training

© Springer Nature Singapore Pte Ltd. 2018
C. Li and J. Wu (Eds.): ACA 2018, CCIS 908, pp. 15–29, 2018.
https://doi.org/10.1007/978-981-13-2423-9_2

algorithms, and the utilization of highly parallel computational resources. All of the three factors show the demand of high computation throughput and memory bandwidth resulting in the developments of general-purpose and specialized accelerators based on highly parallel platform such as GPUs [6,7], FPGAs [12,21], and ASICs [4,6].

After the chasing in accuracy, almost all modern accelerators, especially those hold deep networks, pay more attention on the reduction of power consumption [18]. To achieve better energy efficiency, eliminating unnecessary off-chip memory access and optimizing memory access patterns are effective methods.

Previous studies proposed methods to mitigate the bottleneck of memory access, such as dataflow [2,5], compression [10,13], data quantification [12]. These works gain outstanding performances, but some of them biased towards the adjustments of data formats and processing orders at on-chip or off-chip ends but fail to consider them both simultaneously. The interactions between computation sequences and data layouts have not been considered.

Based on the comparisons between different combinations of computation sequences and data layouts, we propose two optimizations of computation sequences and collocate favorable data layouts in convolutional layers to collaboratively improve the energy efficiency.

To enhance energy efficiency, previous works like [5] focus on the distribution of all types of data movement, such as input data reuse or partial sum accumulation, at different levels of the memory hierarchy. Based on the fact that the data size and the number of off-chip accesses of input feature maps and weights is different in the convolutional layers, our computation sequences that focus on the transformation and balance among different data reuse forms can deliver significant energy saving.

The main contributions of our work include:

- A framework that can model multiple accelerator architectures and evaluate various combinations of computation sequences and data layouts in different convolutional layers.
- Two novel sequences of the convolutional computation called $NHWC_{fine}$ and $NHWC_{coarse}$ and their corresponding data layouts to maximize memory access coalescence and provide sequencial memeory acceess pattern in order to optimize performance and energy efficieny of the memory system.

The experiment result shows that our two computation modes, $NHWC_{fine}$ and $NHWC_{coarse}$, gain higher efficiency in various convolutional layers compared to the basic convolution, with reduction of off-chip latency up to 5.11× and 4.95×, respectively. The two modes also achieve up to 4.10× and 3.98× reduction in total energy consumption of a single convolutional layer. When the networks goes deeper, the reduction ratio will increase accordingly.

The rest of the paper is organized as follows. Section 2 gives the background of CNNs and introduces the related work. Section 3 gives the motivation of this work. We will introduce proposed data layout and optimizations in Sect. 4. Sections 5 and 6 provide a series of experiments to evaluate the memory efficiency of different modes, and this paper concludes in Sect. 7.

2   Background and Related Works

2.1   Convolutional Neural Networks

In machine learning, convolution neural networks, inspired by animal neurons organization of local sensitivity and direction selection, are members of multi-layer feed-forward artificial neural networks. The working principle of CNNs is to extract the local features with special data distributions from high-resolution feature maps and combine them directly into more abstract low-resolution feature maps. Feature extraction and feature mapping operations are completed through two types of layers: convolutional and pooling layers. The last few layers are fully-connected (FC) classifiers that combine all local features to produce the final results.

A convolutional layer extracts local features from input feature maps (ifmaps) via trained filters, and then combines them into the more abstract intermediate activation called output feature maps (ofmaps). Each element of feature maps can be represented into three dimensions: height (H), width (W), and channel index (C). When batch size is more than one to leverage parallelism among different images, there is another dimension N that should be concerned, which represents the different set of ifmaps in their contexts. The computation in the convolutional layers is defined as

$$
\begin{aligned}
ofmaps\,&[z]\,[u]\,[x]\,[y]\\
&= \sum_{k=0}^{Ci-1}\sum_{i=0}^{Fh-1}\sum_{j=0}^{Fw-1} ifmaps\,[z]\,[k]\,[Sx+i]\,[Sy+j]\\
&\times weights\,[u]\,[k]\,[i]\,[j] + bias\,[u]\\
&0\leq z\leq N, 0\leq u\leq Co, 0\leq x\leq Ho, 0\leq y\leq Wo
\end{aligned}
\tag{1}
$$

N is the value of batch size. C_i and C_o are the channel number of ifmaps and ofmaps. H_o and W_o are the height and width of ofmaps. F_h and F_w represent the size of convolution filters. The dimensions of both filters and fmaps are 4D. It means that each filter or ifmap is a 3D structure consisting of 2D planes. In Summary, for an output channel, a 3D ifmap is processed by a 3D filter in convolutional layers. Figure 1 shows the main computation process.

To differentiate data layouts in 4D arrays of fmaps and filters, we will use following notation in this paper: $NCHW$ for fmaps and $C_oC_iF_hF_w$ for filters. There are also two subtypes of $NCHW$ data layout for ifmaps and ofmaps: $NC_iH_iW_i$ and $NC_oH_oW_o$. Data layouts can represent the levels of distance between every two data in the same dimension. For example, in the $NCHW$ data layout, the elements along the lowest dimension W are stored in succession, which continuous elements along the H dimension have a stride of W, and $H*W$ for C dimension, and so on.

2.2   Related Works

Many works are proposed to improve memory utilization in various fields, such as compressions, zero-skip computations [1], data layouts, dataflows, and so on.

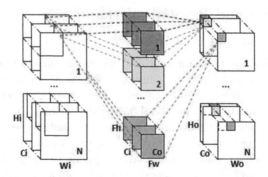

Fig. 1. Computation of a CONV/FC layer. H_i and W_i are the height and width of ifmaps. Other notations are explained behind Eq. 1

DRAM accesses can be reduced by compression techniques such as pruning and quantization [13]. Note that [10] compress a 2D filter to a 1D row for storage at the cost of slower convergence rate, which benefits the optimizations below. Zero-skip computation in [1] ignores the zero bits in activations to eliminate the useless MACs and reduce R/W operations of psums. However, this technique introduces more energy and area problems. Dataflows can be divided into two aspects: intra-layer and inter-layer dataflows. [5] presents various intra-layer dataflow and proposes a dataflow leveraging almost all the data reuses, which is called row-stationary. It receives outstanding memory efficiency. [2] proposes an inter-layer dataflow applied to continuous convolutional layers to reduce the R/W operations of intermediate activations. Data layout, the part that we focus on, can serialize the DRAM accesses to leverage bandwidth and coalescence better. In the view of parallelism, [16] discusses the impacts of all kinds of basic data layouts on GPUs. But, besides neglecting other underlying structures, the relationships between data layouts and computation sequences have also been overlooked.

3   Motivation

3.1   Limited On-Chip Storage Resources

Our basic accelerator's architecture is a design of FPGA-based CNN accelerator for LeNet called *Laius* [17].

LeNet [15] is one of the most traditional neural networks towards light-scale data comparing with advanced networks like VGG. Laius is an FPGA-based accelerator for LeNet.

Benefiting from ping-pong optimization, 8-bit weight precision and weight compression, Laius's inter-layer buffers can save all the output data from the previous layer and provide input to the next layer. If the network model is changed to AlexNet, the data size and the depth of the network will both increase. And then there will be some problems. First, on-chip storage is not enough anymore, and we have to leverage data reuse better to reduce the number of off-chip memory access and save energy. Second, with the deeper going of network structures, there are more convolutional layers with small fmaps and filters. Third, the number of psums produced by parallel contexts is too large to make psums stay in on-chip buffers.

3.2 Data Movement

In most widely used CNNs, such as LeNet [15], AlexNet [14] and VGG [20], convolutional layers account for over 90% of the overall operations and produce a large amount of data movement [5]. Thus, convolutional layers are important for CNNs to gain high performance in throughput and energy efficiency.

There are two issues limiting throughput and energy efficiency of convolution. First, a MAC operation that creates read requests of ifmaps and weights stored in off-chip DRAM results in requirements of high bandwidth and energy consumption. Second, a significant amount of partial sums (*psums*) are produced by limited parallel contexts simultaneously, which introduce additional read or write pressure and energy of access if not accumulated within an acceptable time.

To deal with the first issue, we should leverage different types of data reuse:

- **Sliding reuse.** The value of S (*stride*) is always less than that of F_h and F_w in convolutional layers to slow down the evolution roughening and to gain more information from neighbors. This characteristic makes small amount of ifmaps' pixels become shared across many MAC kernels. Each pixel in ifmaps can be used $F_h \times F_w$ (*with padding*) times in a 2D fmap with 2 directions.
- **Ifmap reuse**
- **Intra-image filter reuse.** According to Eq. 1, each 2D filter can be identified by a couple of an input channel and an output channel. Therefore, convolutional operations of an input channel use only one 2D filter to generate psums of the same output channel. This kind of reuse doesn't exist in FC layers.
- **Inter-image filter reuse.** Each filter can be further reused across the batch of N ifmaps.

The second issue can be handled by scheduling the order of operations to make the psums get final values as soon as possible.

Nevertheless, maximum 2D data reuse and immediate psum reduction cannot be realized completely at the same time. Pixels of a specified output channel is products of a group of C_i 2D ifmap kernels and a group of C_i 2D filters in the same size. All filters in a group must be taken into computation if we want to get the output pixel immediately. But we will read this group of 2D filters in sequence again to compute the value of the next pixel in the same output channel, which is conflicting with the aim of maximum data reuse in a 2D view. As we can see, the reason why these two issues cannot be solved simultaneously is mainly about the independence of each channel.

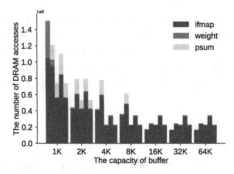

Fig. 2. The number of DRAM accesses of various buffer size. The 5 bars in each cluster represent the 5 CONV layers of AlexNet. With various size of the on-chip buffers, we crawl the output requests of the buffer and record the number of off-chip accesses.

The number of DRAM accesses is an essential factor that directly influences the performance and energy efficiency of a convolutional layer. We analyze this metric's value with its three components, ifmaps/weights/psums, and observe the proportion of each component. As shown in Fig. 2, we find that accessing ifmap pixels is the most significant impact on the total number of accesses in each layer. Failing to leverage access coalescence and ifmap data reuse with limited buffer size makes a large number of repetitive ifmap accesses. When a buffer cannot keep a whole 2D ifmap plane, the two-direction *sliding reuse* of a 2D ifmap plane can always produce repetitive accesses requests in the second direction. Therefore, some methods are needed to convert redundant accesses of ifmap pixels into weights to keep balance and make buffer always hold a 3D filter.

4   Data Layout Optimization

4.1   Computation and Data Layout

When the buffer size is not enough to keep the sum of all the pixels of an input channel, all psums of an output channel and a 2D filter, ifmap pixels are repeatedly read by *sliding reuse* in an HW ifmap plane. According to Eq. 1, we can observe that different heights and widths between filters and ifmaps lead to the two-direction *sliding reuse* in convolutional layers, which creates a long stride to the *sliding reuse* in the second dimension.

Therefore, among dimensions N/H/W/C, we try to find a dimension with the same length owned by both ifmaps and weights to apply single-direction sliding on a 2D plane. Then C_i is found, and we expect to read pixels along C_i dimension first in a specific WC planes. In these planes, kernels will slide along dimension W. To gain a continuous DRAM access sequence, data values along dimension C (C_i/C_o) are supposed to store close to each other in the memory. We change data layouts to $NHWC$ for fmaps based on this single-direction sliding computation mode.

For ofmaps, however, the R/W requests to two adjacent output pixels will experience a long stride of C_o if the data layout is modified to $NH_oW_oC_o$. Fortunately, instead of adding transpose operations, this issue can be solved when we introduce parallel processing to convolutional computation. Details will be discussed in Sect. 4.5.

```
/*NHWC_coarse CONV*/
for (u=0;u<Co;u++)
for (g=0;g<Ci;g=g+tm)
for (x=0;x<Hi;x++)
//vary filters to a plane
for (i=0;i<Fh;i=i+S)
for (y=0;y<Wo;y++)
for (j=0;j<Fw;j++)
for (k=g;k<min(Ci,g+tm);
  k++)
if (((x-i)/S)>=0
  &&((x-i)/S)<Ho)
{
t=input[x][y*S+j][k]
  *weight[u][i][j][k];
output[(x-i)/S][y][u]=
  output[(x-i)/S][y][u]+t;
}
```

```
/*NHWC_fine CONV*/
for (u=0; u<Co; u++)
for (g=0; g<Ci; g=g+tm)
for (x=0; x<Hi; x++)
for (y=0; y<Wo; y++)
//vary filters -a kernel
for (i=0; i<Fh; i=i+S)
for (j=0; j<Fw; j++)
for (k=g; k<min(Ci,g+tm);
  k++)
if (((x-i)/S)>=0
  &&((x-i)/S)<Ho)
{
t=input[x][y*S+j][k]
  *weight[u][i][j][k];
output[(x-i)/S][y][u]=
  output[(x-i)/S][y][u]+t;
}
```

Fig. 3. Kernel code of $NHWC_{coarse}$ (left) and $NHWC_{fine}$ (right) computation process without other opt methods. Notaion g is the number of groups divided along C dimension.

4.2 $NHWC_{coarse}$: A Coarse-grained Optimization of Computation Sequence

If we just change the data layout, there will be a stride along the C_i dimension, which can break the continuity of the access patterns. Other data of the block may be used after a long time resulting in many redundant operations.

We propose a convolution computation sequence that converts *sliding reuse* to intra-image weights reuse. For a specific output channel, each ifmap plane can just be read once and complete all of its operations with a low requirement of storage sources.

As shown in Fig. 3, we will modify computation sequence to maximize the data reuse of ifmap pixels. We first read a WC plane and the corresponding 3D filter to do MAC operations. For each read operation of 2D F_wC filters, this sequence prefers to compute whole WC input plane through the one-direction sliding operations. Then, this WC input plane will be computed with the subsequent 2D filters corresponding to the same output channel. We can only read a WC plane once, if there are sufficient on-chip storage resources.

After we change the loop sequence to fit the new data layout NHWC, the 2D convolutional kernels for the same output pixel will be linked closely. However, different from the traditional sequence computing with F_hF_w ifmap kernels, our new sequence compute with larger WC planes, which brings pressure to on-chip buffers. In other words, due to its long distance before using the same ifmap kernel again with a different 2D filter, this version may perform worse when the free capacity of buffers is not enough to hold a 2D WC ifmap plane. In this situation, the kernels read before might have been replaced and will be asked to read again.

4.3 $NHWC_{fine}$: A Fine-grained Optimization of Computation Sequence

With the computation sequence $NHWC_{coarse}$, expanding of both the overlapping parts of ifmaps and the granularity of filters C_i times highly increase the pressure of on-chip buffers. So we need to change the computation sequences further to apply in a fine granularity and balance them.

As shown in Fig. 3, we first read a 2D fmap kernel of the WC plane and the corresponding 3D filter to do MAC operations. Instead of WC plane in $NHWC_{coarse}$, the 2D kernel will participate in MAC operations F_h times with F_h 2D filters in ascending order of their indexes when $S = 1$, and output pixels will be located in descending order along H dimension. For example, with an assumption that $F_h = F_w = 3$ and $S = 1$, there will be three 2D filters matching with a single 2D fmap kernel whose index along H dimension is assumed to be x. The first 2D filter will compute with the kernel to produce a psum located in the current output pixel(x). The second will produce a new psum located in the last output pixel(x-1), and the third will compute for the pixel before last(x-2).

Through this way, we convert the *sliding reuse* along a direction to inter-image 3D weights reuse, which further reduces the sensitivity of ifmap access times to small buffer size.

4.4   Segmentation

Unfortunately, the length of C_i becomes larger as going deeper along the network, which results in the increasing size of the 2D WC kernel mentioned above. The pressure of buffer is significantly getting larger due to this size increasing. To handle this issue, we divide the 2D WC kernel into some groups along dimension C. The peculiarity that no *sliding reuse* exist along dimension C makes the segment easy to achieve. But the number of input channels per group should be selected carefully.

As shown in Fig. 4, we find that the point where the segment presents a good performance is related to the ratio of block size to data precision. Therefore, four channels for each group will minimize the access times without redundant R/W operations in NHWC data layout.

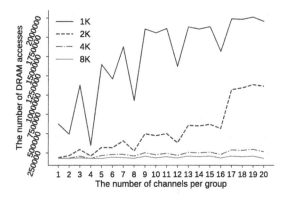

Fig. 4. DRAM accesses of various numbers of channels per group in CONV2 of LeNet. The groups are equally divided along C_i dimension. With various size of the on-chip buffers as shown in legend, we crawl the output requests of the buffer and record the number of off-chip accesses. A block contains four addressed values in this figure.

4.5   Parallelization

We know that there are three intra-image independent dimensions could be paralleled (C_o, H_o, and W_o) from Polyhedral model [22]. Inter-image dimension N, which indicates batch size, is also a good choice.

We prefer to select C_o as the first choice of parallelization for three reasons. First, in the view of maximizing data reuse, the parallelism partition in C_o dimension is easy and efficient. For parallelism partition in C_o dimension, each context will use a same 3D ifmap. The ifmap for these contexts can be read only once all through. Second, in consideration of data size, the contribution of sharing a 3D ifmap, especially for our max-ifmap-reuse optimizations, is much higher than that of sharing a 3D filter in the same reuse granularity. Finally, as for the $NHWC$ layout, the adjacent elements along C dimension can be accessed serially and coalesced, which benefits the reduction of access times and the improvement of memory access patterns.

5   Experiment Setup

5.1   Benchmark and Baseline

As shown in Table 1, we use three widely used networks, LeNet, AlexNet, and VGG, to evaluate the proposed optimization methods. These three networks cover a wide range of network size and memory-efficiency demand rank. Table 1 presents the configurations for different types of convolutional layers selected from the three networks. These layers with different configurations will be used in evaluation among three modes.

– The **base mode** is the traditional convolution, as shown in Eq. 1, with *NCHW* data layout, which is regarded as a basic control mode.

Table 1. The CNNs and their layers used in our experiments.

Layer	Ci	Ho/Wo	Fh/Fw	Co	S
LeNet_CONV1	3	24	5	20	1
LeNet_CONV2	20	8	5	50	1
AlexNet_CONV1	3	55	11	96	4
AlexNet_CONV2	96	27	5	256	1
AlexNet_CONV3	256	13	3	384	1
VGG_CONV1	3	224	3	64	1
VGG_CONV2	64	112	3	128	1
VGG_CONV3	128	56	3	256	1

- **NHWC1 mode** consists of $NHWC_{coarse}$ convolutional computation sequence and $NHWC$ layout.
- **NHWC2 mode** consists of $NHWC_{fine}$ convolutional computation sequence and $NHWC$ layout.

We apply these three modes to the convolutional layers in Table 1 and compare the performance and energy efficiency by four metrics: DRAM access times, latency, and energy consumption. To fit the fact of limited storage resources, We also perform the sensitivity test to buffer size among these four metrics.

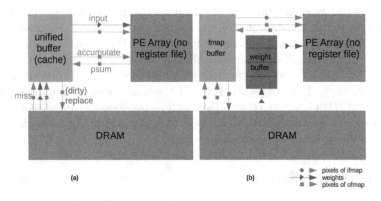

Fig. 5. Top-level structures of CNN accelerators. (a) Unified buffer: uses a unified buffer to make different data on chip compete resources. (b) Split buffer: divides weight buffers out.

5.2 Experiment Framework

Two top-level structures for experiments are illustrated in Fig. 5. On-chip buffers represent the total storage resources on chip including global buffer, FIFO registers, and register files in PEs. There are two modes of on-chip buffer configuration, unified buffer and split buffer, in our experimental structures. A unified buffer can store all types of data. It improves the resource utilization but might introduce more conflicts and redundant replacements. To reduce the redundant accesses of weights, we split global buffer into fmap buffer and weight buffer to hold fmap pixels and 3D filters respectively.

The computation of PE is implemented by the simulator based on *Laius* inference engine to output the behaviors of convolutional operations. The buffers are implemented through a cache mechanism. For the structure with a unified buffer, we feed all the output requests of inference engine into a buffer. And for the structure with split buffers, we feed fmap and weight requests into corresponding buffers respectively. The size of buffers is recorded in total value. We modify DRAM simulator DRAMSim2 [19] to implement and simulated the DRAM module. We use the DRAM configuration of 1.5 ns per DRAM cycle and 16 parallel devices with 4-bit width each.

6 Experiment Results

We simulate the two novel modes and compare their performance with the base mode under same but various buffer size and processing parallelism constraints. To save space, We just show the results of partial representative layers of the networks shown in Table 1.

6.1 The Number of Off-Chip DRAM Accesses

DRAM accesses are supposed to make a significant impact on the energy consumption since their energy cost is significantly higher than on-chip data movements.

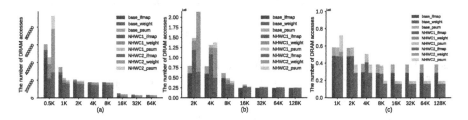

Fig. 6. DRAM accesses of various unified buffer size in CONV layers: (*a*) CONV2 of LeNet, (*b*) CONV2 of AlexNet, (*c*) CONV1 of VGG.

Unified buffer. Figure 6 shows the number of DRAM accesses in different unified buffer size. From the comparisons in the same layer, we can find three features. First, the accesses of ifmap are in the majority among the three modes, and NHWC2 mode can efficiently reduce the number of them except for few cases due to some unexpected replacements in small buffers. Second, NHWC2 mode performs worse than other modes when the buffer size is too small to persistently hold a 3D filter. The reduction of ifmap accesses is covered by the increase of weight accesses. Third, NHWC1 mode relieves the situations described in the second point. It reduces the replacements of weights introduced by limited capacity, which pays the price of increasing ifmap accesses.

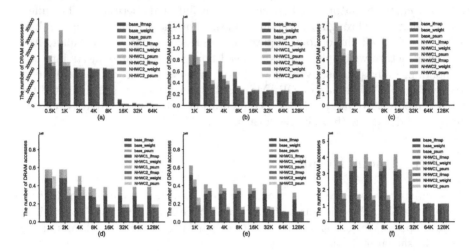

Fig. 7. DRAM accesses of various split buffer size in CONV layers: (*a*) CONV2 of LeNet, (*b*) CONV2 of AlexNet, (*c*) CONV3 of AlexNet, (*d*) CONV1 of VGG, (*e*) CONV2 of VGG, (*f*) CONV3 of VGG.

Split buffer. We split a unified buffer into a fmap buffer and a weight buffer to make sure that a 3D filter cannot be replaced until all its operations for the specified image have been finished. Among the layers shown in Fig. 7, $NHWC_{fine}$ (NHWC2 mode) always introduces less off-chip accesses (reduce up to 3.59× in VGG) mainly due to its maximized utilization of ifmaps. $NHWC_{coarse}$ (NHWC1 mode) does worse than the base mode sometimes due to its coarse-grained ifmap reuse. The effects become more significant as the scale of data and the pressure of buffers grow larger, which meets the trend of CNNs development.

6.2   Total Latency of Off-Chip DRAM Accesses

We record the total number of DRAM cycles spent in the period from receiving the first request to finishing the last R/W operation of various convolutional layers. The latency is the sum of many parts such as cycle time among row address strobe (RAS), column address strobe (CAS), precharge, and refresh commands.

As shown in Fig. 8, the $NWHC2$ mode can always achieve less latency than basic mode with ratios from 1.02× to 3.31× for AlexNet and from 1.07× to 5.11× for VGG, which are expected to grow higher with larger data size.

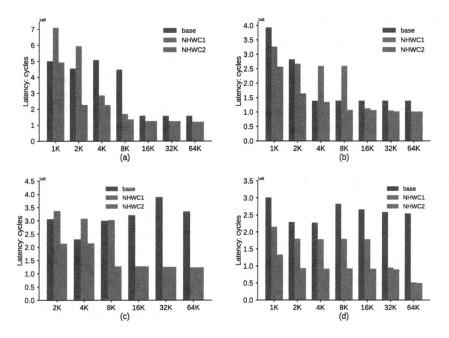

Fig. 8. Total DRAM latency of various split buffer size in CONV layers: (*a*) CONV2 of AlexNet, (*b*) CONV3 of AlexNet, (*c*) CONV1 of VGG, (*d*) CONV2 of VGG.

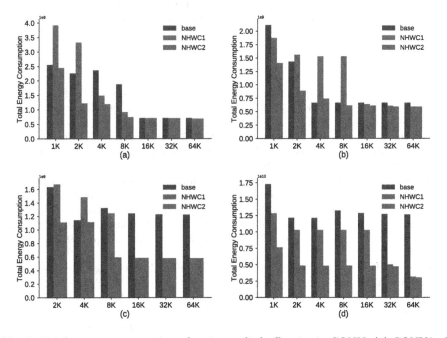

Fig. 9. Total energy consumption of various split buffer size in CONV: (*a*) CONV2 of AlexNet, (*b*) CONV3 of AlexNet, (*c*) CONV1 of VGG, (*d*) CONV2 of VGG.

6.3   Energy Consumption

Figure 9 provides the total DRAM energy consumption of the three modes in different convolutional layers with split buffers. NHWC2 mode is always in lower energy consumption, especially in convolutional layers of VGG, comparing with base mode (up to 4.10× reduction). NHWC1 mode gets bad results in small buffer size due to its large number of redundant ifmap accesses. The results indicate that a fine-grained C-first computation mode is more suitable and energy efficient for the structure with limited split buffers.

7   Conclusions and Future Works

To make effective use of limited on-chip storage resources and reduce off-chip energy consumption, this work presents two convolutional modes that combine computation sequences ($NHWC_{fine}$ and $NHWC_{coarse}$) with their suitable data layouts $NHWC$. These two modes maximize input data reuse, especially the reuse of input feature maps, and minimize read/write operations of psum accumulation.

We use various convolutional layers of three networks, LeNet and AlexNet and VGG, as benchmarks. Compared with the base mode of traditional convolution and NCHW layout, our two novel modes, especially NHWC2 mode, still get good performance with limited buffers and achieve low DRAM latency (up to 5.11× reduction) with low energy consumption(up to 4.10× reduction). The reduction is expected to be more significant with larger data size.

References

1. Albericio, J., et al.: Bit-pragmatic deep neural network computing. In: Proceedings of the 50th Annual IEEE/ACM International Symposium on Microarchitecture, pp. 382–394. ACM (2017)
2. Alwani, M., Chen, H., Ferdman, M., Milder, P.: Fused-layer CNN accelerators. In: 2016 49th Annual IEEE/ACM International Symposium on Microarchitecture (MICRO), pp. 1–12. IEEE (2016)
3. Bastoul, C.: Code generation in the polyhedral model is easier than you think. In: Proceedings of the 13th International Conference on Parallel Architectures and Compilation Techniques, pp. 7–16. IEEE Computer Society (2004)
4. Chen, T., et al.: Diannao: a small-footprint high-throughput accelerator for ubiquitous machine-learning. In: ACM Sigplan Notices, vol. 49, pp. 269–284. ACM (2014)
5. Chen, Y.-H., Emer, J., Sze, V.: Eyeriss: a spatial architecture for energy-efficient dataflow for convolutional neural networks. In: 2016 ACM/IEEE 43rd Annual International Symposium on Computer Architecture (ISCA), pp. 367–379. IEEE (2016)
6. Chen, Y., et al.: Dadiannao: a machine-learning supercomputer. In: Proceedings of the 47th Annual IEEE/ACM International Symposium on Microarchitecture, pp. 609–622. IEEE Computer Society (2014)

7. Cireşan, D.C., Meier, U., Gambardella, L.M., Schmidhuber, J.: Deep, big, simple neural nets for handwritten digit recognition. Neural Comput. **22**(12), 3207–3220 (2010)
8. Collobert, R., Weston, J.: A unified architecture for natural language processing: deep neural networks with multitask learning. In: Proceedings of the 25th International Conference on Machine Learning, pp. 160–167. ACM (2008)
9. Deng, L., et al.: Recent advances in deep learning for speech research at microsoft. In: 2013 IEEE International Conference on Acoustics, Speech and Signal Processing (ICASSP), pp. 8604–8608. IEEE (2013)
10. Ding, C., et al.: C IR CNN: accelerating and compressing deep neural networks using block-circulant weight matrices. In: Proceedings of the 50th Annual IEEE/ACM International Symposium on Microarchitecture, pp. 395–408. ACM (2017)
11. Fowers, J., Brown, G., Cooke, P., Stitt, G.: A performance and energy comparison of FPGAs, GPUS, and multicores for sliding-window applications. In: Proceedings of the ACM/SIGDA International Symposium on Field Programmable Gate Arrays, pp. 47–56. ACM (2012)
12. Gupta, S., Agrawal, A., Gopalakrishnan, K., Narayanan, P.: Deep learning with limited numerical precision. In: Proceedings of the 32nd International Conference on Machine Learning (ICML-15), pp. 1737–1746 (2015)
13. Han, S., Mao, H., Dally, W.J.: Deep compression: compressing deep neural networks with pruning, trained quantization and huffman coding. arXiv preprint arXiv:1510.00149 (2015)
14. Krizhevsky, A., Sutskever, I., Hinton, G.E.: Imagenet classification with deep convolutional neural networks. In: Advances in Neural Information Processing Systems, pp. 1097–1105 (2012)
15. LeCun, Y., Bottou, L., Bengio, Y., Haffner, P.: Gradient-based learning applied to document recognition. Proc. IEEE **86**(11), 2278–2324 (1998)
16. Li, C., Yang, Y., Feng, M., Chakradhar, S., Zhou, H.: Optimizing memory efficiency for deep convolutional neural networks on GPUS. In: SC16: International Conference for High Performance Computing, Networking, Storage and Analysis, pp. 633–644. IEEE (2016)
17. Li, Z., et al.: Laius: an 8-bit fixed-point CNN hardware inference engine. In: 2017 15th IEEE International Symposium on Parallel and Distributed Processing with Applications (ISPA), pp. 143–150. IEEE (2017)
18. Reagen, B., et al.: Minerva: enabling low-power, highly-accurate deep neural network accelerators. In: Proceedings of the 43rd International Symposium on Computer Architecture, pp. 267–278. IEEE Press (2016)
19. Rosenfeld, P., Cooper-Balis, E., Jacob, B.: Dramsim2: a cycle accurate memory system simulator. IEEE Comput. Arch. Lett. **10**(1), 16–19 (2011)
20. Simonyan, K., Zisserman, A.: Very deep convolutional networks for large-scale image recognition. arXiv preprint arXiv:1409.1556 (2014)
21. Wang, C., Gong, L., Qi, Y., Li, X., Xie, Y., Zhou, X.: Dlau: a scalable deep learning accelerator unit on FPGA. IEEE Trans. Comput. Aided Des. Integr. Circuits Syst. **36**(3), 513–517 (2017)
22. Wei, X., et al.: Automated systolic array architecture synthesis for high throughput CNN inference on FPGAs. In: 2017 54th ACM/EDAC/IEEE Design Automation Conference (DAC), pp. 1–6. IEEE (2017)

Research on Parallel Acceleration for Deep Learning Inference Based on Many-Core ARM Platform

Keqian Zhu and Jingfei Jiang[(✉)]

National Laboratory for Parallel and Distributed Processing,
National University of Defense Technology, Changsha, China
zhukeqian94@163.com, jingfeijiang@126.com

Abstract. Deep learning is one of the hottest research directions in the field of artificial intelligence. It has achieved results which subvert these of traditional methods. However, the demand for computing ability of hardware platform is also increasing. The academia and industry mainly use heterogeneous GPUs to accelerating computation. ARM is relatively more open than GPUs. The purpose of this paper is to study the performance and related acceleration techniques of ThunderX high-performance many-core ARM chips under large-scale inference tasks. In order to study the computational performance of the target platform objectively, several deep models are adapted for acceleration. Through the selection of computational libraries, adjustment of parallel strategies, application of various performance optimization techniques, we have excavated the computing ability of many-core ARM platforms deeply. The final experimental results show that the performance of single-chip ThunderX is equivalent to that of the i7 7700 K chip, and the overall performance of dual-chip can reach 1.77 times that of the latter. In terms of energy efficiency, the former is inferior to the latter. Stronger cooling system or bad power management may lead to more power consumption. Overall, high-performance ARM chips can be deployed in the cloud to complete large-scale deep learning inference tasks which requiring high throughput.

Keywords: Parallel acceleration · Deep learning inference · Many-core ARM

1 Introduction

The research boom of deep learning can be traced back to 2012. AlexNet [1] appeared in the ImageNet competition, achieving high classification accuracy, greatly surpassing the traditional methods and gaining the attention of researchers around the world. After that, the depth method not only developed rapidly in the field of computer vision, but also extended to a larger range of machine perception, including speech recognition, natural language understanding, voice recognition, and so on.

In order to improve the perception of the algorithm, researchers tend to widen and deepen the network model, such as from AlexNet to GoogLeNet [2]. While the algorithm is optimized, the demand for computing ability is also increasing. Especially in the end-to-cloud architecture, the cloud has to undertake large-scale training and

© Springer Nature Singapore Pte Ltd. 2018
C. Li and J. Wu (Eds.): ACA 2018, CCIS 908, pp. 30–41, 2018.
https://doi.org/10.1007/978-981-13-2423-9_3

inference tasks at the same time. It must have sufficient computing ability to achieve the desired throughput rate.

Using heterogeneous GPUs to accelerate deep neural network [3] can achieve higher energy efficiency than simply relying on traditional x86 CPUs. In this architecture, the computational load is shifted to high-performance GPU card or cluster. The CPU is responsible for distributing computing tasks and controlling data transfer. The entire ecology of GPU heterogeneous acceleration has been very perfect. However, due to the lack of competition in high-performance GPU manufacturing, users need to bear higher hardware costs.

ARM is also entering the field of high-performance computing. CAVM released ThunderX series ARM chips, focusing on data center and cloud applications. This article aims to study the performance of this chip under large-scale deep learning inference tasks. First of all, it is necessary to grasp the hardware features. Then combine it with the features of the deep learning algorithm to fully exploit its computing capabilities. Lastly, ARM is compared with mainstream high-performance x86 CPUs, to judge its prospects in the field of high-performance computing.

There is already a large amount of work on the ARM platform performing inference tasks. In 2017, Tencent opened the Ncnn [4] deep learning inference framework that optimized for mobile platform. Taking into account the limited hardware resources of mobile platforms, developers have implemented elaborate memory management and data structure design. In addition, ARM NEON assembly-level optimization is also implemented. Ncnn mainly supports acceleration for convolutional neural network. In addition, most of its optimization are developed for the mobile platforms, making it difficult to exploit the computing ability of many-core ARM platforms.

Jetson TX2 is an embedded platform for artificial intelligence launched by NVIDIA. Onboard computing resources are a Pascal GPU with 256 CUDA cores and a 4-core ARM A57 chip. The collaborative heterogeneous computing of GPU and ARM can complete small-scale inference tasks rapidly [5]. However, if only use the 4-core ARM chip, the performance is not as good as the C6678 DSP chip [6].

The above research status shows that the research on deep learning inference acceleration of many-core server-class ARM platforms is insufficient. This article hopes to do some exploratory work in this area.

2   The Many-Core ARM

ARM company is one of the leaders in microprocessor technology and has introduced a series of microprocessor IP cores for different application scenarios. Introduced in 2012, ARMv8 is the new platform for the enterprise market and is the first architecture supporting 64-bit instruction sets. The main features of the ARMv7 architecture are retained or further expanded in the ARMv8 architecture, such as TrustZone security technology, virtualization technology, and NEON SIMD technology.

Cavium is the leading provider of multi-core MIPS and ARM processors on the world. The latest ThunderX series ARM processors are developed by Cavium for the HPC market. Many technical specifications are at the leading level in ARM manufacturing.

ThunderX is fully compatible with the ARMv8 architecture. Single chip has 48 cores, and frequency of each core is up to 2.5 GHz. Dual-chip configuration is supported, and CPPI technology is used to achieve full cache consistency between dual-chips, greatly simplifying application development. A powerful cache architecture and high-speed main memory controller can meet the needs of many-core memory access bandwidth. Each physical core on the chip has 78 KB of instruction cache and 32 KB of data cache, and shares 16 MB of L2 cache. In addition, it supports up to four 72-bit 2400 MHz DDR4 main memory controllers. ThunderX is optimized for high compute loads and is targeted at cloud-based HPC applications.

3   Parallel Resources of ARM

Deep learning models are generally highly parallelizable, so they can exploit hardware parallel computing capabilities. On the ARMv8 platform, the available parallel resources are multi-core MIMD and NEON SIMD coprocessor.

ARM's research on multi-core processor technology is very mature. The big. LITTLE technology and the latest DynamiQ technology have solved the power and performance tradeoffs by integrating multiple cores with different architectures into a single chip. ThunderX is a server-class chip and computing performance is the primary design goal. The cores integrated in the chip are isomorphic, and all belong to the standard high-performance ARMv8 architecture.

NEON first appeared in the ARMv7-A and ARMv7-R architecture as an extension attribute, which is an advanced SIMD architecture extension essentially. The purpose of this technology is to improve the user experience of multimedia applications, and to accelerate audio and video decoding, 2D/3D image processing. NEON can also be used to accelerate digital signal processing, computer vision, and deep learning. In the ARMv8-A architecture, the length of each NEON register is 128, so a NEON ALU instruction can complete the operation between two groups of 8 FP16 or 4 FP32 or 2 FP64 simultaneously. The use of NEON components can theoretically improve computing performance in several ways. Firstly, the number of instructions is greatly reduced. Secondly, NEON components contains multiple 128-bit registers. These register files can be regarded as buffers controlled by compiler.

Developers can use NEON resources at multiple levels. The highest level is to integrate the NEON library directly into applications, which is very simple and efficient. If there is no library can provide the required functionality, developers can use NEON built-in functions. Built-in functions are provided by the compiler, which is equitant to one or more NEON instructions. At the lowest level, developers can write assembly code directly, which can control NEON register allocation and instruction pipeline precisely, to maximize NEON performance.

4 Parallel Computing Library of ARM

In order to maximize the computing performance, we do not use a high-level deep learning framework. Instead, we implement various depth models based on lower-level library to optimize the code manually. At present, the HPC library for deep learning of ARM platform includes Arm Compute Library (ACL), Arm Performance Library (APL), OpenBLAS and so on.

We must make the best choice among the above three major computing libraries. The CaffeOnACL Performance Report states that the ACL-based Caffe framework performs better than OpenBLAS in many deep learning tasks. Especially in the LRN task, ACL greatly exceeds OpenBLAS. The algorithm in common use also determines that OpenBLAS cannot play the full performance of a specific platform. So in the deep learning application of ARM platform, ACL is better than OpenBLAS.

In addition, we tested the GEMM interface of ACL and APL. For the multiplication of two single-precision floating-point matrices with sizes of 10000 * 4096 and 4096 * 4096, test result shows that ACL is still more efficient. Besides, ACL is open source, which offers the possibility to further optimize the code (Table 1).

Table 1. Comparison of matrix multiplication between ACL and APL.

	ACL	APL
Single core	56 s	58 s
48 cores	3 s	3.8 s

5 Target Applications

We chose three deep learning models with different structure as the object of acceleration, to evaluate the computing ability of the target hardware platform comprehensively.

5.1 RNNs-LSTM Model

The first depth model is RNNs-LSTM. RNNs are modeled for sequence and introduce a directional loop within the network structure. The input of the hidden layer consists of the output of the previous layer at the current time and the output of the layer itself at the previous time. This design allows RNNs to perceive sequence semantics. RNNs-LSTM is an improved variant of the traditional RNNs. It ameliorates the gradient disappearance and explosion problem of RNNs, lead to improve the training convergence and inference accuracy under longer sequence. We obtained a pre-trained small LSTM model directly from paper [7]. This model is used for word prediction. The input is a vectored word and the output is a probability vector.

The model consists of an input layer, two LSTM hidden layers, and a Softmax output layer. From a computational point of view, the LSTM hidden layer consists of a GEMM operation and some complex operations that updates the internal state of the hidden layer. The Softmax layer also contains a GEMM operation, and a Softmax normalization process.

5.2 Fully Connected Model

Then we consider using a depth model that only contains a fully connected structure. AlexNet is a classic CNNs model applied for image classification. The last two hidden layers of the network are fully connected layers. GEMM is the core of deep learning computing, and its platform-independent and platform-related computational optimization has been very mature. Therefore, it is very objective and important to select the full-connection layer to evaluate hardware computing performance.

5.3 Confusion Tree Model

Finally, we also noticed the direction of the optimization of network structure in the field of deep learning. The purpose of optimizing the network structure is to improve the performance of the network or reduce the computational complexity. In practical applications, the computational performance is influenced by the specific hardware architecture. Therefore, studying the inference acceleration of the optimized model can not only evaluate the computing performance of the hardware platform more comprehensively, but also analyze the value of network structure optimization from practice.

The confusion tree [8] is an optimization model for the fully connected layer, which greatly reduces the computation complexity. Relative experimental results show that the accuracy of the image classification is comparable to that of the original model, and even improves. This article uses a confusion tree that is designed for AlexNet, as shown in Fig. 1.

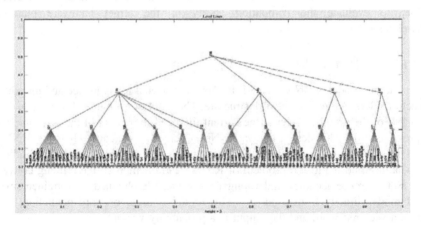

Fig. 1. Structure of confusion tree for AlexNet.

The confusion tree presents a tree structure as its name suggests. Leaf nodes are calculated as prediction probability for each category. Each non-leaf node represents a multi-class SVM that is implemented by combining multiple binary SVMs. The number of binary SVMs is the same as the number of node branches.

For the image to be classified, its feature vector starts from the root node of the tree. The multi-classification results at the root node determine the branches of the feature flow. This calculation process is repeated until the feature vector reaches one of the leaf node.

Each layer of the tree can be understood as a cluster of categories. This tree contains four layers, so a total of four clusters are represented. The above three layers are logical clusters, and the lowest layer is the actual cluster. The root node is the first level, which represents the logical entire category. All image is in this entire category. The second level of nodes represents the second logical cluster, and the third level represents the third logical cluster. The fourth layer is the leaf node, which represents the clusters of 100 categories. From this point of view, the inference process of confusion trees is a process of category breakdown.

6   The Design of Experiments

6.1   Settings of Platform Comparison

We use the high-end Intel i7 7700 K as a comparison platform. The main performance indicators are quad-core eight threads, 4.2 GHz frequency, 256 KB L1 cache, 1 MB L2 cache, 8.0 MB L3 cache, SSE SIMD coprocessor. In order to make the results more persuasive, all depth models are also implemented based on lower-level computing libraries to excavate more computing performance. We chose MKL as Intel platform parallel computing library. MKL is the fastest and most commonly used math library on the Intel platform. It contains a series of basic algorithms such as BLAS, FFT and DNN.

6.2   Parallel Granularity

In setting the scale of inference, we considered the actual scenario where the server platform frequently performs large-scale inference tasks. In the LSTM application, we set the mini-batch size to 9600. In the full connected model and confusion tree, we set the mini-batch size to 10000.

The scale of data has been set, then the main factor affects implementation is parallel model. For deep learning tasks, data parallelism is commonly used because it can achieve high load balance. Data parallelism has two implementations, fine-grained parallelism and coarse-grained parallelism. Parallel granularity is defined as the ratio of computing and communication. Parallel granularity affects load balance, communication overhead, storage requirements and cache locality utilization. The choice of parallel granularity depends on the characteristics of the model, and we will discuss it separately.

6.3   Parallel Scheme for RNNs-LSTM

The fine-grained data parallelism for the LSTM model is shown in the Fig. 2. In this case, multiple cores work together to complete a mini-batch inference task. a sequence of word contains 7 inferences, and each inference contains 9 inference stages. If this parallel scheme is adopted, the cores need to be synchronized 63 times during one inference process.

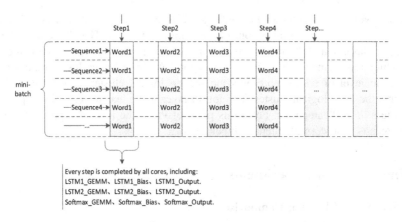

Fig. 2. The fine-grained data parallelism for RNNs-LSTM model.

The coarse-grained data parallel scheme is shown in Fig. 3. Each core completes a whole mini-batch inference task. There will be no logical communication among cores, but the use of cache locality is inferior to the former scheme. We will implement two parallel models at the same time to quantify communication overhead and cache competition costs, and obtain the best experimental results.

6.4   Parallel Scheme for Full Connected Model

The full-connection layer of AlexNet model contains a significantly smaller number of inference stages than the RNNs-LSTM model. Having fewer inference stages means that the synchronization overhead is small. Moreover, the main operation of the full connected model is GEMM, the cache-friendly features of the fine-grained parallel scheme will bring more benefits.

6.5   Parallel Scheme for Confusion Tree Model

The biggest difference between the confusion tree model and the previous two models is that there are branches, which has a great impact on the parallel strategy selection. The branches in the model add dynamicity to the data processing. That is, the data flowing to the same branch can be processed at the same time, but it may flow to different branches in the next phase. If a separate processing method is applied to the

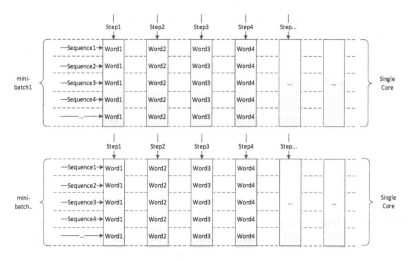

Fig. 3. The coarse-grained data parallelism for RNNs-LSTM model.

feature vectors of each image, only the vector-matrix multiplying operation can be used, which is difficult to exert the full performance of the NEON SIMD components.

A better parallel strategy is to convert the vector-matrix multiplication into matrix-matrix multiplication by handling all data that flows to the same branch. The drawback of this approach is that combining the feature vectors into a matrix will lead to memory copy overhead. We call this parallel strategy as Reorganization Parallelism.

We can ignore the existence of branches. Since all calculations in the confusion tree are looking for the right branch, the data itself will not be changed. Then we can perform calculation on all the nodes for each feature vector, and finally judge the flow of feature vector in the confusion tree. This makes the entire inference process break down into a GEMM operation and the final result statistics. It avoids memory copy overhead. Although the amount of computation is increased, it is still about 1/18 compared to the full connected model. We call this parallel strategy as Intact Parallelism.

6.6   Optimization Technology

The optimization techniques we apply on the ARM platform are: 1. ACL cache optimization to reduce the cache miss rate. 2. Make full use of NEON components to exponentially increase operating speeds.

Cache Optimization for ACL

The ACL library is open source software. After deeply researching the source code, we find out that it performs optimization on the cache. Based on the hypothesis of the hardware cache size, the amount of data for each iteration is controlled to reuse the cached data and thus reduce the cache miss rate. If the hypothesis is too small, the cache is not fully utilized. If the assumption is too large, the cache is insufficient to cache all data, which directly leads to an increase of the cache miss rate.

However, the ACL library only have a default cache size assumption, which is inconsistent with the hardware platform we studied. So we added an interface to the ACL to set the cache size, setting the L1 data cache and L2 cache size to match with ThunderX. After that, the performance of the multi-core GEMM was improved by 114%, as shown in Table 2.

Table 2. Comparison of GEMM performance after ACL cache optimization (time unit: s).

	Original ACL	Modified ACL
Single core	56	56
48 cores	3	1.4

NEON Related Optimization

The optimization of GEMM has been completed, and other operations can rely on NEON components to further increase the speed of calculation, such as the internal state update phase of the RNNs-LSTM model, which contains a large number of sigmoid and tanh operations. We implemented two versions: scalar calculations and vector calculations. After SIMD optimization, performance increased by 139%, as shown in Table 3.

Table 3. NEON-optimized operations of RNNs-LSTM model (unit of time: us).

	Scalar version	SIMD version	Performance increase
Time	20800	8700	139%

7   Experimental Results

7.1   Results of RNNs-LSTM Model

On the ThunderX platform, the coarse-grained parallel scheme achieves higher parallel efficiency in both single-chip and dual-chip cases. The coarse-grained parallel model has 81.9% parallel efficiency under 48 cores and 75.7% under 96 cores (Table 4).

Table 4. ThunderX platform RNNs-LSTM model experiment results (time unit: ms).

	Single core	48 cores fine-grained	48 cores coarse-grained	96 cores fine-grained	96 cores coarse-grained
Time	149093	4528	3788	3900	2050
Speedup ratio	1.0	32.9	39.3	38.23	72.7

The i7 7700 K has 4 physical cores. After the Hyper-Threading feature is enabled, it has 8 logical cores. Experimental results show that parallel performance of 8 threads is better than 4 threads. The final time of the i7 7700 K platform is 3637 ms.

For this model, communication overhead of the fine-grained parallel seriously affects the speedup ratio. The parallel efficiency of the coarse-grained parallel model is ideal. Although i7 7700 K only has 4 physical cores, with the support of hyper-threading, high clock speed, and multi-level cache, it shows strong computing ability. The final experimental results show that single-chip ThunderX is equivalent to the i7 7700 K, and the dual-chip performance is 1.77 times that of the latter.

7.2   Results of Full Connected Model

We divided the last two full-connection layers of AlexNet into multiple phases. The first fully connected layer consists of GEMM, Bias addition, and Relu activation. The second fully connected layer consists of GEMM and Bias addition. The final result is shown in Table 5.

Table 5. ThunderX platform full-connect model experiment results (time unit: ms).

Thread count	FC1 GEMM	FC1 Bias	Relu	FC2 GEMM	FC2 Bias	Total time	Speedup ratio
1	56053	243	205	1556	4	58061	1
4	14339	95	87	392	1	14914	3.89
8	7344	59	54	202	0.6	7659	7.58
16	3732	28	27	110	0.4	3897	14.90
48	1448	17	18	46	0.4	1529	37.97

For the i7 7700 k platform, we found that the overall efficiency is higher when incorporating Bias addition operations into GEMM. The final result is shown in Table 6.

Table 6. i7 7700 K platform full-connect model experiment results (time unit: ms).

FC1 GEMM	Relu	FC2 GEMM	Total time
974	274	113	1361

Experimental results show that the parallel efficiency of ARM is 79.1%, and the single chip performance is 0.89 times that of i7 7700 K.

7.3   Results of Confusion Tree Model

Table 7 shows the experimental results of the Reorganization Parallelism for the ThunderX platform. It can be seen that the matrix reorganization time accounts for 42% to 54% of the whole processing time, which seriously reduces the overall computing performance.

Table 7. Reorganization parallelism results for ThunderX platform (Time Unit in ms).

Thread count	Time of GEMM	Time of Bias addition	Time of matrix reorganization	Total time	Speedup ratio
1	2375	1.9	1748	4129	1
4	607	0.4	365	1042	3.96
8	319	0.2	199	524	7.88
16	166	0.1	143	323	12.78
48	86	0.1	152	283	14.59

Then Intact Parallelism is applied, whose results are shown in Table 8. It can be seen that although the GEMM time has increased, it is no longer necessary to perform matrix reorganization. Compared to Reorganization Parallelism, performance increased by 136%.

Table 8. Intact parallelism results for ThunderX platform (Time Unit in ms).

Thread count	Time of GEMM	Time of result statistics	Total time	Speedup ratio
1	3415	11	3426	1
4	914	11	925	3.70
8	450	5	455	7.53
16	247	8	255	13.44
48	115	5	120	28.55

Table 9. Intact Parallelism results for i7 7700 K platform (Time Unit in ms).

Time of GEMM	Time of result statistics	Total time
129	38	167

In the i7 7700 K platform, Intact Parallelism is adopted directly. The experimental results are shown in Table 9.

Experimental results of the confusion tree show that the performance of single-chip ARM is 1.39 times that of i7 7700 K.

7.4 Energy Efficiency Comparison

A power socket is used to measure the whole machine power consumption of these two platforms. The power of ThunderX is 270 w under no-load and 297 w under single-chip full-load and 316 w under dual-chip full-load. The power of i7 7700 K is 38 w under no-load and 112 w under full-load. In terms of energy efficiency, the former is inferior to the latter.

The Cavium ThunderX does pretty badly here, and one of the reason is that power management either did not work, or at least did not work very well. Besides, the cooling system of server is much stronger than desktop, which causing more power consumption.

8   Conclusion

Combining the experimental data of three deep learning models, performance of single-chip ThunderX is comparable to mainstream high performance x86 platforms. Performance of dual-chip can reach 1.77 times that of the latter. This suggests that high-performance ARM chips can be deployed in the cloud to complete large-scale deep learning inference tasks.

References

1. Krizhevsky, A., Sutskever, I., Hinton, G.E.: Imagenet classification with deep convolutional neural networks. In: Advances in Neural Information Processing Systems, pp. 1097–1105 (2012)
2. Szegedy, C., Liu, W., Jia, Y., et al.: Going deeper with convolutions. In: CVPR (2015)
3. Lee, V.W., Kim, C., Chhugani, J., et al.: Debunking the 100X GPU vs. CPU myth: an evaluation of throughput computing on CPU and GPU. ACM SIGARCH Comput. Arch. News **38**(3), 451–460 (2010)
4. Ni, H.: Ncnn: a high-performance neural network inference framework optimized for the mobile platform (2017). https://github.com/Tencent/ncnn
5. Rungsuptaweekoon, K., Visoottiviseth, V., Takano, R.: Evaluating the power efficiency of deep learning inference on embedded GPU systems. In: 2nd International Conference on Information Technology (INCIT) 2017, pp. 1–5. IEEE (2017)
6. Zhu, K., Jiang, J.: DSP based acceleration for long short-term memory model based word prediction application. In: 2017 10th International Conference on Intelligent Computation Technology and Automation (ICICTA), pp. 93–99. IEEE (2017)
7. Zaremba, W., Sutskever, I., Vinyals, O.: Recurrent neural network regularization. arXiv preprint arXiv:1409.2329 (2014)
8. Jin, R., Dou, Y., Wang, Y., et al.: Confusion graph: detecting confusion communities in large scale image classification. In: Proceedings of the 26th International Joint Conference on Artificial Intelligence, pp. 1980–1986. AAAI Press (2017)

Research on Acceleration Method of Speech Recognition Training

Liang Bai, Jingfei Jiang[⊠], and Yong Dou

National University of Defense Technology, Changsha, China
{bailiang12,yongdou}@nudt.edu.cn,
jingfeijiang@126.com

Abstract. Recurrent Neural Network (RNN) is now widely used in speech recognition. Experiments show that it has significant advantages over traditional methods, but complex computation limits its application, especially in real-time application scenarios. Recurrent neural network is heavily dependent on the pre- and post-state in calculation process, and there is much overlap information, so overlapping information can be reduced to accelerate training. This paper construct a training acceleration structure, which reduces the computation cost and accelerates training speed by discarding the dependence of pre- and post-state of RNN. Then correcting the recognition results errors with text corrector. We verify the proposed method on the TIMIT and Librispeech datasets, which prove that this approach achieves about 3 times speedup with little relative accuracy reduction.

Keywords: Speech recognition · Accelerating training · Text correction

1 Introduction

Communicating with machines and letting machines understand what you say is something that people have long dreamed of. Speech recognition has been a hot topic in recent decades. Before 2000, many core technologies related to speech recognition emerged, such as Gaussian Mixture Mode (GMM), Hidden Markov model (HMM), Mel-Frequency Cepstral Coefficients (MFCC) and its difference, n-gram language Models, discriminative training and various adaptive technologies. These technologies have greatly promoted the development of automatic speech recognition (ASR) and related fields. In recent years, various types of Recurrent Neural Networks (RNNs), such as Long Short Term Memory (LSTM) [1, 2] and Gated Recurrent Unit (GRU) [3–5] began to be used in automatic speech recognition and achieved better performance relative to feed-forward neural networks. The main reason is that recurrent neural network can remember information which cover the long history of the speech sequence, while the feed-forward neural network uses context information within a limited-length window.

However, the connection of recurrent neural networks is more complex than that of feed-forward neural networks, which leads to a greater amount of calculations and results in slower training. This limits the application of recurrent neural networks in tasks that require high real-time performance. In order to pursue better results, many of

C. Li and J. Wu (Eds.): ACA 2018, CCIS 908, pp. 42–50, 2018.
https://doi.org/10.1007/978-981-13-2423-9_4

state-of-the-art methods in deep learning focus on increasing model capacity and calculations, which often involve in using a large number of hyperparameters and setting larger and deeper networks. We know that growing number of network layers and greater hyperparameters significantly increase training time. For example, training a state-of-the-art translation or speech recognition system has to take several days [6–8]. Computation has become the bottleneck of deep learning development. One way to solve this problem is to reduce the size of neural networks, such as reducing the number of network layers or the number of nodes in each layer. However, using a smaller neural network will obviously affect the accuracy of system, so it is necessary to keep the network at a reasonable size [9, 10]. Another way is to modify the structure of the neural network, reducing the amount of computation by modifying neural network. In order to achieve the purpose of accelerating the calculation, this paper uses the SRU network structure to eliminate the dependencies of pre- and post-state, speed up the training speed of the neural network, and correct the recognition results to improve the accuracy. Finally, we finish the entire speech recognition acceleration system.

2 Methods

2.1 Acoustic Characteristics

The response of the human ear to the sound spectrum is non-linear. Processing audio in a way similar to human ear can improve the performance of speech recognition. For speech recognition tasks, common acoustic features are Fbank, MFCC. The extraction of MFCC features is obtained by conducting discrete cosine transform on the basis of Fbank features. MFCC has better discrimination and is more suitable for characterizing sounds. The Fbank feature is close to the human ear response characteristics, its features are highly correlated (adjacent filter groups have overlap), and neural networks can use these correlations to express better feature better.

2.2 Network Model

2.2.1 RNN Network

RNN's ability to learn and transform data over a long period of time makes them stand out from other machine learning methods, and has a significant effect on speech recognition [11]. However, ordinary RNNs are prone to gradients disappearing or exploding during training. Therefore, RNN variants such as LSTM, GRU, etc. are proposed. These variants control the flow of information through gates, which can alleviate the problem of gradient disappearance and explosion. And they have better performance on a variety of tasks. But it also increases the computation complexity while improving RNN performance. RNN needs to use the output state h_{t-1} of the previous state in the current state calculation. For instance, the forget vector would be calculated by $f_t = \sigma\left(w_f x_t + r_f h_{t-1} + b_f\right)$. The inclusion of $r_f h_{t-1}$ breaks independence and parallelism: each dimension of the hidden state depends on other, so the calculation of h_t must wait until the entire h_{t-1} is available. Lei Tao et al. [12] optimized the main calculation part of each time step so that it doesn't need to wait the calculation of the previous state. Thus it can be easily parallelized. The relevant equations for the SRU are given below.

$$\tilde{x}_t = wx_t \tag{1}$$

$$f_t = \sigma\left(w_f x_t + b_f\right) \tag{2}$$

$$r_t = \sigma(w_r x_t + b_r) \tag{3}$$

$$x'_t = w_h x_t \tag{4}$$

$$c_t = f_t \odot c_{t-1} + (1 - f_t) \odot \tilde{x}_t \tag{5}$$

$$h_t = r_t \odot g(c_t) + (1 - r_t) \odot x'_t \tag{6}$$

According to the above equations, the structure is described as follow:

From Fig. 1 and Eq. (6), we can see that its advantages are reducing the dependency of pre- and post-state compared with the traditional RNN networks,and each state can be calculated simultaneously.

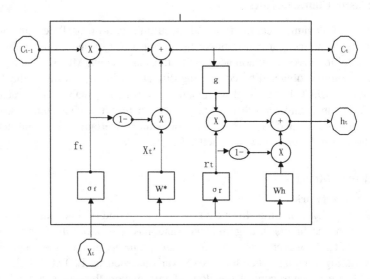

Fig. 1. A block diagram of the SRU structure and flow chart.

2.2.2   Speech Recognition Architecture

It is difficult to give a label to a frame of speech recognition data, but it is easy to identify the corresponding pronunciation labels on tens of frames data. In the traditional speech recognition model, we must always strictly align text with the speech before we train the speech model. This has two disadvantages. First, strict alignment requires manpower and time. Second, the label predicted by model is only the result of local classification and cannot give the result of the entire sequence after strict alignment. It needs to process label to get desired result. The dimensions of the RNN output are obviously inconsistent with really matched label dimensions, so there must be some redundant information in output of the RNN. For example, we actually predicted same category in the two adjacent moments. Alex et al. proposed Connectionist Temporal Classification (CTC) [13] method, which effectively solves this problem. Its core idea is to add blank in output text of the RNN and use a dynamic programming algorithm to solve. We build a complete identification acceleration network module based on this.

The network structure diagram is shown in Fig. 2. It contains three main modules. A convolutional neural network for feature extraction, a recurrent neural network for speech recognition, and a text correction module. The input feature sequence [xt-m, ..., xt, ..., xt + n]is Fbank feature from speech preprocessing. Because CNN's convolutions have translation invariance in the frequency domain, CNN can be used to extract better feature using correlation. After the features are acquired, then we input them into RNN network. Because the calculation of post state depends on output of previous state, traditional RNN networks destroy parallelism and independence of calculations. We see that Eq. (1) $\sim$ (3) are calculated with removing the dependence on h_{t-1} and they are only relevant to input x_t of this state. So each state can be calculated simultaneously in parallel, which significantly increasing the computational strength and GPU utilization. Equation (4) adds a highway connection for retaining information. Equations (5) and (6) are calculated in terms of elements, so it is easy to calculate. Now, the bottleneck of calculation is the four matrix multiplications of Eqs. (1) $\sim$ (4). The solution is to combine the four matrix multiplications into a matrix multiplication calculation, and then compile all the element operations into one kernel function, which makes calculation just call one function each time so that each layer has less computational complexity and higher processing speed, and reducing the training computation overhead.

2.3   Text Correction

Error correction in speech recognition is an important task in speech understanding.

Due to the limited accuracy of speech recognition, the results of speech recognition often have errors, which will hinder the follow-up work of speech understanding and increase the difficulty of speech understanding. The error correction can correct some error results, which help improve the accuracy of speech recognition. According to the Bayesian theory, we can get correct word closest to the recognized word. Assume that recognized word is w_e and we need to find correct word w_c in all candidate words so that the conditional probability for w_e is the greatest, that is, Obtaining $argmaxP(w_c|w_e)$ is equivalent to the Bayesian theory above:

$$argmax_c\ P(w_e|w_c)P(w_c)/P(w_e)$$

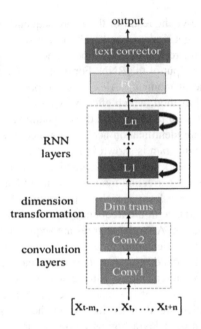

Fig. 2. Speech recognition acceleration network structure.

Since the result of the recognition can be any word, for any w_c, the probability $P(w_e)$ of appearing w_e is the same, so we ignore it in the above formula and write as follow:

$$argmax_c \, P(w_e|w_c)P(w_c)$$

We obtain $P(w_c)$ by training the probability model with a huge corpus, and then we need to determine the correct spelling of the word set. We use the editdistance to measure. According to the study, about 80–95% of misspellings are within 1 editdistance. Based on statistical observations of the recognition results, we decided to use words with an edit distance of two. We can consider a limited number of cases where the editing distance is allowed to be 3. For example, we can only insert a vowel next to the vowel, or replace the vowel, etc. These basically cover All situations. Error correction through text can effectively solve the errors in the recognition result.

3   Experiments

We use Pytorch to implement entire acceleration network and test it on the timit and Librispeech datasets. Timit dataset is an acoustic-phonetic continuous speech corpora constructed by Texas Instruments (TI), the Massachusetts Institute of Technology (MIT), and the Stanford Research Institute (SRI). The speech sampling frequency is 16 kHz, which contains of 6300 sentences. All the sentences are manually segmented at phone level. Timit is relatively small, which can complete whole experiment in a short time, and it is sufficient to show the performance of the system. Librispeech is a large-scale speech dataset that can be downloaded for free. LibriSpeech has its own training, validation and testing models. We use about 100 h of audio files to train and validate our model and original 16 kHz sampling rate. We use a 20 ms sliding window and a 10 ms step size to calculate power spectrum features. We report the letter error rate (LER) on the Librispeech and phoneme error rate (PER) on the timit.

3.1   Result

Table 1 reports the performance of different RNN networks with Fbank feature under the timit and Librispeech datasets. Timit has phoneme-level annotations and we report PER. Librispeech does not have phoneme-level annotation, so we use LER indicators to measure. We found that the accuracy of the SRU dropped by about 2-3%. The reason is that SRU eliminate the state dependency pre- and post-state of RNN. The post state don't remember useful information retained by the previous state. Although the highway connection was used to retain the information. However, the input information is retained instead of the information remembered by previous state, and useful information will loss. Therefore, the accuracy will decrease. After adding text corrector, we found that the accuracy rate increased by about 4%.

Table 1. Recognition accuracy of different RNN networks.

RNN structure	PER on timit (%)	LER on Librispeech (%)
LSTM	17.2	16.9
GRU	17.9	17.4
SRU	23.5	23.7
SRU (with text-corrector)	19.3	19.9

Figure 3(a) reports PER for different RNN networks under the timit dataset. We found that the convergence speed of SRU network is mostly the same as that of GRU. And the initial convergence speed of LSTM is slow. The possible cause is that network parameters are not initialized properly, which resulting in poor network performance. 3 (b) reports LER under Librispeech. We found that our accelerating network's performance is well, and recognition accuracy rate does not have much impact.

Table 2 compares the training time of different RNN networks under timit and Librispeech. We find that our accelerating network training speed is about 3 times faster than LSTM and GRU.

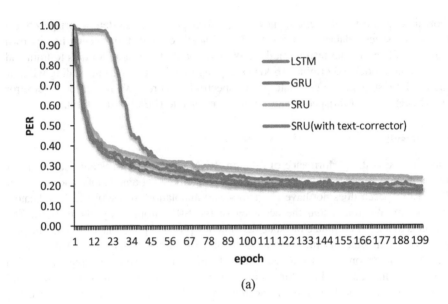

(a)

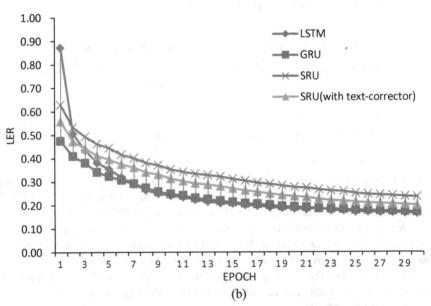

(b)

Fig. 3. (a) Recognition accuracies (y-axis) of LSTM, GRU, SRU and SRU(with text corrector) on Timit dataset and (b) is on Librispeech dataset. X-axis: training epoch (in seconds). They are performed on PyTorch and a desktop machine with a single Nvidia GeForce GTX 1050Ti GPU, Intel Core i7-7700 K Processor.

Table 2. Comparison of average training time between different RNN structures.

RNN structure	Average training time/epoch(s)	
	Timit	Librispeech
LSTM	169.009321854	3041.68586606
GRU	150.906946650	2879.05314912
SRU	55.318402860	1086.64929295

4 Conclusion and Future Work

We introduce a simple end-to-end speech recognition network that combines a convolutional neural network, a recurrent neural network, and a text error corrector. We aim to improve the training speed of the neural network on the premise of ensuring its accuracy. We test timit and Librispeech datasets respectively and find that training speed of the neural network has been greatly improved with little accuracy loss. Since text corrector uses basic corpus, correction doesn't have good performance. In the future, we can build a corpus with more statistical information, such as the probability of identifying errors based on the statistical similarity of phonemes, and improve the recognition accuracy.

References

1. Goodfellow, I., Bengio, Y., Courville, A.: Deep Learning. MIT Press, Cambridge (2016). Book in Preparation
2. Hochreiter, S., Schmidhuber, J.: Long short-term memory. Neural Comput. **9**(8), 1735–1780 (1997)
3. Yao, K., Cohn, T., Vylomova, K., Duh, K., Dyer, C.: Depth-gated recurrent neural networks. arXiv preprint arXiv: 1508.03790v2 (2015)
4. Jozefowicz, R., Zaremba, W., Sutskever, I.: An empirical exploration of recurrent network architectures. In: International Conference, pp. 2342–2350 (2015)
5. Chung, J., Gulcehre, C., Bengio, Y.: Empirical evaluation of gated recurrent neural networks on sequence modeling. arXiv preprint arXiv: 1412.35556 (2014)
6. Vaswani, A., Shazeer, N., Parmar, N., Polosukhin, I.: Attention is all you need. arXiv preprint arXiv:1706.03762 (2017)
7. Wu, Y., Schuster, M., Chen, Z.: Google's neural machine translation system: bridging the gap between human and machine translation. arXiv preprint arXiv:1609.08144 (2016)
8. Sak, H., Senior, A., Françoise, F.: Long short-term memory recurrent neural network architectures for large scale acoustic modeling. In: INTERSPEECH (2014)
9. Frank, S., Li, G., Yu, D.: Conversational speech transcription using context-dependent deep neural networks. In: 12th Annual Conference of the International Speech Communication Association (Interspeech 2011), pp. 437–440, Florence, Italy (2011)
10. Michael, S., Yu, D., Wang, Y.: An investigation of deep neural networks for noise robust speech recognition. In: 2013 IEEE International Conference on Acoustics, Speech and Signal Processing (ICASSP), Vancouver, Canada, pp. 7398–7402 (2013)
11. Graves, A., Jaitly, N.: Towards end-to-end speech recognition with recurrent neural networks. In: International Conference on Machine Learning, pp. 1764–1772 (2014)

12. Lei, T., Zhang, Y., Artzi, Y.: Training RNNs as fast as CNNs. arXiv preprint arXiv:1709. 02755 (2017)
13. Graves, A., Gomez, F.: Connectionist temporal classification: labelling unsegmented sequence data with recurrent neural networks. In: International Conference on Machine Learning, pp. 369–376 (2016)
14. Zhang, Y., He, P.L., Xiang, W., Li, M.: A discriminative reranking approach to spelling correction. J. Softw. **19**(3), 557–564 (2008)
15. Toutanova, K., Moore, R.C.: Pronunciation modeling for improved spelling correction. In: Proceedings of Annual Meeting of the Association for Computational Linguistics, pp. 144–151 (2002)

New Design Explorations

A Post-link Prefetching Based on Event Sampling

Hongmei Wei[1], Fei Wang[2(✉)], and Zhongsheng Li[2]

[1] School of Electronic Information and Electrical Engineering, Shanghai Jiao
Tong University, Shanghai 200030, China
wei-hong-mei@163.com
[2] Jiangnan Institute of Computing Technology, Wuxi 214083, China
weedyblues@126.com, lizhsh@yeah.net

Abstract. Data prefetching is an effective approach to improve performance by
hiding long memory latency. Existing profiling feedback optimizations can do
well in pointer-based linked data structure prefetching. However, these optimizations, which instrument and optimize source code during compiling or post
link, usually incur tremendous overhead at profiling stage. Furthermore, it is a
mission impossible for these methods to do optimization without source code.
This work designs and implements an Event Sampling based Prefetching
Optimizer, which is a post-link prefetching based on hardware performance
counters event sampling. Evaluation on SW26010 processor shows that with the
proposed prefetching approach, 9 out of 29 programs of SPEC2006 can be
speeded up by about 4.3% on average with only less than 10% sampling
overhead on average.

Keywords: Data prefetching · Stride profiling · Sampling
Post-link optimization

1 Introduction

As predicted by the Moore's Law, last 30 years have seen a trend that the performance
gap between processor and memory becomes bigger and bigger, which severely
throttles the performance of current computer systems. Although multi-level caches
have been introduced by processor vendors to alleviate this impact, Memory wall
remains the major bottleneck that hinders the improvement of processor performance.
Particularly, previous research shows that close to 60% of processor stalls are caused
by the long memory access latency [1].

It is well known that data prefetching technology is a very effective way to hide
memory access latency. Based on static compiling analysis, Mowry [2] and Bernstein
[3] explored data prefetching techniques, which mainly aim at the regular array access
in the loop. However, there is a large number of chained data structures (irregular
access) based on pointers, such as linked lists, trees, graphs, etc., in the current
applications. It is difficult to prefetch these pointer accesses on the heap using static
compiling methods. Fortunately, Chilimbi [4] and Wu [5] found that although the
pointer addresses are hard to analyze during compiling, these accesses often show

© Springer Nature Singapore Pte Ltd. 2018
C. Li and J. Wu (Eds.): ACA 2018, CCIS 908, pp. 53–65, 2018.
https://doi.org/10.1007/978-981-13-2423-9_5

regular stride-access patterns at runtime. With the inspiring patterns of the irregular memory accesses, prefetching instructions can be opportunistically inserted to improve the performance of applications.

Existing profiling feedback optimizations profile dynamic memory access with the help of instrumented functions, which are instrumented during compiling [5, 16] or post-link [6]. These approaches introduce significant overhead when programs are profiled, and depend on the source code of programs. In the SW26010-based compiler, both classic static prefetching and profiling feedback prefetching have been deployed.

In this paper a new lightweight event sampling based profiling feedback prefetching, Event Sampling based Prefetching Optimizer (ESPO), is proposed to overcome the above disadvantages and implemented in the post-link part of the SW26010 system. The proposed prefetching can optimize the target program without the present of source code, and the profiling overhead can be throttled within an ideal level by adjusting the sampling frequency.

Specifically, thanks to the hardware performance counters and the configurable sampling frequency mechanism, the sampling overhead of ESPO could be trivial. Experimental results show that the overhead of this sampling is less than 10% of the execution time of the target program on average. Besides that, compared with the existing methods based on instrumentation, ESPO is non-intrusive and does not modify the executable file. And benefit from the trivial sampling overhead, ESPO is able to follow the original execution behavior during profiling progress.

The input of ESPO is the linked executable program. No source code of the target program is needed. Recompiling progress is also unnecessary. In another word, ESPO is independent of compilers and does not affect the previous optimization.

The main contributions of this work are listed as follows:

1. An Event Sampling based Prefetching Optimizer is proposed. Instead of inserting additional source code to do profiling, ESPO greatly reduces the sampling overhead with the help of the hardware performance counters and the configurable sampling frequency mechanism.
2. Based on the profiling information and the variance analysis on samples, ESPO inserts prefetch instructions in programs according to the stride-access patterns at runtime. As this technique works during post-link, it can optimize the legacy target programs without the present of source code.
3. ESPO has been deployed on the Chinese home-made processor, SW26010, which is the key part of the Sunway Taihu Light supercomputer system [19]. Evaluation shows that on SW26010 processor, the proposed prefetching improves the performance of 9 out of 29 SPEC2006 benchmarks by about 4.3% on average, which is due to the 4% reduction of the processor stall periods caused by memory access of ROB head.

The rest of the paper is organized as follows. Section 2 introduces the related work. Section 3 describes the composition and design of the event sampling based profiling feedback prefetching in details. Section 4 presents our evaluation method and performance metrics. Experimental results and analysis are proposed in Sect. 5. Section 6 concludes the paper.

2 Related Work

Long memory access latency is one of the major obstacles to improve performance of modern microprocessors. For example, one access miss on last level cache usually incurs up to hundreds cycles delay. As instructions are sequential submitted in most existing processors, the long-delay access miss can block a large number of associated instructions, and in some case, the processor may be stalled. The prefetching technology is proposed to load data from memory to cache in advance to reduce cache miss rate, and to hide the access latency caused by prefetching itself with appropriate scheduling strategy. Prefetching has attracted the attention of experts in the fields of compilers, Java virtual machines, static post-link optimization and dynamic optimization systems.

Mowry [2] proposed a classic data prefetching method based on compiling analysis. The method inserts prefetch instructions by local analysis and performs the scheduling of loop unrolling. It works well when prefetching data with regular access pattern. Pointer-based linked data structures usually depend on memory allocation interference, such as malloc, to get the heap space. Due to the existence of the same stride between the addresses of the adjacent nodes, in another word, the difference between the memory access addresses in two consecutive iterations of the same instruction is constant, profiling can be used to effectively find these strides and then data can be prefetched. Inspired by this fact, Wu [5] and Qi [16] implemented the profiling feedback compiling optimization based on instrumentation in compiler.

Data prefetching is also an important method on improving the performance of Java applications. Because Java is an object-oriented language, frequently memory access to the heap data introduces the major overhead of an application. To improve the performance of Java application, people profiles memory access to heap data on Java virtual machine, and dynamically prefetch heap data. Zou et al. [7, 18] proposed an adaptive algorithm based on instrumental analysis, which could effectively reduce the overhead caused by over-instrumentation. Tabatabai et al. [8] profiled cache miss information by sampling hardware performance events, depended on garbage collector to maintain the stride of target addresses, and designated JIT compiler to insert prefetch instructions.

Regarding the work of data prefetching in the static post-link optimization system, C.K. Luk et al. implemented post-link prefetching optimization at the target code level in some tools respectively, such as pixie, spike of Alpha [6], and Ispike of Itanium [11]. The idea is to obtain the stride of memory access with the help of profiling, and then prefetching instructions are inserted directly into the target code. However, the instrumentation-based profiling approach introduces significant overhead.

The work on data prefetching in dynamic optimization system is also abundant. Chilimbi et al. implemented a dynamic data prefetching method for hot data stream in Vulcan, including 3 iterative phases: burst sample profiling, analysis optimization, and persistent execution [4]. Lu et al. proposed a runtime data prefetching strategy in the ADORE dynamic optimizer. Firstly, the strategy sampled programs by the performance monitoring components of the target machine. Then, it identified the loops with a large amount of cache miss, and analyzed the data access pattern of these loops to prefetch data [9]. Beyler et al. designed a performance-driven data prefetching scheme in their homemade dynamic software optimization system. By associating each load instruction with a finite state automaton which is periodically monitored, the prefetching instructions can be inserted or dropped in a cycle according to requirements.

Recent years, with the rapid development of multi-core processors, people become more and more interesting on data prefetching on multi-core systems. For example, Kamruzzaman et al. [13] forked another threads to prefetch data needed by the main thread. The main thread is able to switch among cores in the order of prefetching paths, and to get the data that has already been prefetched. On the latest mainstream processor platforms, Mehta et al. [14] investigated the impact of different micro-architectures on prefetching strategy. Inspired by the research on Intel Sandy Bridge processor and Intel Xeon Phi processor, they proposed an architecture-related, multi-level and hardware/software coordinated prefetching method, which prefeches data to different memory/cache levels to improve processor performance.

Zhang et al. [15] proposed an event driven self-repairing dynamic prefetching method on the Trident platform. This method adopted a hardware/software collaboration strategy and proposed some requirements for the hardware architecture, such as adding Watch table and Delinquent load table. These additional hardware components are used to monitor the execution behavior of programs and to obtain the hot run paths of the program, including Delinquent reference information on these paths. One of the advantages of this method is that it can dynamically correct the prefetching distance. Although this adaptive approach inevitably adds some hardware overhead, it still delivers 12% performance improvement over those ways fixed prefetching distances. Compared with the method proposed by Zhang et al., ESPO is a software solution and there is no need to deploy additional hardware components.

Above all, it can be seen that profiling feedback data prefetching is usually implemented with the help of instrumentation. Instrumentation based prefetching can profile any data access information and improve prefetching accuracy. However, one of the disadvantages is the tremendous overhead of profiling in the first run. For example, the experimental results on the SPEC2000 benchmark suite show that the profiling overhead of the post-link optimizer Spike proposed by Luk et al. [6] is 15–30 times longer than the execution time, whereas the profiling overhead of the linked data structure prefetching technology based on profiling feedback compilation proposed by Wang [17] is up to 40 times longer than the execution time. Besides that, the profiling feedback compiling optimization needs to instrument and recompile the target program, which means the program cannot be optimized when its source code is unavailable.

3   Post-link Prefetching Based on Event Sampling

In previous works, we have implemented a profiling feedback compilation for prefetching linked data structure [16, 17]. However, as described in Sect. 2, there are two drawbacks in these existing methods: huge profiling overhead and source code requirements. In this wok, an Event Sampling based Prefetching Optimizer, a.k.a. ESPO, is proposed.

When ESPO works, there are three stages, which are Event based Sampling (Sect. 3.1), Sample Analysis (Sect. 3.2) and Inserting Prefetch Instructions (Sect. 3.3). Event based Sampling samples programs based on hardware performance counters, instead of inserting additional source code. Sample Analysis analyzes the output of the first stage to find those hot-spot instructions in which the cache accesses are missed frequently, and to obtain the memory access patterns of these instructions. At the last stage, an optimizer SWLTO is proposed to insert prefetch instructions.

The following sections describe how each component of ESPO is designed, and how ESPO works in details.

3.1   Event Based Sampling

SW26010 processor provides supports of multiple performance counters, such as DCache access miss, SCache access miss, D-TLB access miss, and so on. When performance counters overflow, interrupts are enabled to handle these exceptions.

As shown in Fig. 1, in the sampling phase, the target program is loaded by *Sample. run*. Then, the program runs in an operating system environment which supports interrupts when performance counters overflow. *Sample.run* selects events and initializes performance counters with APIs provided by *PerfMon*. Particularly, in this work, ESPO samples the access miss of last level cache. When the number of access miss exceeds the threshold, a.k.a. the performance counter overflows, an interrupt occurs and *Sample.run* profiles the samples of the target program.

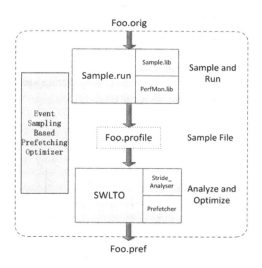

Fig. 1. Component and flowchart of ESPO

Figure 2 shows the sample format. One sample contains three key elements, including R.pc, R.addr and R.latency. R.pc represents the PC value of the memory access instruction R in the access miss event. R.addr indicates the memory address of the PC. R.latency is the delay between two samples for access miss event, and the delay can be represented as the number of cycles.

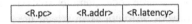

Fig. 2. Sample format

A dynamically configurable *Threshold* is supported in *Sample.run*. When the number of cache miss exceeds *Threshold*, the target program is sampled. The setting of *Threshold* impacts the quality of sampling significantly. The setting principles are shown as follows.

1. In order to effectively throttle the sampling overhead, the value of *Threshold* cannot be too small, that is, the samples should not be too dense.
2. To ensure the accuracy of sampling, the value of *Threshold* cannot be too large; otherwise it will make the samples too sparse to meet the sampling requirement.

Empirically, *Threshold* is set as 800 misses according to the complex environment in this work.

Evaluation shows that it is not necessary to perform a completely uniform sampling when the program is running. In view of this, the sampling periods can be classified as two alternative phases, sleep phase and active phase. The two phases work in an alternative way.

As shown in Fig. 3, in the sleep phase, an interrupt is triggered when there are *Cs* access miss events. According to the aforementioned principles, the value of *Cs* usually needs to be large enough to effectively reduce the sampling overhead. In the active phase, an interrupt is triggered when there are *Ca* access miss events. This method, which uses different sampling parameters respectively during sleep and active phases, can throttle the sampling cost within an ideal level.

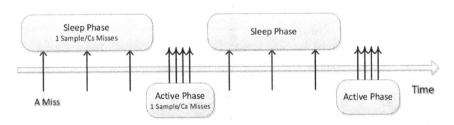

Fig. 3. Two-phase sampling

3.2 Sample Analysis

After the first sampling, *Foo.profile* is generated. At this step, *Foo.profile* is analyzed to find those hot-spot instructions in which the cache accesses are missed frequently, and to obtain the memory access patterns of these instructions. A sample analysis module called *Stride_Analyser* is implemented in the post-link optimizer SWLTO on the SW26010 processor. The analysis mode works in two analysis phases: determining the candidate prefetch instructions and calculating the address stride of the cache miss access.

Determining the Candidate Prefetch Instructions

In the case that a memory access instruction (a.k.a. *Delinquent References* [12]) is frequently executed, and the cache accesses of the instruction are often missed, prefetching usually brings satisfying performance benefits. Sorting the samples according to the frequency of PC, it can be seen that the higher the frequency is, the more frequently the cache miss occurs. If a memory reference with a high frequency shows some access patterns, prefetching will be performed. In this work, *Delinquent References* whose number of miss exceeds a certain threshold are taken as examples to analysis memory access patterns.

Firstly, as shown in Fig. 4, for each *Delinquent Reference*, the collection of the stride address of access miss, represented as set *S*, is formed.

Fig. 4. Compute miss address stride

Empirically, if a memory reference within a loop accesses data in a regular pattern and it has not been prefetched or optimized, then the address stride of miss accesses will show some regular pattern. However, practically, memory access behavior is complicated, and system noise makes it harder to find any regular pattern. In order to obtain accurate information from the sample set *S*, an algorithm is introduced to calculate the mean and variance of the sample set *S*, which are respectively denoted by M (*S*) and D (*S*) as shown in formula (1) and (2).

$$M(S) = \frac{S_1 + S_2 + ... + S_n}{n} \tag{1}$$

$$D(S)^2 = \frac{(S_1 - M)^2 + (S_2 - M)^2 + ... + (S_n - M)^2}{n} \tag{2}$$

The smaller D(*S*) is, the smaller fluctuation of the stride is. In another word, the memory access pattern will be more stable if D(*S*) is smaller. The candidate prefetch instructions are determined by excluding the *Delinquent References* with larger variances.

Calculating the Address Stride of Miss Access

For each candidate prefetch instruction selected in the above stage, the addresses of cache access misses are analyzed in the sample. Existing studies show that there is a regular stride pattern when accessing dynamically allocated heap data in the irregular code segment. In this section, the method proposed by Luk et al. [11] is used to calculate the stride of miss addresses. Firstly, the difference between adjacent addresses is calculated. Then, the greatest common divisor among the differences is obtained. Because sampling only profiles cache miss address, rather than the actual access address, it is impossible to determine the stride between the actual memory access addresses in two consecutive iterations by sampling. Fortunately, if there is a regular stride pattern, in most cases, these strides will equal to the greatest common divisor GCD of the address difference or equal to the multiple of GCD.

As shown in Fig. 5, the four consecutive samplings result in three different address differences. The greatest common divisor of these differences is *stride*. Therefore, it can be determined that the size of the access *stride* for this candidate prefetch instruction is *stride* bytes or a multiple of stride bytes.

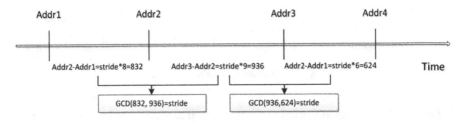

Fig. 5. Using *GCD* to discover strides from miss addresses

3.3 Inserting Prefetch Instructions

The prefetch module (*Prefetcher* shown in Fig. 1) is implemented in the optimizer SWLTO. It receives candidate prefetch PC instructions and the hot-spot stride information from the sample analyzer *Stride_Analyser*. Then, prefetch distance is calculated and prefetch instructions are emitted and inserted in the source code.

$$\text{Prefetch address } = (\text{base\_addr} + \text{distance} * \text{stride}) \qquad (3)$$

As shown in above formula, *base_addr* indicates the base address of the memory access instruction, *stride* is the stride value provided by *Stride_Analyser*, and distance represents the prefetch distance which means the number of iterations prefetched in advance.

Inspired by the previous work [2], we set the general formula of calculating prefetch distance as:

$$\text{Distance} = L/W \qquad (4)$$

Where *L* is the overhead of cache miss represented by the number of clock cycles, *W* represents the execution time of a loop iteration, which can be considered as the estimated time between two consecutive executions of one instruction. Likewise, the unit of *W* is clock cycle.

The following heuristic algorithm is used to calculate *W*:

```
If (Stride > Cache_Line_Size) {
W=M(R.Latency)/sample_ratio;
} else {
    W=M(R.Latency)/(sample_ratio*Stride);
}
```

M(*R.Latency*) can be obtained according to the following calculation steps:

1. First, take the collection of *R.latency* from the sample in active phase.
2. Then, the noise reduction process is carried out to eliminate outliers in the set.
3. Finally, the average of *R.latency*, that is, M(*R.Latency*) can be calculated.

Based on the prefetch distance, prefetch instructions are emitted and inserted before the corresponding memory access instructions.

4 Experiment Settings

SPEC2006 benchmark suite is used to evaluate the performance of single core on a Chinese home-made processor, SW26010. The processor is a 64-bit RISC processor with 32 K L1 data cache, and supports software prefetching instructions. The compiler used in this evaluation is SWCC (SHENWEI Compiler Collection, SWCC), which is designed for SW26010 processor.

Firstly, cache miss rate is recorded. The access number of L1 data cache is represented as *Reference_counts*, and *Miss_counts* means the number of cache miss. So, the cache miss rate can be represented as Formula (5) shows. As shown in Fig. 6, compiled with –O3, 9 out of 29 SPEC2006 programs show at least 10% cache miss rate, and the highest cache miss rate is 38.44%, which is reported in 429.mcf case.

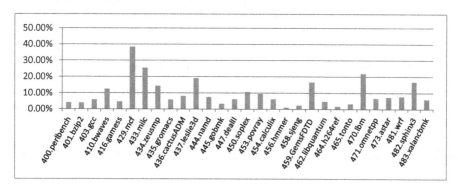

Fig. 6. SPEC2006 DCache miss ratio

$$miss\_ratio = \frac{Miss\_counts}{Reference\_counts} \qquad (5)$$

According to previous works [1], 60% of pipeline halts are caused by LIMCOS (Loads Incurring Majority Commit Stalls). However, no work evaluates the influence of LIMCOS on SPEC2006 benchmark suite so far. With the help of the performance counters of SW26010, the periods of executing uncompleted memory instructions in ROB are recorded. In Fig. 7, the evaluation result confirms that the programs in SPEC2006 have the similar memory access feature as that caused by LIMCOS, and it also shows that due to the memory stall, the memory accessing performance of the program with higher DCache miss rate is lower than the others.

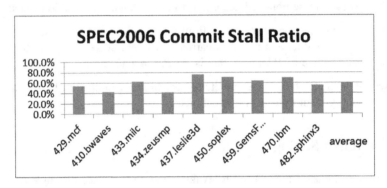

Fig. 7. SPEC2006 Commit Stall ratio caused by uncompleted load in ROB

In Fig. 7, it can be seen that the average proportion of stall ratio caused by uncompleted load in ROB is 59.9%. In the following analysis, this average proportion is considered as the metric to evaluate the degree of performance improvement.

5   Evaluation

An event-sampling based prefetching optimization, ESPO, which is a part of post linker, is implemented as described in Sect. 3. The following subsections show the results of the optimized prefetching and the overhead of the first sampling.

5.1   Performance Evaluation of the Optimized Prefetching

ESPO inserts optimized object codes into the –O3 compiled program, which has significant commit stall ratio. As shown in Fig. 8, compared the performance of original programs, the performance of optimized programs is improved 4.3% on average.

To illustrate the effect of prefetch optimization, the average commit stall ratio of these 9 benchmarks caused by uncompleted load in ROB with prefetching is compared

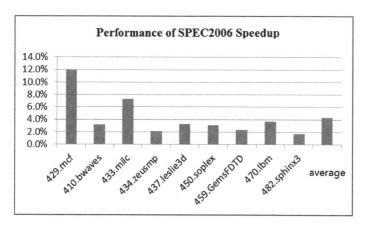

Fig. 8. Performance of SPEC2006 Speedup

with that of the original ones. As shown in Fig. 9, the prefetch optimization reduces the average commit stall ratio from 59.9% to 55.9%.

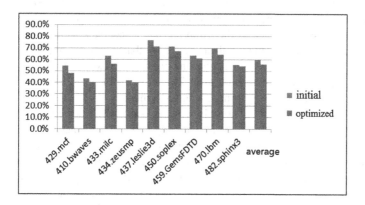

Fig. 9. Reduction of Commit Stall ratio

5.2 The Evaluation of the Sampling Overhead

In ESPO, sampling consists of sleep phase and active phase. The two phases are carried out alternately, which makes the sampling overhead lower than 10% of the program execution. In Fig. 10, the average sampling overhead of the 9 cases is about 9.5%.

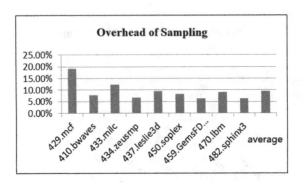

Fig. 10. Overhead of sampling

6 Conclusion

The work applies the hardware performance counter based sampling in the post-link optimizing system, and optimizes the prefetching of linked data structure. According to our best knowledge, this is the first work to apply software prefetching optimization with the help of performance counters on Chinese home-made SW26010 processor. The prefetching method proposed in this work optimizes legacy code without the existence of source code. Due to the sampling based feedback technology, and noise elimination powered by variance analysis on the feedback data, the overhead of the first sampling is dramatically reduced comparing with the existing software prefetching technologies on the single core processor. The experiment on SPEC2006 shows that this work brings impressive performance improvement.

This work prefetches instructions in a static way, which means the prefetching distance is constant. Therefore, in the periodically variable stride access case, programs cannot be speeded up as expected. In the future work, an auxiliary-thread based prefetching will be deployed on multi-core SW26010 processor to support more flexible optimization. The other way to enhance the current work is to try some another optimizations, such as reducing DTLB miss, branch optimization, and so on, to squeeze more and more performance benefits with the help of the hardware performance counters of SW26010 processors.

Acknowledgement. The authors would like to thank all colleagues who provide inspiring suggestions and helpful supports. The material was based upon work supported by National Science and Technology Major Project (NSTMP) (Grant No. 2017ZX01028-101). Any opinions, findings, and conclusions or recommendations expressed in this material are those of the authors and do not necessarily reflected the views of NSTMP.

References

1. Manikantan, R.: Performance oriented prefetching enhancements using commit stalls. J. Instr. Level Parallelism **13**, 1–28 (2011)
2. Mowry, T.C.: Tolerating latency through software-controlled data prefetching, Ph.D. thesis. Stanford University, March 1994
3. Bernstein, D., Cohen, D., Freund, A., Maydan, D.E.: Compiler techniques for data prefetching on the PowerPC. In: Proceedings of the 1995 International Conference on Parallel Architectures and Compilation Techniques, June 1995
4. Chilimbi, T.M., Hirzel, M.: Dynamic hot data stream prefetching for general-purposes programs. In: Proceedings of the 2002 ACM SIGPLAN Conference on Programming Language Design and Implementation, June 2002
5. Wu, Y., Serrano, M., Krishnaiyer, R., Li, W., Fang, J.: Value-profile guided stride prefetching for irregular code. In: Horspool, R.Nigel (ed.) CC 2002. LNCS, vol. 2304, pp. 307–324. Springer, Heidelberg (2002). https://doi.org/10.1007/3-540-45937-5_22
6. Luk, C.-K., Muth, R., Patil, H., Lowney, P.G., Cohn, R., Weiss, R.: Profile-guided post-link stride prefetching. In: Proceedings of 2002 International Conference on Supercomputing, pp. 167–178, June 2002
7. Zou, Q., Li, X.F., Zhang, L.B.: Runtime engine for dynamic profile guided stride prefetching. J. Comput. Sci. Technol. **23**(4), 633–643 (2008)
8. Adl-Tabatabai, A.R., Hudson, R.L., Serrano, M.J., Subramoney, S.: Prefetch injection based on hardware monitoring and objects metadata. In: Proceedings of the ACM SIGPLAN 2004 Conference on Programming Language Design and Implementation (2004)
9. Lu, J., Chen, H., Yew, P.-C., Hsu, w.-C.: Design and implementation of a lightweight dynamic optimization system. J. Instr. Level Parallelism **6**, 1–24 (2004)
10. Beyler, J.C., Clavss, P.: Performance driven data cache prefetching in a dynamic software optimization system. In: Proceedings of the 36th International Conference on Supercomputing, pp. 202–209 (2007)
11. Luk, C.-K., Muth, R., Patil, H., Cohn, R., Lowney, G.: Ispike: a post-link optimizer for the intel itanium architecture. In: Proceedings of the International Symposium on Code Generation and Optimization (2004)
12. Collins, J., et al.: Speculative precomputation: long-range prefetching of delinquent loads. In: Proceedings of the International Symposium on Computer Architecture, July 2001
13. Kamruzzaman, Md., Swanson, S., Tullsen, D.M.: Inter-core prefetching for multicore processors using migrating helper threads. In: ASPLOS 2011, 5–11 March 2011
14. Mehta, S., Fang, Z., Zhai, A., Yew, P.-C.: Multi-stage coordinated prefetching for present-day processors. In: ICS 2014, pp. 73–82 (2014)
15. Weifeng, Z., Calder, B., Tullsen, D.M.: A self-repairing prefetcher in an event-driven dynamic optimization framework. In: Proceedings of the International Symposium on Code Generation and Optimization, pp. 50–64. IEEE Computer Society (2006)
16. Qi, F.B., Wang, F., Li, Z.S.: Feedback directed prefetching optimization for linked data structure. J. Softw. **20**(Suppl.), 34 − 39 2009. (in Chinese)
17. Wang, F., Wei, H.M., Qi, F.B.: Prefetching optimization based on profiling compilation. High Perform. Comput. Technol. **186** (2007). (in Chinese)
18. Zou, Q., Wu, M., Hu, W.W., Zhang, L.B.: An instrument-analysis framework for adaptive prefetch optimization in JVM. J. Softw. **19**(7), 1581–1589 (2008). (in Chinese)
19. Fu, H., Liao, J., Yang, J., et al.: The sunway taihulight supercomputer: system and applications. Sci. China Inf. Sci. **59**(7) (2016)

The Design of Reconfigurable Instruction Set Processor Based on ARM Architecture

Jinyong Yin[1], Zhenpeng Xu[1(✉)], Xinmo Fang[1], and Xihao Zhou[2]

[1] Jiangsu Automation Research Institute,
Lianyungang 222061, People's Republic of China
xuzhenpeng@jari.cn
[2] Nanjing University of Post and Telecommunication,
Nanjing 210094, People's Republic of China

Abstract. In embedded system, performance and flexibility are two of the most important concerns. To solve the problem of the flexibility of GPP (General Purpose Processor) and the performance of ASIC (Application Specific Integrated Circuit), an ARM based RISP(Reconfigurable Instruction Set Processor) architecture is proposed in this paper which adopts partial reconfiguration and coprocessor mechanism to realize the dynamic online reconfiguration of the processor instruction. A prototype system of the architecture is implemented on Xilinx KC705 FPGA and reconfigurable resource management software is designed and developed for the prototype system. DES encryption/decryption algorithms are tested with prototype, and the test results show that the architecture has the both flexibility of GPP and the performance of ASIC, so it has a wide application prospect.

Keywords: RISP · Partial reconfiguration · Coprocessor
Reconfigurable resource management

1 Introduction

With the rapid development of digital technology and network technology, embedded system has been widely used in various aspects such as scientific research, engineering design, military technology, people's daily life and so on. The rapid development of embedded technology makes it become an important branch of computer and electronic technology. So the design and application of embedded processor is the core of embedded technology, which is paid more and more attention.

The traditional computing mode can be divided into two kinds: GPP mode and ASIC mode [1]. In the GPP mode, program code can be compiled into a sequence of processor instructions, and the processor completes the computing task by executing these instructions. This model is flexible enough that when the function of the computing system is changed, the user only needs to modify the program without altering the underlying hardware environment. However, the GPP performance is low because of serialization instruction. In the ASIC mode, specialized hardware integrated circuit is designed for a particular application to accomplish computing tasks. This mode can provide the optimized data path for the operation of the computing task through the

© Springer Nature Singapore Pte Ltd. 2018
C. Li and J. Wu (Eds.): ACA 2018, CCIS 908, pp. 66–78, 2018.
https://doi.org/10.1007/978-981-13-2423-9_6

special hardware design, and support the parallel execution of multiple operations, so can achieve the best computational performance. However, the development period of ASIC is very long, the development cost is too high, and the function is single, which can't adapt to the various computing requirements.

In order to balance the performance and flexibility, reconfigurable computing technology based on programmable logic devices was developed and applied to the design of the RISP [2]. RISP can make use of the hardware programmability of reconfigurable logic devices to customize the optimal instruction for different application features, so as to meet the different application requirements of embedded field effectively [3–6].

The research of RISP is a hotspot in the field of processor design and processor architecture, and is regarded as the next generation processor architecture. Beeck studied a configurable RISP model in paper [7] and in the model, different constraint requirements of RISP can be realized by designing spatial search method. The Xirisc studied in paper [8] is a loading/storage architecture in which all data accesses are carried out through shared register files and use only very simple two extension instructions. The RT-RISP in paper [9] regards each instruction as an independent module which can be dynamically swapping in and out according to the requirement of the current running application through the support of partial reconfigurable technology. Thus the processing performance is improved. The Molen in paper [1] is different from that of most RISP, it does not need to modify the processor core to support reconfigurable logic, nor does it use the method of hardware and software collaborative design. In paper [10], the hardware reconfiguration process is used as part of the processor design, and the computational task applied to the reconfigurable logic is regarded as atomic operation, which is realized by the form of reconfigurable microcode.

2 RISP Architecture

The general RISP hardware architecture is shown in Fig. 1. Logically, a RISP chip is divided into two parts: the basic processor core and the reconfigurable logic. The architecture of the basic processor core is similar to that of the traditional processor. It belongs to the fixed part of the RISP and is used to execute the processor instruction which provides the software programmability for the system application. At the same time, the processor core as the main control part, manages the entire RISP application processing process. The design of the internal architecture of the reconfigurable logic relies on the specific application performed on the RISP. The design of RISP hardware architecture includes two aspects: the design of reconfigurable logic itself and the interface design of reconfigurable logic and other components in the RISP.

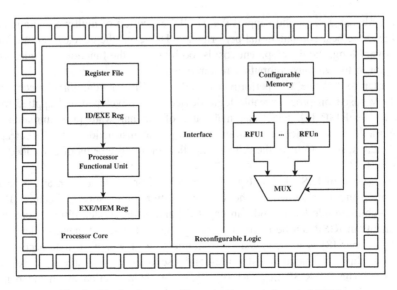

Fig. 1. The hardware architecture diagram of general RISP

3 Hardware Design of RISP

Based on the existing ARM processor core and coprocessor interface, a RISP prototype is constructed on the Xilinx Kintex 7 FPGA Development Board with partial reconfigurable technology. The prototype mainly includes the basic processor, the reconfigurable instruction interface and the online configuration circuit and so on.

The block diagram of RISP is shown in Fig. 2, which mainly includes processor core, AHB bus, clock and reset circuit, DDR3 memory controller, SD card controller, ESRAM, ICAP reconfigurable module, APB Bus, DMA controller, timer, serial controller, interrupt controller and other modules.

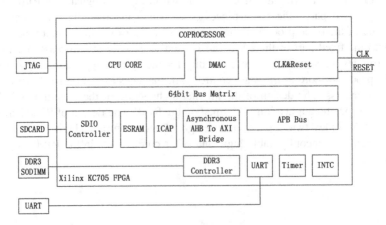

Fig. 2. The block diagram of RISP

3.1 Basic Processor Design

The basic processor uses the 32-bit ARM11 soft core, which has the instruction, the data and the system bus respectively, and they all use the AHB bus interface. The processor may read, write and configure each peripheral through AHB MATRIX. The design of basic processor mainly includes the design of clock reset circuit, AHB Bus and DDR3 controller.

The block diagram of clock tree is shown in Fig. 3.The input source of the clock is the 200 MHz double along clock (sys_clk_p/sys_clk_n) which is brought by FPGA Development Board. The 200 MHz memory controller clock (CLK_PLL), 800 MHz double along DDR clock (clk_mem_pll/clk_rd_base) and 200 MHz reference Clock (clk_ref) are output by the FPGA internal PLL. Further from the CLK_PLL clock to get the bus clock (BUS_CLK) and the processor core clock. Since the DDR3 has a minimum frequency requirement, it works with the processor and peripherals at different frequencies, using asynchronous design between the processor and the memory to ensure normal data transmission.

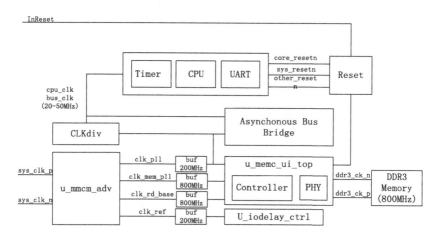

Fig. 3. The clock tree

The reset source of the system comes from the InReset key of the Development Board, The DDR controller is initialized after power up, and the reset signal is sent to the Reset module when the DDR initialization is completed, then the processor and other peripherals come into work state.

The main system bus is AHB BUS MATRIX, and the architecture is shown in Fig. 4. Four master ports and six slave ports are configured. The master ports are used to connect the ARM core and the DMA controller, and the slave ports are used to connect the APB bus and other peripherals.

The address of each device in the system is shown in Table 1 and the address in the table is a physical address and can be accessed directly (Table 2).

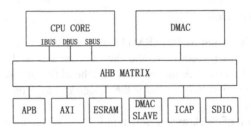

Fig. 4. Matrix bus structure

Table 1. Address assignment.

Device	Start address	End address
DDR	0x50000000	0x8fffffff
Interrupt controller	0x40000000	0x40000fff
Timer	0x40003000	0x40003fff
UART	0x40004000	0x40004fff
DMAC	0x11000000	0x11ffffff
SDIO	0x10000000	0x10ffffff
ESRAM	0x00000000	0x0003ffff
HWICAP	0x4000c000	0x4000cfff

Table 2. Interrupt vector ID.

Device	Vector ID
UART	56
Timer	62
DMAC	61
SDIO	60

3.2 Reconfigurable Instruction Interface

The reconfigurable instruction unit communicates and collaborates with the master processor in a coprocessor manner. It mainly includes reconfigurable instruction interface module and reconfigurable instruction function module. The reconfigurable instruction function module is user-defined instruction function module, which can be dynamically loaded by partial reconfiguration circuit.

The logical relationship of the main processor core, the reconfigurable instruction interface and the reconfigurable instruction functional unit is shown in Fig. 5. The reconfigurable instruction interface adopts arm coprocessor mechanism, which is the interface between the reconfigurable instruction unit and the processor core to do the instruction decoding and data transmission. The main function of reconfigurable instruction interface is to parse the coprocessor interface signal from the processor core and complete the interaction with the processor core data.

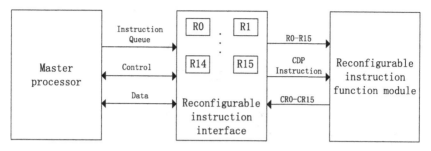

Fig. 5. The logic relation of processor core, reconfigurable instruction interface and reconfigurable instruction function unit

The reconfigurable instruction interface module, shown in Fig. 6, includes data FIFO, instruction FIFO, decoding logic, execution logic and so on. Data and instruction FIFO are used to storage data and instruction queue respectively. The instruction queue is checked whether it is a coprocessor instruction when is pushed. If it is a coprocessor instruction, it is pushed, otherwise, it is discarded. The decoding logic decodes the instructions in FIFO, and transmits the operation code to the execution module.

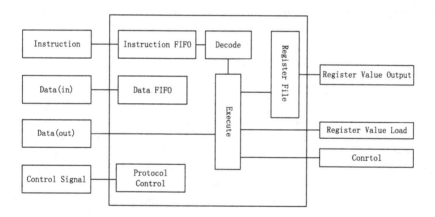

Fig. 6. Reconfigurable instruction interface module

3.3 Design of Reconfigurable Instruction Configuration Circuit

Reconfigurable instruction dynamic configuration module is shown in Fig. 7. In this system, the reconfigurable function is realized by the Hwicap module using partial reconfigure technology of Xilinx Company. The Hwicap module can be regarded as the internal configuration interface of the APB protocol in FPGA, which mainly includes the sequence conversion of the APB protocol to the ICAPE2 interface. The ICAPE2 provides a 32-bit configuration interface in which the data are converted by bit and sent to the ICAP module.

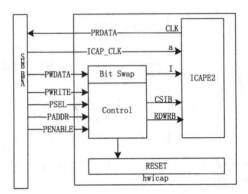

Fig. 7. The block diagram of reconfigurable instruction configuration module

4 Design of Management Software

There are significant differences between the architecture of reconfigurable processors and the common processor architecture, which require the improvement of existing management software, mainly operating systems. Based on existing Linux operating systems, reconfigurable resource management, hybrid task scheduling and reconfigurable instruction loading are the redesigned.

4.1 Reconfigurable Resource Management

The task scheduler and reconfigurable resource manager introduce the reconfigurable instruction preconfigured mechanism and the caching mechanism respectively in order to reduce the reconfiguration overhead and reduce the influence of reconfigurable instruction configuration time on system performance. The reconfigurable instruction preconfigured algorithm predicts the reconfigurable instruction to be executed and configures it to the free slot on the FPGA in advance. When a reconfigurable instruction completes, the reconfigurable resource manager does not physically delete the reconfigurable instruction immediately, but simply marks the slot of the reconfigurable resource it occupies, indicating that it is available. If the reconfigurable instruction is called again, simply cancel the tag without reconfiguring it.

The reconfigurable resource can only be in four states, and the state transition is shown in Fig. 8:

- Blank state: Resource not yet occupied.
- Configuration state: The resource is configuring now.
- Run state: The reconfigurable instruction is executing.
- Cache state: The reconfigurable instruction is configured and is not executed or it is complete and is not deleted.

The management of reconfigurable resources requires the management of the state transitions of these reconfigurable slots. When the reconfigurable instruction are called,

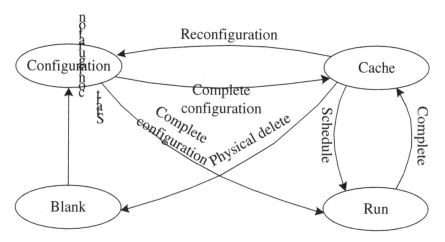

Fig. 8. Reconfigurable resource state

they are allocated the most appropriate resources, refer to as the state of these resources and the resource requirements of the hardware functions.

4.2 Reconfigurable Instructions Loading

The reconfigurable instruction configuration is the process of loading a reconfigurable instruction configuration file onto the FPGA while the system is still running. Because of the configuration file size, a configuration algorithm is designed whose flow graph is shown in Fig. 9. The configuration algorithm first opens the configuration file, reads the configuration file to a cache buffer, determines the location of the configuration data and the number of data by analyzing the configuration file structure, and determines the number of loops and remaining quantities based on the amount of configuration data. It opens the configuration device and writes the start configuration sequence to the configuration device. The start configuration sequence is a special string which indicates that the following data is configuration data. The following process is to write configuration data to the configuration RAM in the FPGA, and finally to write end configuration sequence. The end configuration sequence is also a special string which indicates that the configuration data is terminated and the configuration device and configuration file is closed.

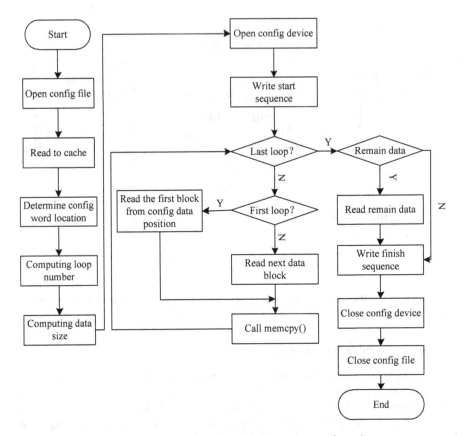

Fig. 9. The flow of reconfigurable instruction configuration

5 Experiments

5.1 Demo Environment

Demo environment includes hardware platform and system software.

Hardware platform is a Xilinx KC705 FPGA Development Board, as shown in Fig. 10. When the system is powered, the RISP is configured from the ROM. The system software includes the developed operating system, configuration program, and demo software which support instruction reconfiguration.

Construct the environment: (1) Connect the KC705 FPGA Development Board to the development workstation via serial port or USB download line and download the image to the FPGA. (2) Insert the system boot SD card into the SD card slot of the FPGA Development Board. (3) Reset the FPGA Development Board. (4) The information as shown in Fig. 11 is displayed on the development workstation serial terminal which indicates that the system software started successfully.

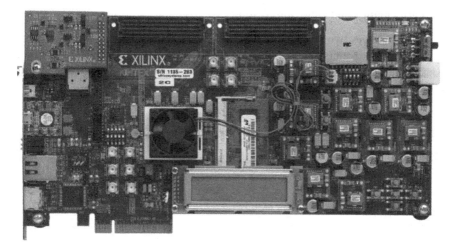

Fig. 10. Hardware platform

```
Serial-COM8
Start reading file image to 0x50008000
Initialize MMC controller!
Read From MMC!
..............................................................................................
...............................................................
Read 10836832 Bytes OK !
Setup linux parameters at 0x50000100
linux command line is: "console=ttyS user_debug=1"
## Starting application at 0x50008000 ...
inux version 2.6.32 (njdnzy@njdnzy-virtual-machine) (gcc version 4.3.2 (Sourcery G++ Lite 2008q3-72) ) #135
 Wed Oct 28 20:48:35 CST 2015
CPU: ARMv6-compatible processor [4117b365] revision 5 (ARMv6TEJ), cr=00c5387f
CPU: VIPT nonaliasing data cache, VIPT nonaliasing instruction cache
Machine: SEUEVB
ATAG_INITRD is deprecated; please update your bootloader.
Memory policy: ECC disabled, Data cache writeback
Built 1 zonelists in Zone order, mobility grouping on.  Total pages: 130048
Kernel command line: console=ttyS user_debug=1
PID hash table entries: 2048 (order: 1, 8192 bytes)
Dentry cache hash table entries: 65536 (order: 6, 262144 bytes)
Inode-cache hash table entries: 32768 (order: 5, 131072 bytes)
Memory: 512MB = 512MB total
Memory: 508544KB available (1780K code, 479K data, 8676K init, 0K highmem)
SLUB: Genslabs=11, HWalign=32, Order=0-3, MinObjects=0, CPUs=1, Nodes=1
Hierarchical RCU implementation.
NR_IRQS:64
=-101
Console: colour dummy device 80x30
Mount-cache hash table entries: 512
CPU: Testing write buffer coherency: ok
NET: Registered protocol family 16
bio: create slab <bio-0> at 0
Switching to clocksource jiffies
io scheduler noop registered (default)
Serial: 8250/16550 driver, 1 ports, IRQ sharing disabled
serial8250.0: ttyS0 at MMIO 0x40004000 (irq = 56) is a 16550A
console [ttyS0] enabled
mice: PS/2 mouse device common for all mice
SEP0611 MMC Driver v1.2
Freeing init memory: 8676K
mmc0: host does not support reading read-only switch. assuming write-enable.
mmc0: new high speed SDHC card at address 1234
blk_queue_max_segment_size: set to minimum 4096
mmcblk0: mmc0:1234 SA04G 3.68 GiB
 mmcblk0:
 p1
/ #
```

Fig. 11. System software start information

5.2   Performance and Function Testing

The system reserves two reconfigurable slots that can be configured with two recon-figurable instruction units. You can use the./reconfigure xx.bit command to configure the instruction unit and query the reconfigurable slot state by the./configure -i com-mand, as shown in Figs. 12 and 13.

```
Serial-COM8

/mnt #
/mnt #
/mnt # ./reconfigure config_2_U_AHB1_SUB_U_ARM1136_cptop_u_des_p7_des_p7_second_
partial.bit
reconfigure_ok!
reset_ok!
time: 2.300000s
Resize:
SLICE:720
DSP48:16
RAMB18:8
RAMB36:4
/mnt #
```

Fig. 12. Reconfigurable instruction configuration process

```
Serial-COM8

/mnt # ./reconfigure -i
report
p7:adder
p8:adder
/mnt #
```

Fig. 13. Reconfigurable zone state

With DES encryption/decryption algorithms as the typical application, the RISP prototype, the main processor in this system and Intel Core I5 processor which is the current mainstream processor are tested. 64bit data is encrypted and decrypted 50000 times by RISP, ARM processor and Intel Core I5 processor respectively, and the execution time is 0.38s, 1850s and 2.5s. RISP is faster 4868 times and 6.5 times than ARM processor and Core I5 processor. The test results are shown in Table 3.

Table 3. Accelerated ratio table.

Item	RISP	ARM processor	Core I5 processor
Execution time	0.38s	1850s	2.5s
RISP speed UP	1	4868	6.5

The test process is divided into three parts:

1. Use the LDC instruction to load the data in memory into the coprocessor registers.
2. Use the CDP instruction to send the operation code, where 0 represents encryption operation and 1 represents the decryption operation.
3. After a fixed-period delay, the result in the coprocessor registers is read into memory and the encryption/decryption operation is completed.

6 Conclusion

Based on the ARM processor and Linux operating system, a reconfigurable computing system is developed in this paper and it is verified in FPGA hardware platform. Because a soft ARM core is used in the system, the processor frequency is only 100 MHz, so the overall performance is not high. To further improve the system computing performance, the future work will be the hardcore or development of SOC chip.

References

1. Pivezhandi, M., Eshghi, M.: ASIP design for two dimensional cordic based DFT and DCT algorithms. In: 2016 6th International Conference on Computer and Knowledge Engineering (ICCKE), pp. 269–273. Mashhad (2016)
2. Kavitha, V., Ramakrishanan, K.V.: Study of multigrain MRPSoC. In: 2016 3rd International Conference on Computing for Sustainable Global Development (INDIACom), pp. 2534–2538. IEEE, New Delhi (2016)
3. Hussain, W., Chen, X., Ascheid, G., Nurmi, J.: A reconfigurable application-specific instruction-set processor for fast fourier transform processing. In: 2013 IEEE 24th International Conference on Application-Specific Systems, Architectures and Processors, pp. 339–345. Washington, DC (2013)
4. Zhang, B., Mei, K., Zheng, N.: Reconfigurable processor for binary image processing. IEEE Trans. Circuits Syst. for Video Technol. 23(5), 823–831 (2013)
5. Bauer, L., Grudnitsky, A., Damschen, M., Kerekare, S.R., Henkel, J.: Floating point acceleration for stream processing applications in dynamically reconfigurable processors. In: 2015 13th IEEE Symposium on Embedded Systems for Real-time Multimedia (ESTIMedia), pp. 1–2. Amsterdam (2015)
6. Chen, X., Minwegen, A., Hussain, S.B., Chattopadhyay, A., Ascheid, G., Leupers, R.: Flexible, efficient multimode MIMO detection by using reconfigurable ASIP. IEEE Trans. Very Large Scale Integr. VLSI Syst. 23(10), 2173–2186 (2015)
7. de Beeck, P.O., Barat, F., Jayapala, M., Lauwereins, R.: CRISP: a template for reconfigurable instruction set processors. In: Brebner, G., Woods, R. (eds.) FPL 2001. LNCS, vol. 2147, pp. 296–305. Springer, Heidelberg (2001). https://doi.org/10.1007/3-540-44687-7_31

8. Barat, F., Jayapala, M., Vander Aa, T., Lauwereins, R., Deconinck, G., Corporaal, H.: Low power coarse-grained reconfigurable instruction set processor. In: Y. K. Cheung, P., Constantinides, G.A. (eds.) FPL 2003. LNCS, vol. 2778, pp. 230–239. Springer, Heidelberg (2003). https://doi.org/10.1007/978-3-540-45234-8_23

9. Barat, F., Jayapala, M., de Beeck, P.O., Deconinck, G.: Reconfigurable instruction set processors: an implementation platform for interactive multimedia applications. In: Conference Record of Thirty-Fifth Asilomar Conference on Signals, Systems and Computers, vol. 1, pp. 481–485. Pacific Grove, CA, USA (2001)

10. Barat, F., Lauwereins, R., Deconinck, G.: Reconfigurable instruction set processors from a hardware/software perspective. IEEE Trans. Softw. Eng. 28(9), 847–862 (2002)

Stateful Forward-Edge CFI Enforcement with Intel MPX

Jun Zhang[1,2,4(✉)], Rui Hou[3], Wei Song[3], Zhiyuan Zhan[3,4], Boyan Zhao[2,4], Mingyu Chen[2,4], and Dan Meng[3]

[1] Hubei University of Arts and Science, Xiangyang, China
[2] State Key Laboratory of Computer Architecture, ICT, CAS, Beijing, China
{zhangjun02,zhaoboyan,cmy}@ict.ac.cn
[3] Institute of Information Engineering, CAS, Beijing, China
{hourui,songwei,zhanzhiyuan,mengdan}@iie.ac.cn
[4] University of Chinese Academy of Sciences, Beijing, China

Abstract. This paper presents a stateful forward-edge CFI mechanism based on a novel use of the Intel Memory Protection Extensions (MPX) technology. To enforce stateful CFI policies, we protect against malicious modification of pointers on the dereference pathes of indirect jumps or function calls by saving these pointers into shadow memory. Intel MPX, which stores pointer's bounds into shadow memory, offers the capability of managing the copy for these indirect dereferenced pointers. There are two challenges in applying MPX to forward-edge CFI enforcement. First, as MPX is designed to protect against every pointers that may incurs memory errors, MPX incurs unacceptable runtime overhead. Second, the MPX defense has holes when maintaining interoperability with legacy code. We address these challenges by only protecting the pointers on the dereference pathes of indirect function calls and jumps, and making a further check on the loaded pointer value. We have implemented our mechanism on the LLVM compiler and evaluated it on a commodity Intel Skylake machine with MPX support. Evaluation results show that our mechanism is effective in enforcing forward-edge CFI, while incurring acceptable performance overhead.

Keywords: Code-reuse attacks · Control-flow integrity
Shadow stack · Shadow memory · MPX · LLVM

1 Introduction

Code-reuse attacks (CRA) [1–5] exploit memory corruption vulnerabilities to redirect the intended control-flow of applications to unintended but valid code sequences. As these attacks require no code injection, they can defeat the defenses in mainstream computing devices [6], such as StackGuard [7], DEP [8] and ASLR [9]. Control-flow integrity (CFI) [10,11] is considered as a general and promising method to prevent code-reuse attacks. CFI restricts the control transfers along the edges of the programs's predefined Control-Flow Graph (CFG),

© Springer Nature Singapore Pte Ltd. 2018
C. Li and J. Wu (Eds.): ACA 2018, CCIS 908, pp. 79–94, 2018.
https://doi.org/10.1007/978-981-13-2423-9_7

which is constructed by statically analyzing either the source code or the binary of a given program. The control-transfers caused by indirect jumps and function calls are corresponding to forward-edge control-flow. Backward-edge control-flow represents transfers caused by `ret` instructions.

Shadow stack is considered as an essential mechanism to enforce stateful backward-edge CFI policies [10,12]. It keeps track of the function calls by storing the return addresses in a dedicated protected memory region. Most of the forward-edge CFI enforcement technologies follow a two-phase process. During the analysis phase, all the legal targets of each indirect control-transfer are abstracted from the protected program's CFG. The enforcement phase ensures that each control-transfer target belongs to the legal targets set. However, even the context/field sensitive static analysis still over-approximates the targets of indirect control-transfers [12–14]. Recent researches show that just the intended legal targets are enough for a successful attack [12–14]. The weakness of current forward-edge CFI mechanisms is that conformance to the CFG is a stateless policy [12]. To conduct control-flow hijack attacks without violate the CFG restriction, attackers still have to maliciously overwrite (craft) the targets of indirect control-transfers [12,14]. Malicious modifications can be detected by verifying the runtime control-flow information [15,16].

In this paper, we introduce a novel stateful forward-edge CFI mechanism. Unlike the traditional CFI mechanisms, which check only whether each control-transfer target belongs to legal targets set [10,11,17–20], our mechanism checks the integrity of all pointers on the dereference pathes of indirect jumps and function calls. We call the pointers on the dereference pathes of indirect jumps and function calls as control-transfer related pointers. To support this method, we protect against malicious modification on control-transfer related pointers by saving these pointers in a disjoint shadow memory[1] when they are stored into memory. When a control-transfer related pointer is dereferenced, its copy is loaded from the shadow memory and compared with itself. If the integrity check passes, no action is taken; if the check fails, the program control transfers to the error handler. This process is similar to shadow stack. To facility the copy management and integrity checking, we implement our mechanism based on a new, commercially available hardware feature called Memory Protection Extensions (MPX) on Intel CPUs [24–26]. In MPX, every pointer stored in memory has its associated bounds stored in a shadow memory, which is only accessible via `bndstx` and `bndldx` instructions.

In particular, we make the following contributions:

- We design a stateful forward-edge CFI mechanism, which protects the control-transfer related pointers by saving a copy into shadow memory. When a control-transfer related pointer is dereferenced, the copy is used to check its integrity similar to the shadow stack.
- Intel MPX is reused to manage the copies of control-transfer related pointers. We implement our mechanism on the LLVM compiler framework. A compiler

---

[1] Shadow memory is a memory space paralleling the normal data space [21–23].

pass is developed to identify the control-transfer related pointers and instrument integrity check codes for them. A runtime library is developed to facility the MPX hardware initialization and check code instrumentation.
- We evaluated our mechanism on a commodity Intel Skylake machine with MPX support. The evaluation shows that our mechanism is effective in enforcing stateful forward-edge CFI, while incurring acceptable performance overhead.

2   Intel MPX

Intel MPX [24–26] was first announced in 2013 and became available as part of the Skylake microarchitecture in late 2015. The purpose of Intel MPX is to protect against memory errors and attacks. When Intel MPX protection is applied, bounds-check codes are inserted to detect out-of-bounds accesses. To realize this goal, each level of the hardware-software stacks is modified to support the Intel MPX technology.

At the hardware level, new MPX instructions [25] are introduced to facilitate the bounds operations. These instructions are summarized in Table 1. To reduce the register pressure on the general-purpose registers (GPRs), MPX introduces a set of 128-bit bounds registers. The current Intel Skylake architecture provides four bounds registers named bnd0-bnd3. Each of the bounds registers stores a lower 64-bit bound in bits 0–63 and an upper bounds in bits 64–127. MPX also introduces #BR exception to facilitate the exceptions thrown by the bounds operations.

Table 1. Intel MPX instruction summary

Intel MPX Instruction	Description
bndmk bndx, m	create LowerBound and UpperBound
bndcl bndx, r/m	check the pointer value in GPR/memory against the lower
bndcu bndx, r/m	check the pointer value in GPR/memory against the upper
bndmov bndx, bndx/m	move pointer bounds from bnd/memory to bnd
bndmov bndx/m, bndx	move pointer bounds from bnd to bnd/memory
bndldx bndx, mib	load pointer bounds from memory
bndstx bndx, mib	store pointer bounds to memory

The memory of bounds and #BR exceptions are managed by the OS. Bounds are stored in shadow memory, which is dynamically allocated by the OS in a similar way of paging. Each pointer has an entry in a Bounds Table (BT), which is comparable to a page table. The addresses of BTs are stored in a Bounds Directory (BD), which corresponds to a page directory in analogy. As the bounds registers are not enough for real-world programs, bounds have to be stored/loaded to/from BT by the `bndstx`/`bndldx` instructions. When a BT does not exist, the CPU raises #BR and traps into the OS. Then the OS allocates a new BT for the bounds. Furthermore, the OS is in charge of bounds check violation.

At the compiler level, new MPX transformation passes are added to insert MPX instructions to create, propagate, store and check bounds. Additional runtime libraries provide initialization/finalization routines, statistics and debug info, and wrappers for functions from standard C libraries [28]. Until now, both GCC and ICC compilers have native support for Intel MPX [24,26]. The LLVM compiler only adds the MPX instructions and bounds registers to its Backend [29].

There are at least two challenges in applying MPX to implement our mechanism. First, MPX is designed to protect every pointers that may incur memory errors. To enforce our mechanism, we have to identity the control-transfer related pointers before the instrumentation. Second, MPX utilizes the `bndldx` instruction to load bounds from the BT. When the content of the index register of `bndldx` instruction matches with the pointer value stored along with bounds in the BT, the destination MPX register is updated with the loaded bounds. However, if a mismatch is detected, the destination MPX register is updated as always-true (INIT) [24–26]. This creates holes in MPX defense. Thus, we need to address the problem of how to check the integrity of control-transfer related pointers based on the loaded bounds.

3   Threat Model

In this paper, we only focus on user-space forward-edge CFI and assume that the backward-edge CFI has been efficiently enforced by previous solutions. Since bounds memory and #BR exceptions are managed by the OS, we assume adversaries have no control over the OS kernel. This assumption prevents adversaries from directly tampering with our enforced protection. We assume that (1) attackers can not control the program loading process; (2) the system deploys the memory protection, which forbids code section and read only data to get written at run time, and forbids a memory region to be writable and executable at the same time. These assumptions ensure the integrity of the loaded program and prevent code injection attacks. We assume attackers can arbitrary read application's code, and has the full control over the program's stack and heap. In other words, attackers have the following capabilities: (1) attackers can launch information attacks and defeat the protection of ALSR; (2) they can corrupt control data such as return address and function pointers. Our assumptions are as strong and realistic as prior work in this area.

4   Stateful Forward-Edge CFI

The goal of this paper is to enforce stateful forward-edge CFI mechanism, which is similar to shadow stack [10,12] and incurs acceptable runtime overhead. In this section we set up a stateful forward-edge CFI model, and discuss the enforcement method based on this model.

To check the integrity of forward-edge control-flow, we need to understand the low level process of control-flow transfers caused by indirect jumps and function calls. A function call through pointer dereference is shown in Fig. 1(a). The source code is in black and the disassembly is in blue. At line 8, a pointer, which is a return value from *malloc*, is assigned to *p1*. At lines 11–12, the execution makes *p2* point to the address of *p1*. At lines 15–17, the address of function *func1* is assigned to a structure member *sfunc_ptr*, which is found by dereferencing pointer *p2* twice. At that program point, the pointer relationships holding between the variables and functions are illustrated in Fig. 1(b). At lines 19–23, function *func1* is called by dereferencing pointer *p2*. We call this dereference path as a Dereferenced-Pointers-Flow (DPF), which is analogous to a linked list. DPF consists of a series of elements (such as structures, arrays, pointers). Each contains (or is) a pointer to a element containing its successor. We call these pointers as control-transfer related pointers. The last level control-transfer related pointer points to a function or a address.

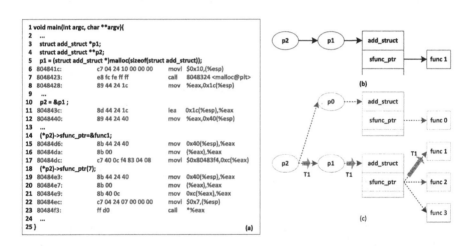

Fig. 1. Stateful forward-edge CFI model

For the whole program, the pointer relationships related to pointer *p2* can be abstracted by statically analyzing. As shown in Fig. 1(c), the relationships can be represented as a tree. Every node contains (or is) a control-transfer related pointer. The root node is pointer *p2*, and the leaf nodes are functions with the same type. There are multiple pathes (indicated as dotted lines) from *p2* to the leaf nodes. But there are only one DPF (indicated by the shadow blue arrow) at moment *T1*. If we can make sure that every pointer on the DPF is trusted, we call this forward control-flow is integrity. As shown in Fig. 1(a), the DPF is selected by assigning proper value (e.g., location of a function, return pointer from *malloc*, or one address in the stack) to the control-transfer related pointer. If any pointer in the code-pointer tree is overwritten by attackers, the pointer dereference will use another DPF, and the control-flow transfers to target controlled by attackers. We come exactly to the conclusion that the correctness of function call or jump through a pointer dereference depends on the integrity of the DPF at a moment. A pointer dereference satisfies the integrity property iff its value equals to the last legal update. We say an indirect control-transfer satisfies the CFI property iff the DPFs are protected. If all DPFs are protected, it is sufficient to prevent forward-edge control-flow hijack attacks.

For fine-grained CFI (such as IFCC and VTV [19]) mechanisms, they prevent control-flow hijack attacks by ensuring that the target address of each indirect branch is within the predefined targets set. The targets sets are computed by static program analysis. Thus *func0-func3* are all valid targets for the control transfer at line 23 in Fig. 1 at a moment. Actually, there are only one dereference path at a moment. For example, when the program in Fig. 1(a) executes at line 23, there is only one DPF as shown in Fig. 1(c) at moment *T1*. The false negative of fine-grained CFI mechanisms can be attributed to their stateless target checking. In other words, the target of a control transfer depends on the DPF which is selected by the control-transfer related pointers at a moment.

5   Implementation

We implement our stateful forward-edge CFI mechanism on the LLVM compiler framework [29]. As shown in Fig. 2, we add an optimization pass (DFI pass) during the optimization stage, and link the object codes with the runtime library at the link stage.

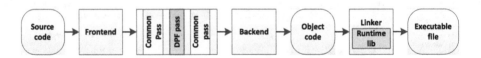

Fig. 2. The process of our stateful forward-edge CFI mechanism implementation. It first identifies the DPF nodes and inserts integrity checking codes by the DPF pass, and finally links the object codes with the runtime library.

Integrity Check Based on MPX Instructions: The method of checking the integrity of control-transfer related pointers is shown in Fig. 3. Function bound_set is designed to store the pointers into shadow memory. Function bound_set is designed load the copies of pointers and verify their integrity. The input of these functions are the location and the value of one pointer. To deal with the defense holes of MPX (the seconde challenge mentioned in Sect. 2), we store the pointer value into the lower bound. As shown in Fig. 3(a), the function bound_set creates bounds at line 4. Since we set the base register of bndmk instruction as ptr_value, ptr_value is stored in the lower bound bnd0.LB. As shown in Fig. 3(b), when we call bound_assert to check the integrity of ptr_value loaded from ptr, we firstly load its bounds to bnd0 at line 15. Then, we move the bounds from bnd0 to the memory space indexed by the pointer ptr_tmp at line 17, and assign the lower bound to ptr_rst at line 18. Finally, we compare the loaded pointer value ptr_value with the lower bound at line 22. If a mismatch is detected between them, the control transfers to the error_lable() function.

```
1 __MPX_INLINE void __llvm__bound_set (void **ptr, void *ptr_value){
2 unitprt_t offset;
3 offset = 4;
4 __asm__ __volatile__ ( "bndmk (% 2, % 1),   %% bnd0\n\t"
5                        "bndstx %% bnd0,   (% 0, % 2)"
6                                  :
7                        : "r" (ptr), "r" (offset), "r" (ptr_value)
8                        : "% bnd0" )
9 }                                                          (a)
```

```
10 __MPX_INLINE void __llvm__bound_assert (void **ptr, void *ptr_value){
11 __llvm__bounds  bounds;
12 __llvm__bounds* ptr_tmp;
13 ptr_tmp = &bounds;
14 int ptr_rst;
15 __asm__ __volatile__ ( "bndldx (% 1, % 2),   %% bnd0\n\t"
16                        "mov      %3,         %% rax\n\t"
17                        "bndmov %%bnd0,   (%% rax)\n\t"
18                        "mov      (%% rax),   %0"
19                        : "=r" (ptr_rst)
20                        : "r" (ptr), "r" (ptr_value), "r" (ptr_tmp)
21                        : "% bnd0" )
22 if(ptr_rst != ptr_value) error_lable();                    (b)
23 }
```

Fig. 3. Integrity checks based on MPX instructions.

Runtime Library: As described in the above paragraph, the bound_set() function and bound_assert() function are added as intrinsic function calls. We implement these functions into a runtime library. Besides these integrity checking functions, we also add some functions to initialize the MPX hardware at program startup. These functions are migrated from the libmpx library of GCC compiler. We compile these functions into a object file and link with this object file at the link stage.

DPF Pass: We implemented the static analysis and instrumentation as an optimization pass. The optimization pass operates on the LLVM intermediate representation (IR), which is a low-level strongly-typed language-independent program representation tailored for static analyses and optimization purpose [29]. The LLVM IR is generated from the C/C++ source code by clang, which preserves most of the type information that is required in our analysis. When our stateful mechanism is applied, the DPF pass works as the following: (1) DPF pass performs type based static analysis to identify any pointers that are control-transfer related. As shown in Fig. 1, control-transfer related pointers are pointers to functions, pointers to struct or other composite types which contain control-transfer related pointers. This method is similar to CPI [40]. (2) Once the control-transfer related pointers are identified, the DPF pass creates appropriate function calls to the intrinsic functions. When a value is assigned a control-transfer related pointer, a call to bound_set is created before the store instruction. Function bound_set saves the pointer's value in the shadow memory in the form of bounds. When a control-transfer related pointers is used[2], a call to bound_assert is created before this instruction. Function bound_assert check the pointer's integrity before being used. An example of instrumented codes are shown in Fig. 4.

6   Evaluation

6.1   Effectiveness Evaluation

To evaluate our mechanism's effectiveness, we use the RIPE benchmark [30] which is developed to provide a standard way of testing the coverage of a defense mechanism against memory errors. This program contains 850 attack forms. Our experiment is on the Ubuntu 16.04. To make more attacks work, we disabled the ASLR and compiled it without stack protection and data execution protection. Even though, many exploits failed because of built-in system protection mechanisms, such as changes in the runtime layout, as well as compatibility issues due to the usage of newer-version libraries. At last, 64 attacks works. These attacks can be divided into forward-edge control flow hijacks and backward-edge control flow hijacks. After implementing our stateful forward-edge CFI mechanism, only 6 attacks work. These attacks belong to backward-edge hijack attacks. It is shown that our mechanism is effective in forward-edge control flow enforcement.

The above evaluation is based on the assumption that the copies of control-transfer related pointers are unmodified by attackers. Actually, as the shadow memory of Intel MPX is allocated in the user address space, the Bounds Tables could be found and corrupted by memory corruption vulnerabilities. Since attackers have to modify the control-transfer related pointers in two distinct locations, checking for a match renders an attack much harder [6]. Thus, our mechanism with unprotected shadow memory still raises the bar of code-reuse attacks.

6.2   Performance Evaluation

To evaluate the performance overhead of our protection mechanism, five applications are selected from the SPEC CPU2006 benchmark suit [31]. As shown in Table 2, these applications have different fractions of instrumented memory operations. Their allocated bounds tables and instruction overhead are also shown

---

[2] The control-transfer related pointers can be used to call functions, used as function parameters, used to load pointers and so on.

```
400fff:   c7 45 fc 04 00 00 00   movl    $0x4, 0x4(,rbp)
401006:   c7 45 f8 02 00 00 00   movl    $0x2,-0x8(%rbp)
40100d:   e8 fe fd ff ff         callq   400e10 <malloc@plt>
401012:   48 8d 7d e8            lea     -0x18(%rbp),%rdi
401016:   48 89 c1               mov     %rax,%rcx
401019:   48 89 ce               mov     %rcx,%rsi
40101c:   48 89 45 d8            mov     %rax,-0x28(%rbp)
401020:   e8 7b 18 00 00         callq   4028a0 < llvm bound_set>
401025:   48 8d 45 e8            lea     -0x18(%rbp),%rax
401029:   48 8d 4d e0            lea     -0x20(%rbp),%rcx
40102d:   48 8b 75 d8            mov     -0x28(%rbp),%rsi
401031:   48 89 75 e8            mov     %rsi,-0x18(%rbp)
401035:   48 89 cf               mov     %rcx,%rdi
401038:   48 89 c6               mov     %rax,%rsi
40103b:   e8 60 18 00 00         callq   4028a0 < llvm bound_set>
401040:   48 8d 45 e0            lea     -0x20(%rbp),%rax
401044:   48 8d 4d e8            lea     -0x18(%rbp),%rcx
401048:   48 89 4d e0            mov     %rcx,-0x20(%rbp)
40104c:   48 8b 4d e0            mov     -0x20(%rbp),%rcx
401050:   48 89 ce               mov     %rcx,%rsi
401053:   48 89 c7               mov     %rax,%rdi
401056:   48 89 4d d0            mov     %rcx,-0x30(%rbp)
40105a:   e8 91 18 00 00         callq   4028f0 < llvm bound_assert>
40105f:   48 8b 45 d0            mov     -0x30(%rbp),%rax
401063:   48 8b 08               mov     (%rax),%rcx
401066:   48 89 ce               mov     %rcx,%rsi
401069:   48 89 c7               mov     %rax,%rdi
40106c:   48 89 4d c8            mov     %rcx,-0x38(%rbp)
401070:   e8 7b 18 00 00         callq   4028f0 < llvm bound_assert>
401075:   48 b8 b0 0f 40 00 00   movabs  $0x400fb0,%rax
          00 00 00
40107c:
40107f:   48 8b 4d c8            mov     -0x38(%rbp),%rcx
401083:   48 83 c1 10            add     $0x10,%rcx
401087:   48 89 cf               mov     %rcx,%rdi
40108a:   48 89 c6               mov     %rax,%rsi
40108d:   e8 0e 18 00 00         callq   4028a0 < llvm bound_set>
401092:   48 8d 4d e0            lea     -0x20(%rbp),%rcx
401096:   48 b9 b0 0f 40 00 00   movabs  $0x400fb0,%rcx
          00 00 00
40109d:
```

Fig. 4. An example of our stateful forward-edge CFI enforcement.

in Table 2. These information is obtained by the profiler tool Perf [32]. We re-compile these applications with Low Level Virtual Machine (LLVM) [29] to apply our stateful protection.

We ran our experiments on an Intel Xeon(R) E3-1280 v5 with 8 cores 3.7 GHz in 64-bit mode with 64 GB DRAM. As shown in Fig. 5a, the y-axis shows that the runtime overhead normalized to the baseline, i.e., the native applications without protection. In average, our protection mechanism incurs 9.1% runtime degradation. The worst-case is 28.1% for `h264ref`. On the one hand, the performance overhead can be attributed to the increase in number of instructions executed in a protected application. Comparing Fig. 5a and the IO column in Table 2, there is a strong correlation between them. As expected, `hmmer`, which has the least instructions increase, has ignorable performance overhead. `h264ref`, which has the most instructions increase, has the worst performance overhead. On the other hand, the performance overhead can be partially attributed to the lower hit rate. Figure 5b shows the impact of our instrumentation on the data cache hit rate. As seen from the figure, most of protected applications have lower data cache hit rate. The exception is `hmmer`, which has ignorable instrumented memory operations.

Table 2. Statistics for the selected applications: FMON represents the fraction of memory operations instrumented; NBT represents the bounds tables allocated for each application; IO represents the instruction overhead normalized to the baseline.

	FMOI	NBT	IO
bzip2	0.25%	1	9.49%
gcc	2.54%	129	17.12%
hmmer	≈ 0	1	≈ 0
h264ref	2.42%	18	33.83%
sphinx3	0.06%	2	0.20%

7   Related Work

7.1   Control-Flow Integrity

CFI is proposed by Abadi *et al.* in 2005 [10]. It restricts the control-transfers along the edge of the program's predefined CFG. The initial implementation of CFI instruments software with runtime label checks to ensure the source and destination of indirect control transfer have the same label. As frequently called function might have a large set of valid target addresses, CFI is generally coupled with a protected shadow stack to ensure backward-edge CFI [12]. Researchers mainly focus on two CFI enforcement techniques: software-based and hardware-assisted mechansims.

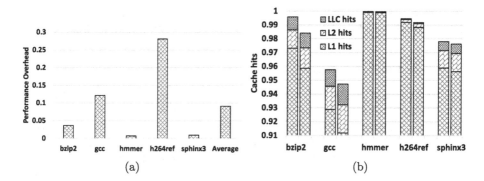

Fig. 5. (a) Performance overhead of our stateful forward-edge CFI mechanism. (b) CPU cache behavior of baseline (bar on the left) and our stateful forward-edge CFI mecahnism (bar on the right).

Software-Based Approaches. Software-based CFI approaches enforce the CFI policies by instrument the source code or legacy binaries. This can be done as part of a compiler optimization pass or binary rewriting. For the compiler-based approaches [15,19,20,34–36], the type information is used to abstract the indirect control transfer targets. Now, the LLVM includes an implementation of a number of CFI schemes [33]. Ge *et al.* [20] leveraged LLVM to enforce fine-grained CFI for FreeBSD and MINIX kernels. The binary rewriting approaches [10,17,18,37–39] derive the CFI policy directly form binaries and insert checks for CFI policies enforcement. While software-based approaches are effective in enforcing CFI, they have to make a tradeoff between efficiency and precision.

Hardware-Assisted Protection. To reduce the performance overhead of software-based approaches, several hardware-assisted CFI approaches have been designed. New CFI instructions and hardware-based shadow stack are introduce to accelerate label checking on each indirect branch [41,41–43]. Intel have added the CFI instructions and shadow stack into their Instruction Set Architecture (ISA) [44]. kBounder [45] and PathARmor [46] utilize the Last Branch Record (LBR) feature to build CFI defense. CFIMon [47] leverages Branch Trace Store (BTS) to record control transfers and implement CFI checks. However, these approaches only implement coarse-grained security policies. To enforce fine-grained CFI, CFIGuard [48] proposes to combine the LBR with the Performance Monitoring Unit (PMU). By program the PMU to trigger an interrupt when the LBR stack is full, CFIGuard could check all executed indirect branches. However, CFIGuard incurs much runtime overhead because of the frequently generated interrupts. FlowGuard [49], GRIFFIN [50] and PT-CFI [51] leverage the Intel Processor Trace (PT) to record the execution trace of a monitored program and perform online control-flow checks based on the offline CFI policies. One advantage of these work is that they are capable of enforcing a variety of stateful CFI policies over unmodified binaries. Comparing to the above hardware-assisted mechanisms, our mechanism reuses the MPX to enforce stateful forward-edge CFI, which do not need to construct the CFG and offline trains.

7.2   Code Pointer Integrity

Memory errors are the root of control-flow hijack attacks. Though many of memory safety mechanisms have been designed, they have not been widely adapted by industry for their high runtime overhead. Kuznetsov et al. [40] propose the Code Pointer Integrity (CPI) mechanism based on the observe that integrity guarantee of code pointers is sufficient to prevent control-flow hijack attacks. They implement CPI by storing sensitive pointers in an isolated memory region, and further use the runtime information (such as bounds of pointers) to check the validation of pointer dereference. There are a large body of research leveraging cryptography to provide security for code pointers. Tuck *et al.* [52] protect the pointer by encrypting the stored value. Their work is designed to protection from buffer overflow and cannot prevent code-reuse attacks. To prevent code-reuse attacks, Cryptographic CFI (CCFI) [15] uses MACs to check the integrity of indirect control-transfer targets. As the MACs contain more runtime information than the encrypted pointers, CCFI provides CFI protection efficiently. Recently, ARM announced the ARMv8.3-A architecture added a pointer integrity mechanism, called Pointer Authentication (PA) [53]. Similar to CCFI, PA use short cryptographic MACs to verify the integrity of pointers. Essentially, we enforce forward-edge CFI by guarantee the integrity of control-transfer related pointers. Different form these CPI mechanisms, we compares one control-transfer related pointer with its copy to verify its integrity. This method is similar to shadow stack. Furthermore, we leverage Intel MPX to facility the integrity checking.

8   Conclusions

This paper presents an efficient stateful forward-edge mechanism based on Intel MPX. We guarantee the integrity of control-transfer related pointers by storing these pointers into shadow memory, which is managed by OS and accessed by the MPX `bndstx` and `bndldx` instructions. To implement our method based on MPX, we design a LLVM pass to identify the control-transfer related pointers and instrument the source code. We also develop a runtime library to facility the instrumentation and initialize the MPX hardware. Our evaluation results show that our method is effective in enforcing forward-edge CFI, while incurring acceptable performance overhead.

Acknowledgments. We thank the anonymous reviewers for their valuable comments. This work was supported by the China National Science Fund for Outstanding Young Scholars under grant No. 61522212; National Key R&D Plan under grant No. 2017YFB1001602; Frontier Science Research Projects, Chinese Academy of Science, under grant No. QYZDB-SSW-JSC010; and National Natural Science Foundation of China (NSFC) under grant No. 61521092 and No. 61502459.

References

1. Shacham, H.: The geometry of innocent flesh on the bone: return-into-libc without function calls (on the x86). In: ACM 14th Conference on Computer and Communications Security (CCS 2007), pp. 552–561 (2007)
2. Hund, R., Holz, T., Freiling, F.C.: Return-oriented rootkits: bypassing kernel code integrity protection mechanisms. In: USENIX 18th Security Symposium (SEC2009), pp. 383–398 (2009)
3. Bletsch, T., Jiang, X., Freeh, V.W., Liang, Z.: Jump-oriented programming: a new class of code-reuse attack. In: ACM 6th Symposium on Information, Computer and Communications Security (ASIACCS), pp. 30–40 (2011)
4. Schuster, F., Tendyck, T., Liebchen, C., Davi, L., Sadeghi, A.R., Holz, T.: Counterfeit object-oriented programming: on the difficulty of preventing code reuse attacks in C++ applications. In: IEEE 36th Symposium on Security and Privacy (S&P 2015), pp. 745–762 (2015)
5. Carlini, N., Wagner, D.: ROP is still dangerous: breaking modern defenses. In: USENIX 23rd Security Symposium (SEC 2014), pp. 385–399 (2014)
6. Szekeres, L., Payer, M., Wei, T., Song, D.: SOK: eternal war in memory. In: IEEE 34th Symposium on Security and Privacy (S&P 2013), pp. 48–62 (2013)
7. Cowan, C., et al.: Stackguard: automatic adaptive detection and prevention of buffer-overflow attacks. In: USENIX 7th Security Symposium (SEC 1998), pp. 63–78 (1998)
8. LNCS Microsoft Corporation: Data Execution Prevention. https://msdn.microsoft.com/en-us/library/windows/desktop/aa366553(v=vs.85)
9. Xu, J., Kalbarczyk, Z., Iyer, R.K.: Transparent runtime randomization for security. In: IEEE 22nd Symposium on Reliable Distributed Systems (SRDS 2003), pp. 260–269 (2003)
10. Abadi, M., Budiu, M., Erlingsson, Ú, Ligatti, J.: Control-flow integrity. In: ACM 12th Computer and Communications Security (CCS 2005), pp. 340–353 (2005)
11. Burow, N., et al.: Control-flow integrity: precision, security, and performance. ACM Comput. Surv. **50**, 16:1–16:33 (2017)
12. Carlini, N., Barresi, A., Payer, M., Wagner, D., Gross, T.R.: Control-flow bending: on the effectiveness of control-flow integrity. In: USENIX 24th Conference on Security Symposium (SEC 2015), pp. 161–176 (2015)
13. Evans, I., et al.: Control jujutsu: on the weaknesses of fine-grained control flow integrity. In: ACM 22nd Conference on Computer and Communications Security (CCS 2015), pp. 901–913 (2015)
14. Conti, M., et al.: Losing control: on the effectiveness of control-flow integrity under stack attacks. In: ACM 22nd Conference on Computer and Communications Security (CCS 2015), pp. 952–963 (2015)
15. Mashtizadeh, A. J., Bittau, A., Boneh, D., Mazières, D.: Ccfi: cryptographically enforced control flow integrity. In: ACM 22nd Conference on Computer and Communications Security (CCS 2015), pp. 941–951 (2015)
16. Zhang, J., Hou, R., Fan, J., Liu, K., Zhang, L., McKee, S.: Raguard: a hardware based mechanism for backward-edge control-flow integrity. In: ACM Computing Frontiers Conference (CF 2017), pp. 27–34 (2017)
17. Zhang, M., Sekar, R.: Control flow integrity for cots binaries. In: USENIX 22th Conference on Security (SEC 2013), pp. 337–352 (2013)

18. Zhang, C., et al.: Practical control flow integrity and randomization for binary executables. In: IEEE 34th Symposium on Security and Privacy (S&P 2013), pp. 559–573 (2013)
19. Tice, C., et al.: Enforcing forward-edge control-flow integrity GCC & LLVM. In: USENIX 23rd Security Symposium (SEC 2014), pp. 941–954 (2014)
20. Ge, X., Talele, N., Payer, M., Jaeger, T.: Fine-grained control-flow integrity for kernel software. In: IEEE 1st European Symposium on Security and Privacy (EuroS&P), pp. 179–194 (2016)
21. Devietti, J., Blundell, C., Martin, M.M.K., Zdancewic, S.: Hardbound: architectural support for spatial safety of the c programming language. In: ACM 13th International Conference on Architectural Support for Programming Languages and Operating Systems (ASPLOS 2008), pp. 103–114 (2008)
22. Nagarakatte, S., Zhao, J., Martin, M.M., Zdancewic, S.: Softbound: highly compatible and complete spatial memory safety for C. In: ACM 30th SIGPLAN Conference on Programming Language Design and Implementation on proceedings (2009 PLDI), pp. 245–258. ACM, Dulin (2010)
23. Nagarakatte, S., Martin, M.M.K., Zdancewic, S.: Watchdoglite: hardware-accelerated compiler-based pointer checking. In: Annual IEEE/ACM International Symposium on Code Generation and Optimization (CGO 2014), pp. 175–184 (2014)
24. Intel Corporation: Intel Memory Protection Extensions Enabling Guide. https://software.intel.com/sites/default/files/managed/9d/f6/Intel_MPX_EnablingGuide.pdf
25. Intel Corporation: Intel memory ptrotection extensions. Intel 64 and IA-32 Architectures Software Developer's Manual, vol. 1, chap. 17 (2017)
26. Oleksenko, O., Kuvaiskii, D., Bhatotia, P., Felber, P., Fetzer, C.: Intel MPX explained: an empirical study of intel MPX and software-based bounds checking approaches. In: Arxiv CoRR, vol. abs/1702.00719 (2017)
27. GCC Wiki: Intel Memory Protection Extensions (Intel MPX) support in the GCC compiler. https://gcc.gnu.org/wiki/Intel%20MPX%20support%20in%20the%20GCC%20compiler
28. gcc-mirror. https://github.com/gcc-mirror/gcc/tree/master/libmpx
29. The LLVM Compiler Infrastructure. http://llvm.org/
30. Wilander, J., Nikiforakis, N., Younan, Y., Kamkar, M., Joosen, W.: RIPE: runtime intrusion prevention evaluator. In: Proceedings of the 27th Annual Computer Security Applications Conference (ACSAC 2011), pp. 41–50 (2011)
31. SPEC CPU2006 Benchmark. http://www.spec.org/cpu2006/
32. Linux kernel profiling with perf. https://perf.wiki.kernel.org/index.php/Tutorial
33. Clang 7 documentation: Control Flow Integrity. https://clang.llvm.org/docs/ControlFlowIntegrity.html
34. Wang, Z., Jiang, X.: HyperSafe: a lightweight approach to provide lifetime hypervisor control-flow integrity. In: Proceedings of the 2010 IEEE Symposium on Security and Privacy (S&P 2010), pp. 380–395 (2010)
35. Niu, B., Tan, G.: Modular control-flow Integrity. In: Proceedings of the 35th ACM SIGPLAN Conference on Programming Language Design and Implementation (OSDI 2014), pp. 577–587 (2014)

36. Niu, B., Tan, G.: Per-input control-flow integrity. In: Proceedings of the 22nd ACM SIGSAC Conference on Computer and Communications Security (CCS 2015), pp. 914–926 (2015)
37. Payer, M., Barresi, A., Gross, T.R.: Fine-grained control-flow integrity through binary hardening. In: Almgren, M., Gulisano, V., Maggi, F. (eds.) DIMVA 2015. LNCS, vol. 9148, pp. 144–164. Springer, Cham (2015). https://doi.org/10.1007/978-3-319-20550-2_8
38. Mohan, V., Larsen, P., Brunthaler, S., Hamlen, K.W., Franz, M.: Opaque control-flow integrity. In: Proceedings of the 2015 Network and Distributed System Security Symposium (NDSS 2015)
39. Elsabagh, M., Fleck, D., Stavrou, A.: Strict virtual call integrity checking for C++ binaries. In: Proceedings of the 2017 ACM on Asia Conference on Computer and Communications Security (ASIA CCS 2015)
40. Kuznetsov, V., Szekeres, L., Payer, M., Candea, G., Sekar, R., Song, D.: Code-pointer integrity. In: USENIX 11th Conference on Operating Systems Design and Implementation (OSDI 2014), pp. 147–163 (2014)
41. Davi, L., et al.: HAFIX: hardware-assisted flow integrity eXtension. In: Proceedings of the 52nd ACM/EDAC/IEEE Design Automation Conference (DAC 2015), pp. 1–6 (2015)
42. Sullivan, D., Arias, O., Davi, L., Larsen, P., Sadeghi, A.-R., Jin, Y.: Strategy without tactics: policy-agnostic hardware-enhanced control-flow integrity. In: Proceedings of the 53rd Annual Design Automation Conference (DAC 2016), pp. 163:1–163:6 (2016)
43. Christoulakis, N., Christou, G., Athanasopoulos, E., Ioannidis, S.: HCFI: hardware-enforced Control-Flow Integrity. In: Proceedings of the 6th ACM Conference on Data and Application Security and Privacy (CODASPY 2016), pp. 38–49 (2016)
44. Intel Corporation: Control-flow enforcement technology preview. https://software.intel.com/sites/default/files/managed/4d/2a/control-flow-enforcement-technology-preview.pdf
45. Pappas, V., Polychronakis, M., Keromytis, A.D.: Transparent ROP exploit mitigation using indirect branch tracing. In: Proceedings of the 22nd USENIX Security Symposium (USENIX Security 2013)
46. van der Veen, V., et al.: Practical context-sensitive CFI. In: Proceedings of the 22nd ACM SIGSAC Conference on Computer and Communications Security (CCS 2015), pp. 927–940 (2015)
47. Xia, Y., Liu, Y., Chen, H., Zang, B.: CFIMon: detecting violation of control flow integrity using performance counters. In: Proceedings of the 22nd ACM SIGSAC Conference on Computer and Communications Security (CCS 2015), pp. 1–12 (2012)
48. Yuan, P., Zeng, Q., Ding, X.: Hardware-assisted finegrained code-reuse attack detection. In: Proceedings of the 18th International Symposium on Research in Attacks, Intrusions, and Defenses (RAID 2015), pp. 66–85 (2015)
49. Liu, Y., Shi, P., Wang, X., Chen, H., Zang, B., Guan, H.: Transparent and efficient CFI enforcement with intel processor trace. In: 2017 IEEE International Symposium on High Performance Computer Architecture (HPCA 2017), pp. 529–540 (2017)

50. Ge, X., Cui, W., Jaeger, T.: GRIFFIN: guarding control flows using intel processor trace. In: Proceedings of the 22nd International Conference on Architectural Support for Programming Languages and Operating Systems (ASPLOS 2017), pp. 585–598 (2017)
51. Gu, Y., Zhao, Q., Zhang, Y., Lin, Z.: PT-CFI: transparent backward-edge control flow violation detection using intel processor trace. In: Proceedings of the 7th ACM on Conference on Data and Application Security and Privacy (CODASPY 2017), pp. 173–184 (2017)
52. Tuck, N., Calder, B., Varghese, G.: Hardware and binary modification support for code pointer protection from buffer overflow. In: Proceedings of the 37th Annual IEEE/ACM International Symposium on Microarchitecture (MICRO 2004), pp. 209–220 (2004)
53. Qualcomm Technologies Inc: Pointer Authentication on ARMv8.3. file:///E:/beifeng/code%20reuse%20attack/PointerAuthentication/whitepaper-pointer-authentication-on-armv8-3.pdf

Analytical Two-Level Near Threshold Cache Exploration for Low Power Biomedical Applications

Yun Liang[1(✉)], Shuo Wang[1], Tulika Mitra[2], and Yajun Ha[3]

[1] Center for Energy-Efficient Computing and Applications (CECA),
School of EECS, Peking University, Beijing, China
{ericlyun,shvowang}pku.edu.cn
[2] School of Computing, National University of Singapore, Singapore, Singapore
tulika@comp.nus.edu.sg
[3] School of Information Science and Technology,
ShanghaiTech University, Shanghai, China
hayj@shanghaitech.edu.cn

Abstract. Emerging biomedical applications generally work at low/medium frequencies and require ultra-low energy. Near threshold processors with near threshold caches are proposed to be the computing platforms for these applications. There exists a large design space for multi-level near threshold cache hierarchies, which requires a fast design space exploration framework. In this paper, we first propose three different two-level near threshold cache architectures with different performance and energy tradeoff. Then, we describe the design space of a two-level near threshold cache hierarchy and develop an accurate and fast analytical design space exploration framework to analyze this space. Experiments indicate that significant energy saving (59%) on average is achieved by our new near threshold cache architecture. Moreover, our analytical framework is shown to be both accurate and efficient.

1 Introduction

Emerging biomedical applications are requiring ultra-low energy dissipation, such as hearing aids, pace-makers and implantable devices. Luckily, these ultra low energy biomedical applications are generally running at low/medium frequencies. Ideally, these applications should be self-powered, relying on scavenging energy from the environment, or at least be sustained by a small battery for a long period like several years. Such a stringent energy budget constraints the total system computation power to be less than tens of microwatts, which poses a great challenge to modern computing architectures and design methodologies. In short, ultra low energy and low/medium frequency are the two features of these biomedical applications.

Near threshold processors [3,5,11,13,15,19,20,22,23] have been proposed to meet the ultra-low energy requirements. They scale their supply voltages VDD

C. Li and J. Wu (Eds.): ACA 2018, CCIS 908, pp. 95–108, 2018.
https://doi.org/10.1007/978-981-13-2423-9_8

along with their operating frequencies. As VDD scales, not only does the processor dynamic energy reduce quadratically, but also the processor leakage current does reduce super-linearly due to the drain-induced barrier-lowering (DIBL) effect. Therefore, the total energy dissipation of a processor can considerably be reduced. Moreover, VDD scaling reduces transient current spikes, hence lowering the notorious ground bounce noise. In contrast to analog circuit design where lowering the VDD to the near threshold region is generally avoided because of the small values of the driving currents and the exceedingly large noise, CMOS digital logic gates can work seamlessly from full VDD to near threshold voltage VT.

Near threshold cache hierarchy is an important part of ultra-low energy processor systems. Compared to traditional cache hierarchy that is designed for performance only, near threshold cache hierarchy is designed for power/energy. Meanwhile, cache design involves various parameters such as line size, associativity etc. The design space of caches is significantly expanded when both near threshold cache design and cache hierarchy are considered. For example, either $L1$ or $L2$ cache can be fabricated to near threshold cache to save energy consumption. Also, the design space of cache hierarchy can not be explored separately, because the $L2$ cache access depends on $L1$ cache access results. Moreover, with novel near threshold circuit designs, near threshold caches are able to achieve the same access latency as that of standard caches, but with the trade-off of a larger silicon area. Thus, given the same silicon area, when it is fabricated to near threshold cache, the cache size (capacity) will be decreased. All these new parameters brought by near threshold caches enlarge the already complex design space of multi-level cache hierarchies and the extended design space of the near threshold cache requires a fast multi-level cache exploration framework.

In this work, we first propose three two-level near threshold cache architectures for lower power biomedical applications. The three architectures are different in use of near threshold cache which results in different tradeoff of performance and energy. Then, we develop an analytical framework for efficient and accurate exploration of cache hierarchy. The exploration results are the optimal configurations (cache architecture, design parameters). Experiments show that our analytical exploration covers all the exact solutions from simulation and new architectures achieves on average 59% energy saving compared to baseline architecture. Furthermore, our analytical analysis is shown to be much more efficient than simulation based approaches.

2   Related Work

Some very interesting prototype chips which function in the sub/near threshold have been built. Among these chips, the most famous are the 180 mV FFT processor in 180 nm CMOS process designed by Alice Wang [20]. Ben Calhoun had designed a 256 kb 10-T dual port SRAM in 65 nm CMOS process [3]. M.I.T group and Texas Instruments had jointly announced the newest sub-threshold MSP430 DSP processor with integrated DC-DC converter [11]. An ultra-low energy multi-standard JPEG co-processor in 65 nm CMOS with sub/near threshold supply voltage [13, 22, 23] has been demonstrated with an ultra low energy dissipation of 1.0 pJ per cycle with a 0.45 V supply voltage working at 4.5 MHz. Near threshold cache architectures have been used in embedded systems to save power/energy consumption [5]. However, the optimal cache configuration is determined by exploring the design space via simulation. The time spent in exploration could be significantly long due to the huge design space for multiple level caches and slowness of simulation.

The design space of caches can be explored via both simulation [6,18] and analytical approaches [7,12,14]. In addition, there are hybrid approaches using both simulation and heuristics [8,9]. Trace-driven simulation is widely used for evaluating cache design parameters [18]. Ghosh and Givargis [7] propose an efficient analytical approach which can generate the set of cache configurations that meet the performance constraints directly. A fast and accurate static analysis for exploring level one instruction cache is presented in [12,14]. Their technique achieves high accuracy and speedup compared to the fastest single pass cache simulator Cheetah [17]. Hybrid approaches are used to explore both single and multi level cache design space in [8,9]. In their technique, heuristics are proposed to prune the cache design space and simulation are used to obtain the cache performance number for the reduced design space only. However, hybrid approaches are still not fast enough, because simulations are still needed.

3   Cache Architecture

We first describe the cache design parameters. The following definition can be applied to either $L1$ or $L2$ cache. A cache memory is defined in terms of three major parameters: *block or line size L, number of sets K* and *associativity A*. Now the cache size is defined as $(K \times A \times L)$. A memory block m can be mapped to *only one* cache set given by $(m \ modulo \ K)$. In addition, we consider least recently used (LRU) replacement policy in this paper. We also assume that the block size and total cache size $L2$ cache must be equal to or greater than the that of $L1$ cache [9], respectively. Finally, we are analyzing non-inclusive multiple level caches [10]. For non-inclusive caches, the following properties hold, (1) a memory reference is searched in the L2 cache if and only if it is a miss in L1 cache. (2) for every miss at level L, the requested memory block is loaded into the cache at level L.

For single level instruction cache, its design space includes various line size, cache sets and associativity. For two-level instruction cache, we can not explore the instruction cache hierarchy independently, because $L1$ cache configuration affects the $L2$ cache access in non-inclusive multiple level caches. Thus, for two-level cache, the design space is about the cross product of the design space of each level. Given a standard cache with size S consisting of N cache configurations (line size, associativity), when it is fabricated to near threshold cache, the cache size (capacity) is decreased to $S \times K$, where $K < 1$, due to the larger cell size of near threshold cache. Thus, we have to explore another N (roughly) cache configurations for cache size $S \times K$ too. The design space is further expanded if near threshold cache is taken into account.

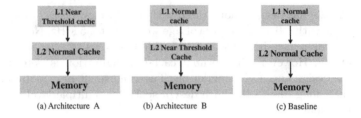

(a) Architecture A   (b) Architecture B   (c) Baseline

Fig. 1. Proposed three cache architectures.

We propose three two-level instruction cache architectures for our low power biomedical applications as shown in Fig. 1. Architecture A is designed to save energy of $L1$ cache; Architecture B is designed to save energy of $L2$ cache; Baseline is good for performance. Although architecture A and B are designed for energy saving, they may not always achieve energy reduction. It is because given the same die size, the fabricated near threshold cache size is smaller than standard cache. Thus, both architecture A and B may introduce more cache misses which results in more access to memory. The energy consumed per access to memory is much more than that of cache access. Thus, energy consumption may be increased by using architecture A and B.

Now, given a cache configuration, it is associated with two categories of parameters: architecture type (one of above three) and cache design parameters (size, block size, etc.) for each level. The design constraints we consider include both energy consumption and performance. To determine the best cache parameters and architectures shown in Fig. 1 for a particular application, the entire design space has to been explored. For any cache configuration, let (P, E) denote the corresponding performance and energy consumption. We are only interested in identifying the set of Pareto-optimal solutions $S = \{(P_1, E_1), \ldots, (P_n, E_n)\}$ that capture the different performance and energy tradeoffs [4]. Each $(P_i, E_i) \in S$ has the property that there does not exist any other cache configuration with a performance and energy tuple (P, E) such at $P \leq P_i$ and $E \leq E_i$, with at least one of the inequalities being strict. Let V be the set of performance and energy tuples corresponding to all cache configurations. Then, for any configuration $(P_i, E_i) \in V - P$ are referred as *dominated* solutions. Furthermore, we are also interested in the architecture type of the Pareto optimal solutions.

4   Analytical Cache Analysis

4.1   Cache Modeling

Given a memory block, it is mapped to only one cache set. Thus, each cache set can be analyzed independently. For one cache set, it can be considered as a fully-associative LRU cache with A cache blocks (A is associativity). Also, for one cache set, we use cache state to describe cache content and cache state c is just a vector $< c[1], \ldots, c[A] >$ of length A where $c[j]$ holds the jth most recently used memory block.

An efficient analytical framework is proposed for rapid and accurate design space exploration of instruction cache [12, 14]. In their work, cache states at each node of the control flow graph is modelled in a probabilistic manner. This is due to the fact that a program point can be reached through multiple program paths leading to a number of possible cache states at that point. Hence, probabilistic cache state is used to capture the cache contents and probabilistic cache state is just a set of possible cache states and each cache state is associated with a probability. The inputs to the analysis is the basic block and control flow edges counts from which the branch probability and loop bound can be derived. The analysis involves two phases traversal of the program and the probabilistic cache state at each program point in the context of entire program is available after the two phases traversal. Given a probabilistic cache state C and a memory block access m, the hit probability of m is just the sum of the probabilities of cache states where m can be found in C. Finally, the cache hit/miss of the entire program can be derived.

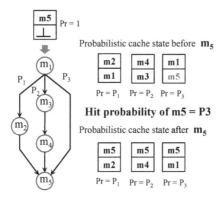

Fig. 2. An example of probabilistic cache state. $\perp$ indicates empty and Pr represents probability. Probabilistic cache state before $m5$ contains three cache states, one for each path. The hit probability of $m5$ is P_3. After accessing $m5$, probabilistic cache state is updated correspondingly with $m5$ as the most recently accessed memory block.

Figure 2 shows an example of probabilistic cache state. Cache is assumed to be a 2-way associative cache and the top memory block is the most recently accessed memory block. In the example, the input probabilistic cache state contains only one cache state and its corresponding probability is 1. Memory block $m5$ can be reached via three paths. Thus, before $m5$ is accessed, the corresponding probabilistic cache state contains 3 cache states and each of them is associated with a probability (path probability). Given the probabilistic cache state, the hit probability of $m5$ is the sum of probabilities where $m5$ can be found which is just P_3 in the example. After $m5$ is accessed, the probabilistic cache state is updated with $m5$ becoming the most recent accessed memory block (top).

4.2   Static Program Analysis

Cache hierarchy is not modelled in [12,14]. In the following, we will extend it for caches with multiple levels.

Separate Cache Analysis. For $L1$ cache, it services every memory reference request. However, this is not true for $L2$ cache, because $L2$ cache is only accessed when the memory reference incurs $L1$ cache misses. Given a memory reference m and its hit rate on level L cache $H_m[L](0 \leq H_m[1] \leq 1)$, we need to consider two scenarios (access and not access) for level $L + 1$.

Let $\odot$ be the cache state update operator defined in [12,14]. Given a probabilistic cache state C (single level), $C \odot m$ returns the probabilistic cache state after accessing $m5$ (See Fig. 2, probabilistic cache state before $m5$ is updated after the access to $m5$). We define $\oplus$ as a merge operator for two probabilistic cache state. $\oplus(C_1, C_2, w)$ will return a new probabilistic cache state C which is the union of all the cache states in C_1 and C_2. w is a weight function of C_1 and C_2, where $w(C_1) + w(C_2) = 1$. As for the probability of each cache state after merging, let P_C^c denote the probability of cache state c in probabilistic cache state C. After merging, $P_C^c = P_{C_1}^c \times w(C_1) + P_{C_2}^c \times w(C_2)$.

Now, let C_m^{in} and C_m^{out} be the $L2$ cache state before and after access to memory block m. In order to handle two-levels cache, we define a new probabilistic cache state update operator $\diamond$

$$C_m^{out} = C_m^{in} \diamond m$$
$$= \oplus(C_m^{in}, C_m^{in} \odot m, w)$$

where the weight function w is defined as $w(C_m^{in}) = H_m[1]$ and $w(C_m^{in} \odot m) = 1 - H_m[1]$. For the base case ($L1$ cache), $\diamond = \odot$.

Analysis of Cache Hierarchy. For a two-level caches, we need to do a top-down cache hierarchy analysis as shown in Fig. 3. We start with $L1$ cache analysis. After $L1$ analysis, the probabilistic $L1$ cache state is available at every point of program and the hit/miss probability of each memory access can be computed. Then, we proceed to $L2$ cache analysis. For $L2$ analysis, the cache state is updated based on the hit/miss probability of $L1$. After $L2$ analysis, the probabilistic $L2$ cache state at every point of program and the corresponding hit/miss probability of each memory access to $L2$ cache can be derived.

Cache Hits Computation. Let us use $\mathbf{B}$ to represent the set of the basic blocks of the program and M_B to represent the set of memory blocks of basic block B. Let $H[L]$ be the number of cache hits of level L for the entire program. For basic block B, let us use N_B to denote its execution count. According to the

Fig. 3. Top-down cache hierarchy analysis

non-inclusive multiple level cache properties, $L2$ cache is accessed if and only if it is a miss in level one cache. Thus, we have:

$$H[1] = \sum_{B \in \mathbf{B}} \sum_{m \in M_B} N_B \times H_m[1]$$
$$H[2] = \sum_{B \in \mathbf{B}} \sum_{m \in M_B} N_B \times (1 - H_m[1]) \times H_m[2] \qquad (1)$$

where $H_m[L]$ is the cache hit rate of memory block m in cache level L. $H_m[L]$ is available after the above separate cache analysis and N_B can be obtained through profiling. In addition, the number of accesses to memory ($L2$ misses) is just $I - H[1] - H[2]$, where I is the number of dynamic executed instructions.

Optimizations. We observe that, in a probabilistic cache state, some of the cache states have very low probabilities. That is, these cache states correspond to rare program paths. Based on this observation, we prune some of the cache states for space and time efficiency. We define the metric *dist* for pruning. Given two cache states c_1, c_2 at the same level, we define $d(c_1, c_2)$ as the measure of the distance between them. It is defined as a function of the number of different memory blocks between them. But higher priority is given to the more recently used memory blocks as shown in Eq. 2.

$$dist(c_1, c_2) = \sum_{\forall i} \begin{cases} A - i + 1, & \text{if } c_1[i] \neq c_2[i] \\ 0 & \text{otherwise} \end{cases} \qquad (2)$$

We apply two merging strategies for each level of cache. First, if the probability of a cache state c is too small ($< T_e$), then it is pruned. But its probability is added to the closest cache state to c (the closest is defined by the *dist* metric) in the probabilistic cache state. Second, if the number of cache states in a probabilistic cache state exceeds a pre-defined limit Z, then Z cache states with highest probability are kept and the others are pruned. As before, the probability of each pruned cache state is added to its closest surviving cache state in the probabilistic cache state defined by the *dist* metric. In practice, we set T_e to 10^{-6} and Z to 4.

5   Experimental Evaluation

5.1   Experiments Setup

We evaluate the accuracy and efficiency of our analytical modeling using Imp-Bench suite [16] which is designed especially for biomedical applications. Imp-Bench contains benchmarks from four categories: *lossless data compression, symmetric-key encryption, data-integrity* and *real applications*. The benchmarks are described in Table 1.

Traditionally, cache design space is explored via trace driven cache simulation. In this paper, we compare with one of widely used trace-driven cache simulation tools Dinero IV [6]. Dinero IV supports both single level and multiple level cache simulation. Given the cache design parameters of two level caches, Dinero IV returns the cache performance number (hits/misses) for each level respectively. The input trace size for each benchmark is shown in Table 1.

We use SimpleScalar toolsets [1] for experiments. We instrument its functional simulator to collect the execution count of basic blocks and control flow edges. Our estimation first disassembles the executable and construct CFG, and then proceeds with the analytical cache analysis and cache hit/miss estimation. We perform all experiments on a 3 GHZ Pentium 4 CPU with 2 GB memory.

Table 1. Benchmark characteristics and exploration time comparison. Exploration time via simulation is shown in column *Dinero*; our analytical analysis time is shown in column *Analysis*.

Benchmarks	Description	Trace (MB)	Time (sec)	
			Dinero	Analysis
Minilzo	Compression	948	8921	23.07
Finish	Compression	1600	14938	45.49
Misty1	Encryption	1300	13788	23.25
RC6	Encryption	643	6223	52.53
Checksum	Data-integrity	359	3316	19.87
Crc32	Data-integrity	2100	19943	17.51
Motion	Real-application	529	4986	24.03
Dmu	Real-application	2200	21440	254.57

5.2   Performance and Energy Model

We assume processor, standard cache and near threshold cache all work at lower frequency mode (10 Mhz) to achieve energy saving. For near threshold cache, its access latency should be slightly slower than standard cache due to the increased cell size, but body-biasing techniques can be used to regain the speed at the cost of additional energy consumption [5]. As for the cache access latency, we assume 1 cycle latency for $L1$ access and 4 cycles latency for $L2$ access. The main memory access is considered to be pipelined. The first access to main memory is 18 cycles, while the subsequent accesses take 2 cycles. For different cache configurations, we model the energy consumption of the memory hierarchy using the CACTI [21] model for 0.13 μm technology. In this paper, our focus is dynamic energy consumption.

As has been mentioned earlier, given the same die size, the fabricated near threshold cache size (capacity) is smaller than standard ones. On the other hand, the consumed energy per access of near threshold cache is less than that of standard cache due to its lower voltage. In this paper, the parameters of the near threshold cache we consider is the same as the one used in [5]. Table 2 shows various parameters for standard and near threshold cache used in this paper. As shown, near threshold cache is with lower voltage but its size (capacity) is only half of the standard cache with the same die area. More importantly, our method is not restricted to these specific parameters and can be applied to other near threshold designs as well.

Table 2. System parameters.

	Voltage	Size
Standard cache	800 mV	S
Near threshold cache	500 mV	$0.5 \times S$

Given a cache configuration C, its energy per access to standard cache is defined as E_s which is obtained from CACTI [21]. According to general energy equation $E_s = C \times V^2 \times f \times t$, when the supplied voltage is decreased to V', the energy consumption per access is changed to $E_s \times (\frac{V'}{V})^2$. Thus, for the same cache configuration C, the energy consumption per access to near threshold cache $E_n = E_s \times (\frac{500}{800})^2$ using the parameters in Table 2. As for the energy consumption for one access to memory, it is assumed to be 50 times of energy consumption of one access to standard level two cache [24].

5.3   Experiment Results

As for the cache design parameters, we choose realistic parameters to reflect the typical design of embedded systems. For $L1$ cache, we consider 1 KB and 2 KB cache sizes, 16 and 32 block (line) size and direct mapped, 2 and 4 way set associativities. For $L2$ cache, we explore 1 K, 2 K, 4 K and 8 K cache sizes, 16 and 32 block size and direct mapped, 2, and 4 way set associativities. However, in reality, the block size and cache size of $L2$ must be equal to or greater than that of $L1$ cache, respectively. In addition, for near threshold cache design, its size is a half of standard cache as shown Table 2. Thus, we need to explore 512B $L1$ cache as well (others have been covered). For $L2$ cache, we do not need to explore 512B cache size, because $L2$ size should be greater or equal to L1 size and we do not have an architecture that both $L1$ and $L2$ are near threshold cache. Totally, Dinero and our analytical analysis have to explore 297 cache configurations and there are 540 design points (architecture type and cache parameters) in the design space.

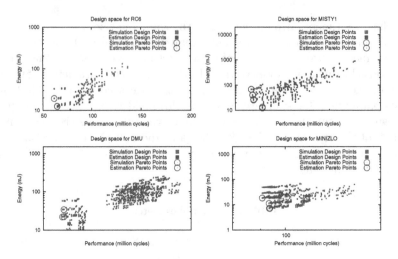

Fig. 4. Performance-energy design space and pareto curves for both simulation and estimation.

Design Space and Pareto Optimal Points. The entire design space regarding to two-level cache design is explored via both simulation (Dinero) and our estimation (analytical analysis). The simulation and estimation results are cache performance numbers (hits/misses) for each cache level. Then, we compute the performance and energy numbers for each cache configuration based on the performance and energy model. The entire design space for both simulation and estimation are shown in Fig. 4. Each point represents a cache configuration (architecture type, $L1$ and $L2$ parameters) and it is associated with corresponding performance and energy consumption. The pareto points regarding to both simulation and estimation are highlighted too. Only 4 benchmarks (*RC6, Misty1, Minizlo, Dmu*) are shown here due to space constraints.

For the entire search space, we are only interested in the pareto optimal points and each pareto optimal point represents a cache configuration (architecture type: baseline, architecture A and B, cache parameters: cache size, line size and associativity). From Fig. 4, we observe that our estimation is close to simulation for these pareto optimal points. We rely on the detailed simulation to evaluate accuracy of our estimation for these pareto optimal points. We use Wattch energy/performance model to obtain the accurate performance and energy of the cache configurations represented by pareto optimal points for both simulation and estimation. Wattach is a micro-architecture level cycle energy/performance simulator [2]. However, Wattch does not model the memory energy. We extend Wattch to include the energy consumption of memory component and modify it to use the parameters shown in Table 2. In this paper, we focus on the instruction cache, so we disable the data cache component in the Wattch simulator.

Now, we have two sets of pareto optimal points (simulation and estimation) from Wattch. To compare them, we rely on the metric in [25]. Let X', X'' be two sets of pareto optimal points,

$$C(X', X'') = \frac{|\{a'' \in X''; \exists a' \in X' : a' \preceq a''\}|}{|X''|}$$

where $a' \preceq a''$ means a' covers (dominate or equal) a''. $C(X', X'')$ is in interval $[0, 1]$, where $C(X', X'') = 1$ means that all solutions in X'' are covered by solutions in X'; $C(X', X'') = 0$ means that none of the solutions in X'' are covered by the set X'. Let sim, est be the two sets of pareto optimal points for simulation and estimation, respectively. Then, we are interested in $C[est, sim]$. For all the 8 benchmarks, $C[est, sim] = 1$. In other words, all the exact solutions (configurations from simulation) are covered by solutions (configurations) returned by our analytical modeling.

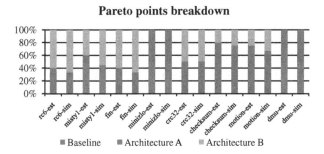

Fig. 5. Pareto points breakdown.

Architectures Comparison. For the set of pareto optimal points, they may be different in terms of cache design parameters (cache size, line size and associativity). Moreover, they may be from different architectures (Baseline, Architecture A and Architecture B). In Fig. 5, the breakdown of pareto optimal points in terms of cache architectures for both simulation and estimation are shown. We observe that for all the benchmarks, the composition of pareto optimal points of estimation is very close to that of simulation.

For benchmarks such as *crc32, checksum* etc., their working set are quite small. In other words, smaller cache can achieve the same performance as bigger cache. Thus, for these applications, to fabricate the same area to smaller size near threshold cache does not affect performance but reduce the energy consumption. Therefore, the pareto optimal points consist only of near threshold design (architecture A and architecture B), not baseline design. For benchmarks such as *misty1, dmu* etc., their working set are not small, reduction in cache size for near threshold cache may help reduce the energy but may lose the performance on the other hand. Thus, both the baseline and architecture (A or B) for near threshold cache are found in the pareto optimal solutions. Normally, architecture A may bring down the energy significantly and meanwhile may degrade the performance much; architecture B may reduce the energy slightly since there are fewer access to $L2$ and meanwhile maintain the performance. These different architectures reflect different design tradeoffs (performance vs energy design). To thoroughly evaluate the design tradeoffs (performance vs energy), all the three architectures need to be explored. More importantly, with the help of architecture A and B, we may find some cache configurations that can meet the design constraints for energy critical biomedical applications, while this may be infeasible only considering baseline architecture due to its large energy consumption.

Energy Reduction. For some biomedical applications, energy saving is more important than performance lose. Here, we focus on the energy consumption only. For baseline architecture, we select the configuration which results in the minimal memory hierarchy energy in the design space. For near threshold architecture (both architecture A and B), we choose the configuration with the minimal energy too. Then, we compare these two minimal energy consumption achieved from different architecture. The results is shown in Fig. 6. It can be seen that energy consumption is reduced significantly by using near threshold cache. On average, near threshold cache architecture shows an 59% reduction in memory hierarchy energy over baseline without near threshold cache.

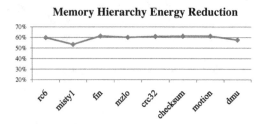

Fig. 6. Memory hierarchy energy reduction compared to baseline architecture without near threshold cache.

Exploration Time. The total time for exploring the entire space using simulation and estimation (our analytical analysis) is shown in Table 1 in column *Time*. As shown, the exploration is reduced from hours (for simulation) to seconds. Overall, our analysis is 84–1003 times faster compared to simulation. Gordon-Ross et al. [8] showed that heuristics can be used to reduce the search space such that only 7% of the space needs to be explored. However, the speedup (about 14 times faster) achieved by their heuristic is still much less than our analytical analysis. More importantly, our analysis can be enhanced with their technique to further improve the efficiency.

6   Conclusion

In this paper, we present an analytical approach for exploring two-level near threshold cache for low power biomedical applications. We first propose three different architectures for performance and energy purposes. Then, we describe an efficient analytical approach to explore multiple levels cache configurations. The experiments results indicate that our analytical analysis cover all the optimal points obtained by simulation. Furthermore, using near threshold cache architectures, we show on average a 59% reduction in energy.

Acknowledgments. This work was supported by the National Natural Science Foundation China (No. 61672048) and Beijing Natural Science Foundation (No. L172004). We thank all the anonymous reviewers for their feedback.

References

1. Austin, T.: Simplescalar: an infrastructure for computer system modeling. Computer **35**(2), 59–67 (2002)
2. Brooks, D., Tiwari, V., Martonosi, M.: Wattch: a framework for architectural-level power analysis and optimizations. In: ISCA (2000)
3. Calhoun, B.H., Chandrakasan, A.P.: A 256 kb subthreshold SRAM in 65 nm CMOS. In: IEEE International Solid- State Circuits Conference (2006)
4. Deb, K., Kalyanmoy, D.: Multi-Objective Optimization Using Evolutionary Algorithms. Wiley (2001)
5. Dreslinski, R.G., et al.: Reconfigurable energy efficient near threshold cache architectures. In: MICRO (2008)
6. Edler, J., Hill, M.D.: Dinero IV trace-driven uniprocessor cache simulator. http://www.cs.wisc.edu/~markhill/DineroIV/
7. Ghosh, A., Givargis, T.: Cache optimization for embedded processor cores: an analytical approach. ACM Trans. Des. Autom. Electron. Syst. **9**(4), 419–440 (2004)
8. Gordon-Ross, A., Vahid, F., Dutt, N.: Automatic tuning of two-level caches to embedded applications. In: DATE (2004)
9. Gordon-Ross, A., Vahid, F., Dutt, N.: Fast configurable-cache tuning with a unified second-level cache. In: ISLPED (2005)
10. Hardy, D., Puaut, I.: WCET analysis of multi-level non-inclusive set-associative instruction caches. In: RTSS (2008)
11. Kwong, J.: A 65 nm sub-vt microcontroller with integrated SRAM and switched capacitor DC-DC converter. IEEE J. Solid-State Circuits **44**(1), 115–126 (2009)
12. Liang, Y., Mitra, T.: Cache modeling in probabilistic execution time analysis. In: DAC, pp. 319–324. ACM (2008)
13. Liang, Y., Mitra, T.: Static analysis for fast and accurate design space exploration of caches. In: CODES+ISSS, pp. 103–108. ACM (2008)
14. Liang, Y., Mitra, T.: An analytical approach for fast and accurate design space exploration of instruction caches. TECS **13**(3), 43 (2013)
15. Nazhandali, L., et al.: Energy optimization of subthreshold-voltage sensor network processors. In: ISCA (2005)
16. Strydis, C., Kachris, C., Gaydadjiev, G.N.: ImpBench: a novel benchmark suite for biomedical, microelectronic implants. In: International Conference on Embedded Computer Systems: Architectures, Modeling, and Simulation (2008)

17. Sugumar, R.A., Abraham, S.G.: Set-associative cache simulation using generalized binomial trees. ACM Trans. Comput. Syst. **13**(1) (1995)
18. Uhlig, R.A., Mudge, T.N.: Trace-driven memory simulation: a survey. ACM Comput. Surv. **29**(2), 128–170 (1997)
19. Verma, N., Chandrakasan, A.P.: A 256 kb 65 nm 8t subthreshold sram employing sense-amplifier redundancy. IEEE J. Solid-State Circuits **43**(1), 141–149 (2008)
20. Wang, A., Chandrakasan, A.: A 180mv subthreshold fft processor using a minimum energy design methodology. IEEE J. Solid-State Circuits **40**(1), 310–319 (2005)
21. Wilton, S.J.E., Jouppi, N.P.: CACTI an enhanced cache access and cycle time model. IEEE J. Solid-State Circuits **31**, 677–688 (1996)
22. Xie, X., Liang, Y., Sun, G., Chen, D.: An efficient compiler framework for cache bypassing on GPUs. In: ICCAD, pp. 516–523. IEEE (2013)
23. Xie, X., Liang, Y., Wang, Y., Sun, G., Wang, T.: Coordinated static and dynamic cache bypassing for GPUs. In: HPCA, pp. 76–88. IEEE (2015)
24. Zhang, C., Vahid, F., Najjar, W.: A highly configurable cache architecture for embedded systems. In: ISCA (2003)
25. Zitzler, E., Deb, K., Thiele, L.: Comparison of multiobjective evolutionary algorithms: empirical results. Evol. Comput. **8**(2), 173–195 (2000)

DearDRAM: Discard Weak Rows for Reducing DRAM's Refresh Overhead

Xusheng Zhan[1,2], Yungang Bao[1(✉)], and Ninghui Sun[1]

[1] State Key Laboratory of Computer Architecture, ICT, CAS, Beijing, China
{zhanxusheng,baoyg,snh}@ict.ac.cn
[2] University of Chinese Academy of Sciences, Beijing, China

Abstract. Due to leakage current, DRAM devices need periodic refresh operations to maintain the validity of data in each DRAM cell. The shorter refresh period is, the more refresh overhead DRAM devices have to amortize. Since the retention time of DRAM cells are different because of process variation, DRAM providers usually set default refresh period as the retention time of those weakest cells that account for less than 0.1% of total capacity.

In this paper, we propose DearDRAM (Discard weak rows DRAM), an efficient refresh approach that is able to substantially reduce refresh overhead using two mechanisms: selectively disabling weak rows and remapping their physical addresses to a reserved region. DearDRAM allows DRAM devices to perform refresh operations with a much longer period (increasing from 64 ms to 256 ms), which reduces energy consumption. It is worth noting that compared to previous schemes, DearDRAM is easy to be implemented, does not modify DRAM chip and only introduces slight modifications to memory controller. Experimental results show that DearDRAM can save refresh energy an average of 76.12%, save total energy about 12.51% and improve IPC an average of 4.56% in normal temperature mode.

Keywords: DRAM · Memory controller · Refresh · Weak cell

1 Introduction

Dynamic Random Access Memory (DRAM) takes nearly 11.7% of peak power usage of hardware systems [1], but a quite fraction of energy is used against leakage current rather than normal accesses to DRAM devices. Basically, DRAM consists of vast charge storage cells that are basic units to control and store each bit of data [2]. Each cell contains a capacitive structure that stores the electrical charge to present each bit of data. Because charge leakage, which is an inherent phenomenon and shortage of the capacitor, will change the stored data over time, a *refresh* operation is needed to maintain data integrity or data correctness.

The maximum time that a DRAM cell maintains data correctness without taking any refresh operations is referred to as *retention time*, also called the

© Springer Nature Singapore Pte Ltd. 2018
C. Li and J. Wu (Eds.): ACA 2018, CCIS 908, pp. 109–124, 2018.
https://doi.org/10.1007/978-981-13-2423-9_9

refresh window, t_{REFW}. The retention time of each DRAM cell is not the same due to process variation and operation temperature. For instance, process variation will lead to a small fraction of weak DRAM cells that have weaker ability to keep data integrity than normal cells [3–5]. The retention time of weak cells might be 64 ms while that of normal cells could be 256 ms. In order to keep data correctness in all cells, DRAM providers usually adopt a conservative yet simple approach, i.e., configuring all cells with a uniform retention time that depends on weak cells. However, it is unnecessary to refresh the vast majority of normal cells in such high frequency, which results in a nearly 20% of extra power consumption [5,6]. Moreover, intensive refresh operations significantly reduce performance of DRAM devices [7], because DRAM ranks under refreshing can not execute any read or write operations.

To reduce large amount of unnecessary refresh operations, several differentiated refresh strategies are adopted to refresh weak cells and normal cells with different frequencies, i.e. adding extra refresh operations for weak cells [5,6,8].

It is clear that above approaches are efficient to reduce refresh overhead, but they have two shortages. On one hand, previous approaches need to modify JEDEC[1] standards to add extra refresh operations. Although it is technically reasonable to modify commands and state diagrams of DRAM devices defined in JEDEC standards, a lot of row activation commands for refreshing rows will take up much command bus bandwidth and lead to bus congestion. On the other hand, current approaches require relatively complicated design to leverage differentiated retention time. For example, usually the distribution of retention time of weak cells as well as normal cells needs to be persevered.

In this paper, we propose a low-overhead refresh approach, DearDRAM (Discard weak rows DRAM). Instead of devising different refreshing policies according to the distribution of retention time, DearDRAM directly discards (or disables) weak DRAM rows that contains weak cells. Such an extreme idea is based on a key observation that weak cells actually account for even less than 0.1% of total capacity of a DRAM chip [5]. For example, a 32GB DRAM chip has fewer than 1000 cells whose retention time is less than 256ms, and only about 30 cells whose retention time is between 64 ms and 128 ms. So it is acceptable to disable those weak cells. By doing so, memory controllers will not send requests to these weak rows. Meanwhile, DRAM devices can perform refresh operations with a much longer period based on the retention time of normal cells, thereby significantly reduce refresh overhead. Moreover, DearDRAM does not require modifications to JEDEC's DDRx specification.

However, directly disabling weak rows leaves holes in physical address space, which raises challenges on OS memory management. To deal with this issue, DearDRAM adopts an address remapping mechanism that maps the addresses of weak rows to a reserved region so that holes of physical address space are filled and OS can still obtain a continuous physical address space.

We implement DearDRAM on DRAMSim2 simulator that is integrated into gem5 [10] and choose 7 memory-intensive workloads from benchmark suites

---

[1] Joint Electron Devices Engineering Council (JEDEC) [9].

SPECCPU2006 [11] for evaluation. Experimental results show that for a 16GB DRAM system, DearDRAM can improve performance by 4.56% (up to 10.57% in high temperature) and save energy consumption by 12.51% (up to 28.84% in high temperature) on average over baseline mode.

In summary, this paper makes the following contributions:

- We propose a low-overhead DRAM refresh scheme DearDRAM that adopts an extreme yet effective idea of disabling weak rows for reducing refresh overhead. The idea is based on a key observation that weak cells account for even less than 0.1% of total capacity of a DRAM chip.
- We design an address remapping mechanism to resolve the address space hole issue so that OS can still obtain a continuous physical address space. The overhead of the remapping mechanism is negligible, requiring only a storage of 8.87 KB extra space in memory controller.
- Our experimental results show that DearDRAM outperforms state-of-the-art approaches. Moreover, it is independent of any refresh modes and is non-intrusive to industry standards. Thus, DearDRAM can be easily and directly integrated into current DRAM systems.

2 Background

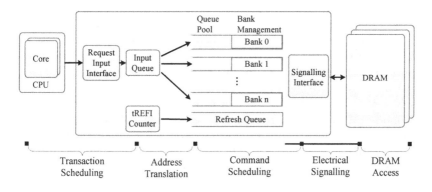

Fig. 1. Basic organization of memory controller.

2.1 Memory Controller

In modern memory systems, a memory controller is the key component that processes data streams into or out of DRAM devices that connect with the controller [2]. As shown in Fig. 1, an abstract architecture of memory controller consists of various components. From CPU to DRAM chips, DRAM requests are processed through the following five stages:

1. Transaction scheduling. Processor cores send read and write requests to Input Queue of memory controller via Request Input Interface [14].

2. Address translation. Operations are mapped to corresponding memory addresses and converted into a series of DRAM commands.

3. Command scheduling. A pool of queues are used to store commands, and each queue can be assigned to one bank or rank. Memory controller also generates refresh operations and stores them in Refresh Queue. Then memory controller uses a pre-defined scheduling policy to select operations among the pool of queues and the refresh queue.

4. Electrical signalling. With the signalling interface, the chosen commands are issued to target DRAM devices.

5. DRAM access. DRAM devices finish the requested operations in this stage.

2.2 DRAM Refresh Modes

Current DRAM devices support two typical refresh modes: auto-refresh (AR) and self-refresh (SR). AR is used to maintain the DRAM working on normal state, while the target of SR is to reduce background energy when DRAM devices stay at idle periods without any operations.

Auto-Refresh Mode. In general, refresh circuits consist of a refresh counter and a timer, where the refresh counter is used to record the address of row that will be refreshed, and the timer is used to increase the refresh counter to trace the rows. Refresh circuits can stay in a memory controller [14] or can be a part of DRAM devices [8]. Memory controller issues refresh operations interleaved with normal memory accesses at regular intervals.

DRAM devices have the ability to flexibly control the refresh operations by themselves, thereby simplifying the structure of memory controller [8]. A typical refresh mode called *all-bank refresh* has been adopted in commercial DRAM chips. It works as follows: First, the memory controller issues AR commands at a fixed refresh interval (t_{REFI}) to all banks in a rank. Second, during the refresh completion interval (t_{RFC}), DRAM device decides the rows to refresh by its internal refresh logic. Due to limited current, banks are refreshed in a pipelined way [2,7] instead of refreshing all banks simultaneously. However, the rank will not receive any memory requests from memory controller during the period of all-bank refresh.

For DDRx devices, t_{REFI} is variable due to operation temperature, while t_{RFC} escalates rapidly with the increasing of device density [5]. DDR4 implements a fine granularity refresh mode to slow down the growth rate of t_{RFC} [9]. In the fine granularity mode, users can use a mode register set (MRS) command to program the t_{REFI} and t_{RFC} in 1x, 2x or 4x mode. Table 1 shows the detailed timing values of t_{REFI} and t_{RFC} for two DRAM generations in different device sizes and operation temperatures.

Table 1. The values of refresh timing parameters for various DDRx devices in different modes and temperatures.

Device (mode)	$t_{REFI}(\mu s)$		$t_{RFC}(\eta s)$			
	$0 \sim 85$ °C	$85 \sim 95$ °C	4 Gb	8 Gb	16 Gb	32 Gb
DDR3	7.8	3.9	300	350	-	-
DDR4(1x)	7.8	3.9	260	350	480	640
DDR4(2x)	3.9	1.95	160	260	350	480
DDR4(4x)	1.95	0.975	110	160	260	350

Self-Refresh Mode. In AR mode, all clock circuits of DRAM devices stay in active state during the whole refresh procedure. In the refresh procedure, the delay locked loop and peripheral logic cost much of background power. In fact, DRAM device will not receive any read/write commands from memory controller, so the energy consumption of background power can be reduced by closing external I/O circuitries, i.e. SR mode. In order to maintain data integrity, each DRAM device has a build-in timer to trace and generate refresh operations. When a DRAM device switches to SR mode, it will disable all related peripheral logic circuitries and delay locked loop.

2.3   DRAM Rows Retention Time

Due to the electric charge leakage phenomenon of DRAM cells, it is needed to charge each cell over time to maintain data integrity. Retention time indicates the maximal time that a row can keep data validation without any charge operations. There are two factors influencing row retention time. First, process variations will lead to different retention time of cells, which are usually divided into weak cells and normal cells. In this work, we use similar timing values to divide cells as prior works [5,6,8]. Specifically, the retention times of normal cells is not less than 256 ms, while the remainder cells are weak cells. The rows containing weak cells are weak rows and others are normal rows.

Second, high operation temperatures speed up the cell leakage. DRAM commercial operating temperatures defined by JEDEC standards are between 0 °C and 95 °C, where the normal temperature mode is between 0 °C and 85 °C and the high temperature mode is between 85 °C and 95 °C. The retention time is 64 ms in normal mode, and 32 ms in high temperature mode.

3   Discard Weak Rows DRAM

We propose a low overhead refresh approach, DearDRAM (Discard weak rows DRAM) which directly discards (or disables) weak DRAM rows. In this section, we will present detailed design of DearDRAM.

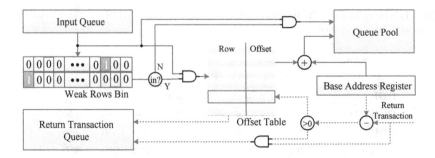

Fig. 2. The architecture of DearDRAM.

3.1   Overview of DearDRAM

DearDRAM disables weak rows by redesigning the address translation stage (as described in Sect. 2.1) of memory controller. The physical address space is divided into two continuous regions, i.e., normal address region and reserved address region, where only the normal address region is visible to OS. Each region consists of a number of continuous DRAM rows. Basically, the normal address region is far larger than the reserved address region and contains a large scale of continuous DRAM rows including weak rows. Thus, memory controller is responsible for mapping the addresses of weak rows into the reserved address region. In particular, if a request accesses the address of a weak row, memory controller will forward it to a normal row in the reserved address region. By contrast, when a request accesses the address of a normal row, it will be processed in traditional way.

To minimize the overhead of address remapping, we pick several successive rows to form a reserved address region, and use the mode of "Base address + Offset" to simplify the complexity of DearDRAM's address remapping design. The detailed architecture of DearDRAM is shown in Fig. 2. Three components, *Weak Rows Bin*, *Offset Table* and *Base Address Register*, are added to memory controller. More information is described as follows:

Weak Rows Bin. This structure is used to store the information of weak rows. It may be the simplest way to store weak row information by associating each row of DRAM with a 1 bit wide status counter in memory controller. However, it will result in excessive storage overhead. To reduce storage cost, we adopts same measures as RAIDR [5]that uses bloom filter, an efficient data structure, to store the information of weak rows with low hardware overhead.

Offset Table. To track the address remapping information for weak rows, we use an offset table to record the indices of weak row and the offset of new mapped normal rows from the start address of the reserved address region. The offset ranges from 0 to $Num_{weak} - 1$, where Num_{weak} is the number of weak rows. The total items of the offset table are not less than the number of weak rows.

Base Address Register. We use a base address register to record the boundary between normal address region and reserved address region, i.e. the start address of reversed address region.

In next subsections, we will elaborate DearDRAM's design.

3.2   Weak Row Address Mapping

In general, it is easier for OS to manage a continuous physical address space than an address space with holes. Unfortunately, DearDRAM disabling weak rows leaves holes in the normal address region, which raises complexity of OS memory management. Thus, to resolve this issue, DearDRAM adopts a weak row address remapping mechanism. Specifically, when a DRAM operation accesses a normal row, its address remains unchanged and is not affected by DearDRAM. Next we will mainly focus on how the requests to weak rows are remapped in the following parts.

In DearDRAM, when a weak row is accessed, it will be redirected to a row in the reserved address region. In order to simplify the mapping between weak rows and the reserved address region, we locate the reserved address region in the end of whole DRAM address space. We use Eqs. (1) and (2) to calculate the size and the start address of reserved address region respectively. The target address of each weak row are computed by Eq. (3).

$$Size_{reserved} = Size_{row} \times Num_{weak} \tag{1}$$

$$Base_{addr} = Max_{addr} - Num_{weak} \tag{2}$$

$$Dest^i_{addr} = Base_{addr} + Offset^i \tag{3}$$

where $Size_{reserved}$ is the size of reserved address region. $Size_{row}$ is the size of a single row. Max_{addr} denotes the maximum physical address of current DRAM configuration. $Base_{addr}$ represents the initial address of the reserved address region. $Dest^i_{addr}$ indicates the mapping address in the reserved address region of $i-th$ weak row.

3.3   Address Translation

In the address translation phase, memory controller will distinguish the destination address of each request received from processors or DMA engines, and process them with different operations. DearDRAM disassembles this phase into following two steps:

The first step is identifying the type of destination address. When memory controller is translating the address of a request, it lookups the destination address in the weak rows bin. If such an address is not found, the target row is a normal row in the normal address region. If the target address is in the weak rows bin, then the target row is a weak row and will be remapped into the reserved address region.

The second step is processing requests. The normal requests will be immediately sent to queue pool as a normal operation. For a request to a weak row, memory controller will use its destination address to get the offset by querying the offset table, then compute the mapping address by Eq. (3) and send it to queue pool.

3.4   Return Transactions

For return transactions, we also need to take differentiated actions to process them. Likewise, memory controller processes all return transactions from DRAM with the following two phases:

The first phase is recognizing the region of each return transaction. Memory controller exploits the return address to minus the value of base address register, then checks the result. For addresses in the normal address region, the differences are larger than '0'. Other results are considered to be from reserved address region.

The second phase is processing return transactions. The return transactions of normal rows are appended to the return transaction queue directly. For other transactions, memory controller uses the result of phase 1 to query the offset table, then recovers the original addresses of return transaction and inserts them into return transaction queue.

3.5   Weak Rows Profiling

In order to identify weak rows from a whole DRAM system, we have to detect each DRAM cell in every row. We adopt a common method which has been used in several previous studies to inspect the row retention time [5,15]. This method disables the refresh operations, then writes a series of data in "all 1s" or "all 0s" pattern, and verifies the intactness of these data in a specified time period.

In DearDRAM mechanism, the memory controller uses default refresh mode to maintain the data correctness before filling the weak rows bin, offset table and base address register. With the above method, OS can examine the retention time of each row and record these information in a file. Then, OS calculates the initial address of reserved address region, generates the offset of each weak row, and saves these results into another file. During the next OS' boot-up, these files are loaded into the memory controller to fill the three key components. Meanwhile, OS will adjust the size of accessible DRAM address space to the size of normal address region.

Variable retention time (VRT) reflects a new phenomenon that several DRAM cells will transform between weak and normal cells [16] Luckily, a recent research [17] discovers that combining profiling techniques with SECDEC-ECC and guardbandings can be an efficient way to avoid VRT-related faults. Our study runs with these profiling techniques on this issue.

3.6   Hardware Overhead Exploration

In our evaluation, we add three components in the memory controller, where the hardware overhead mainly from the weak rows bin and offset table. First, we exploit an efficient technique, bloom filter, as RAIDR [5] to reduce the cost of storing weak row in memory controller. For RAIDR, its cost is mainly affected by the number of bins associated with the DRAM refresh interval. The default RAIDR configuration uses a 256B bin to store the rows that retention time between 64 ms and 128 ms, and uses another 1 KB bin to save the rows that retention time between 128 ms and 256 ms. Unlike RAIDR, DearDRAM only requires one bin to record the information of which are weak cells, so we use a 1 KB as default weak row bin size. Second, we conservatively set 1.5 K items for the offset table to indicate the mapping between weak rows and normal rows in the reserved region, based on the analysis of previous studies [3–5]. For 32-bit address space, each item consumes 43 bits, the whole table takes up 7.87 KB, where 32 bits denote row address and 11 bits present offset. Third, the overhead of base address register and the power overhead of the additional components is negligible compared to the entire DRAM chip. In above analysis, the total extra overhead of DearDRAM is 8.87 KB.

4   Implementation

As introduced in Sect. 2.2, the memory controller has to send more than $\frac{t_{REFW}}{t_{REFI}}$ refresh commands within a t_{REFW}, otherwise DRAM cells will fail to hold data due to the deadline of retention time. For the original all-bank refresh mechanism, it requires at least $\frac{64\,ms}{7.8\,\mu s} \approx 8192$ refresh commands during each retention time. In DearDRAM design, we enlarge the original value of t_{REFW} (64ms) of DDR3 and DDR4 devices to 256 ms. DearDRAM provides two implementation

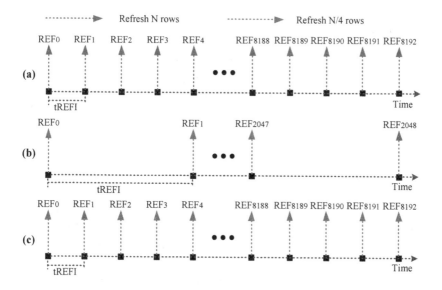

Fig. 3. Different refresh modes.

mechanisms, *extending* and *shortening*, to balance the tradeoff between energy consumption and access latency in different aspects. In this section, we show how they are implemented in all-bank refresh mode. Figure 3 shows the refresh operations of all-bank refresh mode and DearDRAM, where Fig. 3(a) shows the issue pattern of the original refresh operations in all-bank refresh mode.

Extending. The *extending* method does not change the number of rows being refreshed by each command, but enlarge the value of t_{REFI}, i.e. send less refresh operations within t_{REFW}. For an 8Gb x8 DRAM device in all-bank refresh mode, each bank has 65536 rows, and hence each all-bank refresh command has to refresh 8 rows in each bank. With the extending method, each refresh operation still refreshes 8 rows, but t_{REFI} increases from 7.8 μs to 256 ms ÷ 64 ms × 7.8 μs = 31.2 μs. Figure 3(b) shows the issue pattern of the refresh operations using extending method.

Shortening. The *shortening* scheme holds the number of refresh commands being issued within t_{REFW}. Instead, less rows will be refreshed by a refresh command to ensure the correctness of all DRAM cells during each retention time. For the DRAM device mentioned above, shortening scheme will issue 8192 refresh commands within t_{REFW}, and each command only refreshes 2 rows. Figure 3(c) illustrates the issue pattern of the refresh operations using shortening method.

5   Methodology

5.1   Experimental Setup

To evaluate the effectiveness of DearDRAM, we use an open-source cycle-accurate simulator, gem5 [10], to simulate a X86 multi-core platform and integrate another open-source memory system simulator DRAMsim2 [18] into gem5 to simulate the DRAM system. We improve DRAMSim2 to conform the JEDEC DDR4 specification, including several timing parameters and different refresh modes. For all refresh related DRAM timing and current parameters, we use the values similar to [7,8], as listed in Table 2. Where IDD5B is 47 for REFLEX and DearDRAM1, and is 102 for others.

Table 2. The timing and current parameters configuration of DDR4 16 Gb (x16) DRAM device, where the unit of timing values is $1.25\eta s$, except for tCK.

Timing	Value	Current	Value (mA)	Timing	Value	Current	Value (mA)
tCK	1.25	IDD0	24	tRCD	10	IDD1	32
tRAS	28	IDD2P	6.4	tRC	40	IDD2N	10.1
tRP	12	IDD3N	16.6	tRRD	4	IDD4w	58
tWR	15	IDD4R	60	tFAW	20	IDD5B	47/102
tRFC	384	IDD6	6.7	tRFC_4x	208	IDD7	107

Table 3. Configuration of the evaluated system.

Processor	4 OoO cores, 10 MSHRs per core, 3.2 GHz clock frequency
L1 Cache	Private, 4-way associativity, 32 KB, 64 B block size
L2 Cache	Shared, 64 B block size, 4 MB, 16-way associativity
Memory	Close page, line-interleaved address mapping,
Controller	64-entry read/write queue, FR-FCFS scheduling [?]
DRAM	800 MHz Bus frequency, Devices density 16 Gb, 1 channel, 2 rank per channel, 8 banks per rank, 16 subarrays per bank

Table 4. Retention time distribution of the evaluated system.

Retention time range	Number of rows
64 ms–128 ms	28
128 ms–256 ms	978
more than 256 ms	523282

As adopted in former memory studies [20, 21], we complete the cache warm-up via skipping the the initial stages with running 5 billion instruction in fast-forward mode. In addition, we only ensure the fastest core can reach to 100 million instructions. The detailed system configuration is shown in Table 3. To evaluate the performance of multi-core systems, we use Weighted Speedup (WS) [13] as the performance metric.

5.2 Workloads

We select 7 workloads from a single-thread benchmark suite, SPEC2006 [11](lbm, libquantum, mcf, milc, soplex, astar, gobmk), to evaluate our schemes and several related mechanisms with reference input set. These workloads are memory intensive applications and have high last-level cache (LLC) misses per kilo instructions (MPKI). To implement multi-core simulation environment, we replicate and mix these workloads via running a copy or process of an application on each core. We use the following short names to denote all workload combinations: 4 × lbm (M1), 4 × milc (M2), 3 × milclibquantum (M3), 3 × libquantum-mcf (M4), 3 × milc-lbm (M5), 3 × mcf-libquantum (M6), 2 × mcf-libquantum-lbm (M7), 2 × milc-mcf-lbm (M8), lbm-libquantum-mcf-milc(M9), 2 × libquantum-mcf-milc (M10), lbm-libquantum-soplex-astar (M11) and libquantum-milc-gobmk-soplex (M12).

6   Evaluation Results

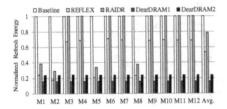

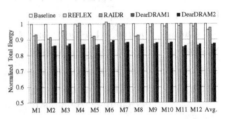

Fig. 4. Normalized refresh energy comparison among All-bank Refresh, REFLEX, RAIDR, DearDRAM1 and DearDRAM2 for a 16 GB DRAM system in normal temperature mode (lower is better).

Fig. 5. Normalized total energy comparison among All-bank Refresh, REFLEX, RAIDR, DearDRAM1 and DearDRAM2 for a 16 GB DRAM system in normal temperature mode (lower is better).

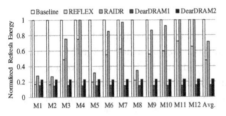

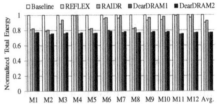

Fig. 6. Normalized refresh energy comparison among all schemes in high temperature mode (lower is better).

Fig. 7. Normalized total energy comparison among different mechanisms in high temperature mode (lower is better).

6.1   Compared Mechanisms

In this section, we evaluate the energy and performance of each refresh policy in both normal and high temperature modes. We compare the performance of DearDRAM with the following mechanisms:

- **All-bank refresh.** As introduced in Sect. 2.2.1, all-bank refresh is the baseline of our experiments.
- **RAIDR.** The Retention-Aware Intelligent DRAM Refresh mechanism groups DRAM rows into different bins according to different DRAM cell retention times, then refreshes rows in different bins with different rates. We quote the DRAM rows distribution from the original literature [5] and list them in Table 4. The original RAIDR is incompatible with all-bank refresh, and it refreshes DRAM with a row-granularity refresh scheme that has not yet been used in modern DRAM. Therefore, we modify it to support the all-bank mode as [6].

- **REFLEX**. The Flexible Auto-Refresh scheme [8] modifies the internal refresh counter of DRAM and add a new command "dummy-refresh" to skip unnecessary refreshes. We focus on REFLEX-4x techniques with all bank refresh.

6.2 Energy Saving

We use DearDRAM1 to denote the *shortening* and DearDRAM2 to present the *extending* (the following figures adopt the same terms). We set the all-bank refresh policy as the baseline and normalize the result of all other mechanisms. In all figures, 'Avg.' is the average of all workloads combinations.

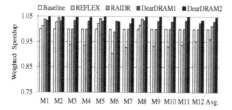
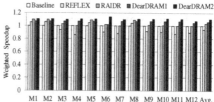

Fig. 8. Normalized performance comparison of all schemes in normal temperature mode (higher is better).

Fig. 9. Normalized performance comparison of all schemes in high temperature mode (higher is better).

Figure 4 compares the DRAM refresh energy consumption of each refresh scheme by running different combinations. Compared to the baseline, all mechanisms can eliminate redundancy refresh operations. For most workloads, the refresh energy consumption of different schemes follows an order (from more to less): baseline, REFLEX, RAIDR, DearDRAM2 and DearDRAM1. REFLEX will decrease about 46.74% extra refresh energy on average, because this policy can reduce the number of row refreshed by each refresh operation, and requires the less current. The modified RAIDR can save 22.69% refresh energy on average (up to 71.12%). However, for those extreme memory-intensive combinations such as *M1*, RAIDR is better than DearDRAM1 primarily because the higher MPKI a workload exhibits, the more bus bandwidth it needed. Thus, when the MPKI reaches a threshold, it occupies much bandwidth and increases latency. On average, DearDRAM1 and DearDRAM2 save refresh energy by 84.39% and 76.12%, respectively. DearDRAM1 save the most refresh energy in all schemes.

Figure 5 shows the total energy consumption on four-core multiprogrammed workloads. The total power consumption of each combination has similar distribution as the refresh power consumption in Fig. 6. DearDRAM1 consumes less total energy than RAIDR for all combinations, due to DearDRAM1 consumes less background energy and easier to enter SR mode when the accesses in a low frequency. DearDRAM1 can achieve up to 14.61% (an average of 13.21%) energy saving. Meanwhile, DearDRAM2 can reach to 14.02% (an average of 12.51%) energy saving.

Figures 6 and 7 show the refresh and total power of different mechanisms, respectively. When the DRAM is operated in high temperature, refresh operations are more frequent and will be doubled. On average, DearDRAM1 and DearDRAM2 save refresh energy by 84.92% and 77.4%, respectively. Despite the percentage of refresh power reduction is not changed much for DearDRAM1 and DearDRAM2 in different temperature mode, they total energy are reduced about 23.86% and 23.15% respectively, due to refresh energy is increased in the proportion of total energy.

No matter in normal temperature mode or high temperature mode, DearDRAM1 and DearDRAM2 can save more energy than other schemes, especially the mechanism DearDRAM1.

6.3   Performance Improvement

As mentioned before, eliminating refresh operations improves effective serving time of DRAM chips, thereby reducing memory access latency. Figure 8 shows the normalized DRAM weighted speedup of each workload with different refresh policies in normal temperature mode. Comparing Fig. 5 and 87, we can find that the weighted IPC of different mechanisms follow the similar pattern as energy saving in general. For most workloads combinations, REFLEX performs worse than baseline, and reduces performance by 3.81% on average. DearDRAM1 improves performance by 3.06% on average while RAIDR achieves an average of 1.3%.

In high temperature mode as shown in Fig. 9, REFLEX performs even worse than the baseline because too many refresh commands are issued so as to occupy the command bus for a long time and delay normal read/write operations. REFLEX and DearDRAM1 are not suitable for memory-intensive application combinations, and are more suitable for evenly distributed memory requests. In high-temperature environment, the refresh operations will increase and the advantages of DearDRAM1 and DearDRAM2 are even more obvious. Overall, DearDRAM2 always performs the most among all schemes, slightly improves the performance of 4.56% on average (up to 5.1%) in normal temperature mode and an average of 10.57% (up to 14.04%) in high temperature mode.

7   Related Work

Liu et al. [5] propose RAIDR, as described in Sect. 6.1. RAIDR reduces unnecessary refresh operations by the fact that different DRAM cells have different retention time. RAIDR refreshes DRAM rows with different refresh rates for different retention times. Cui et al. [22] propose DTail, a refresh reduction scheme that stores the retention time information within the DRAM itself to reduce storage cost. They revise the DDRx protocol and add a new command *silent refresh* that only increases the value of row address counter, instead of executing refresh operation. Wang et al. [6] propose ProactiveDRAM, a new DRAM retention time management that stores weak rows information in the DRAM like [22] and allow the DRAM itself to issue extra refresh to weak rows when necessary. Bhati et al. [8] propose Flexible Auto-Refresh (REFLEX) techniques to reduce unnecessary refresh operations. They also propose *dummy refresh*, a command is similar to *silent refresh* to increase the refresh counter in the DRAM device while skipping refresh operations. Almost all these studies are motivated by leveraging the RAS-only refresh (ROR) which is disused in the current DRAM device for its poor scalability and compatibility. Furthermore, it is not a good tradeoff to take too much cost to maintain the correction of a small number of weak rows.

8 Conclusion

In this work, we present DearDRAM, a novel DRAM system scheme for reducing unnecessary refresh operations and improving the access efficiency with low-overhead modification on the memory controller. DearDRAM is motivated by the observation that the vast majority of DRAM rows have longer retention time than the value offered by JEDEC. DearDRAM no longer maintains the correctness of weak rows and remaps the weak rows addresses to a reserved region to keep the address space contiguous. Our experiments showed that, DearDRAM is a low-cost and efficient scheme to save refresh power consumption and reduce DRAM latency within the whole DRAM system.

References

1. Barroso, L.A., Clidaras, J., Holzle, U.: The datacenter as a computer: an introduction to the design of warehouse-scale machines. Synth. Lect. Comput. Archit. **8**(3), 1–154 (2013)
2. Jacob, B., Ng, S., Wang, D.: Memory Systems: Cache, DRAM, Disk. Morgan Kaufmann (2010)
3. Kim, K., Lee, J.: A new investigation of data retention time in truly nanoscaled DRAMs. IEEE Electron Device Lett. **30**(8), 846–848 (2009)
4. Li, Y., Schneider, H., Schnabel, F.: DRAM yield analysis and optimization by a statistical design approach. IEEE Trans. Circuits Syst. I Regul. Pap. **58**(12), 2906–2918 (2011)
5. Liu, J., Jaiyen, B., Veras, R.: RAIDR: retention-aware intelligent DRAM refresh. ACM SIGARCH Comput. Architect. News **40**(3), 1–12 (2012)
6. Wang, J., Dong, X., Xie, Y.: ProactiveDRAM: a DRAM-initiated retention management scheme. In: 2014 32nd IEEE International Conference on Computer Design (ICCD), pp. 22–27. IEEE (2014)
7. Mukundan, J., Hunter, H., Kim, K.: Understanding and mitigating refresh overheads in high-density DDR4 DRAM systems. ACM SIGARCH Comput. Architect. News **41**(3), 48–59 (2013)
8. Bhati, I., Chishti, Z., Lu, S.L.: Flexible auto-refresh: enabling scalable and energy-efficient DRAM refresh reductions. ACM SIGARCH Comput. Architect. News **43**(3), 235–246 (2015)
9. JEDEC, DDR4 sdram specification (2012)
10. Binkert, N., Beckmann, B., Black, G.: The gem5 simulator. ACM SIGARCH Comput. Architect. News **39**(2), 1–7 (2011)

11. Henning, J.L.: SPEC CPU2006 benchmark descriptions. ACM SIGARCH Comput. Architect. News **34**(4), 1–17 (2006)
12. Kim, Y., Seshadri, V., Lee, D.: A case for exploiting subarray-level parallelism (SALP) in DRAM. ACM SIGARCH Comput. Architect. News **40**(3), 368–379 (2012)
13. Snavely, A., Tullsen, D.M.: Symbiotic jobscheduling for a simultaneous mutlithreading processor. ACM SIGPLAN Not. **35**(11), 234–244 (2000)
14. Stuecheli, J., Kaseridis, D., Hunter, H.C., et al.: Elastic refresh: techniques to mitigate refresh penalties in high density memory. In: 43rd Annual IEEE/ACM International Symposium on Microarchitecture (MICRO), pp. 375–384 (2010)
15. Venkatesan, R.K., Herr, S., Rotenberg, E.: Retention-aware placement in DRAM (RAPID): software methods for quasi-non-volatile DRAM. The Twelfth International Symposium on High-Performance Computer Architecture, pp. 155–165. IEEE (2006)
16. Liu, J., Jaiyen, B., Kim, Y.: An experimental study of data retention behavior in modern DRAM devices: implications for retention time profiling mechanisms. ACM SIGARCH Comput. Architect. News **41**(3), 60–71 (2013)
17. Khan, S., Lee, D., Kim, Y.: The efficacy of error mitigation techniques for DRAM retention failures: a comparative experimental study. ACM SIGMETRICS Perform. Eval. Rev. **42**(1), 519–532 (2014)
18. Rosenfeld, P., Cooper-Balis, E., Jacob, B.: DRAMSim2: a cycle accurate memory system simulator. IEEE Comput. Architect. Lett. **10**(1), 16–19 (2011)
19. Rixner, S., Dally, W.J., Kapasi, U.J.: Memory access scheduling. ACM SIGARCH Comput. Architect. News **28**(2), 128–138 (2000)
20. Kotra, J.B., Shahidi, N., Chishti, Z.A., et al.: Hardware-software co-design to mitigate dram refresh overheads: a case for refresh-aware process scheduling. In: Proceedings of the Twenty-Second International Conference on Architectural Support for Programming Languages and Operating Systems, pp. 723–736. ACM (2017)
21. Malladi, K.T., Lee, B.C., Nothaft, F.A.: Towards energy-proportional datacenter memory with mobile DRAM. ACM SIGARCH Comput. Architect. News **40**(3), 37–48 (2012)
22. Cui, Z., McKee, S.A., Zha, Z., et al. DTail: a flexible approach to DRAM refresh management. In: Proceedings of the 28th ACM International Conference on Supercomputing, pp. 43–52. ACM (2014)

Towards Efficient ML/AI

EffectFace: A Fast and Efficient Deep Neural Network Model for Face Recognition

Weicheng Li[1], Dan Jia[1], Jia Zhai[3,4], Jihong Cai[2], Han Zhang[2], Lianyi Zhang[2], Hailong Yang[1], Depei Qian[1], and Rui Wang[1(✉)]

[1] School of Computer Science and Engineering,
Beihang University, Beijing, China
wangrui@buaa.edu.cn
[2] Science and Technology on Special System Simulation Laboratory,
Beijing Simulation Center, Beijing, China
[3] Communication University of China, Beijing, China
[4] Science and Technology on Electromagnetic Scattering Laboratory,
Beijing, China

Abstract. Despite the Deep Neural Network (DNN) has achieved a great success in image recognition, the resource needed by DNN applications is still too much in terms of both memory usage and computing time, which makes it barely possible to deploy a whole DNN system on resource-limited devices such as smartphones and small embedded systems. In this paper, we present a DNN model named EffectFace designed for higher storage and computation efficiency without compromising the accuracy.

EffectFace includes two sub-modules, EffectDet for face detection and EffectApp for face recognition. In EffectDet we use sparse and small-scale convolution cores (filters) to reduce the number of weights for less memory usage. In EffectApp, we use pruning and weights-sharing technology to further reduce weights. At the output stage of the network, we use a new loss function rather than the traditional Softmax function to acquire feature vectors of the input face images, which reduces the dimension of the output of the network from n to fixed 128 where n equals to the number of categories to classify. Experiments show that, compared with previous models, the amounts of weights of our EffectFace is dramatically decreased (less than 10% of previous models) without losing the accuracy of recognition.

Keywords: Deep learning · Efficient neural network · Face recognition

J. Zhai—This work is supported by National key R&D program of China grants No.2017YFB0202202, No. 2017YFB0203201 and NO. 2017YFC0820100, and by NSFC grant No. 61732002 and No. 61202425.

1 Introduction

Going with the progress of computing technology, the machine learning technology, especially the deep neural network (DNN) technology, is experiencing a breakthrough in recent years. As the levels of the neural networks going deeper, their express ability is going to an unprecedented area, which made DNNs the best choice in an increasing club of applications. As for face recognition, some state-of-art DNN models for image recognition have achieved great success such as the VGGFace [4] which achieves 99.47% of accuracy on LFW.

However, as the cons, DNN models have a very large quantity of weights. As for VGGFace, the size of its weights is up to 520 Mbytes. A large number of parameters require extremely high computing power and high energy cost. As for the resource-limited platforms such as smartphones, it is not easy to share the great success of DNN. Another issue for those models is that all of them use a classifier such as Softmax at the end of the network [5–9], to classify the image and find out which category the object in the image belongs. The downsides of this approach are its indirectness and its inefficiency. The dimension of the output equals to the number of the categories to classify [10–12], which could be very large.

To improve the efficiency of the model, we analyzed many previous models for face recognition such as Cascade CNN [1] and DDFD [2]. We learned that these DNN models all simply pile more convolution layers on the network to achieve the goal see Fig. 1. That makes this method not be able to scale to various devices in terms of computing and storage capability.

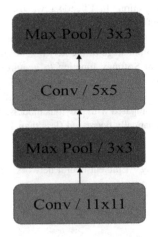

Fig. 1. Previous DNN architecture

Face recognition requires two procedures, face detection (finding out where the face is in a specific image) and face recognition (analyzing the identity of the face).

In this paper, we propose EffectFace, a new DNN model for face recognition designed with speed and efficiency in consideration. Our model is designed for both training as well as inference and consuming much fewer resources of both computation and storage makes it suitable to be deployed on a wide range of resource-limited devices.

In our EffectFace model, we introduce two efficient sub-modules respectively for these two procedures and both are DNN models.

The model we use for face detection is called EffectDet. we use sparse and small-scale filters inspired by NiN [14] (Network-in-Network) for our EffectDet model for face detection, which both theoretically and experimentally proved to reduce the number of weights and size of the feature map of each layer significantly.

Our model for face recognition, named EffectApp, is also designed with speed and efficiency in mind. Based on VGG16, we first use the pruning and weights-sharing technology on the neural networks model to reduce the size of weights for each convolution and fully-connected layer. Then, at the end of the net, we use TripletLoss [13] as loss function rather than traditional Softmax classifier to acquire the feature vector of the aimed face image. At last, with feature vectors of the face images, recognition becomes a simple k-NN classification problem. Through this approach, the output of the EffectApp network is a fixed 128-bit feature vector of the face image and the number of weights is reduced, which is far more efficient than the previous VGG model.

The rest of this paper is organized as follows: Sect. 2 gives brief analysis on related work, Sect. 3 talks about the details of the approach to implement our model and Sect. 4 shows the evaluation data of the model via experiments

2 Related Work

Convolutional Network is the most prevalent Neural Network at present. It has achieved great success in Computer Vision. For instance, LeNet [20] is a typical small Convolutional Network with two Conv layers, two pooling layers and two FC layers which has a good performance on some small-scale datasets such as MNIST and CIFAR. To deal with other large-scale datasets such as ImageNet, a direct way is to add more layers to acquire enough feature such as VGGNet [4]. The disadvantage of this method is obvious. Simply piling layers would make the number of weights increase intensively resulting in numerous usage of the resource of memory and computation.

Architecture like NiN [14] (Network in Network) and Inception [3] are designed to solve the above issue. Both use sparse filters to replace the dense connections of complicated networks and increase the depth of the network with multiple "micro-cores" like 1×1 conv filters.

To further reduce the number of weights, some DNN Compression technologies are used such as pruning and weights-sharing. Early works like [21, 22] prune networks based on Hessian loss function while recent work like [23] successfully prunes some large-scale networks without accuracy penalty. Works like [24–26] use Hash function to group the weights into some Hash bucket and weights in the same bucket share a single value. [27] implements this method on several different datasets keeping the generalization of the model without increasing storage overhead. The Back-Propagation algorithm can naturally be applied to the parameter training of the Hash bucket and the weights-sharing tech can be integrated into other generalized DNN models.

3   Fast and Efficient Face Detection and Recognition

3.1   EffectDet

In our EffectDet model for face detection, we use a network-in-network paradigm introduced by [3] to optimize the network structure, including several relatively small convolution kernels (filters) of different size. The design of the Inception [3] architecture is inspired by the research of the visual neural model of animals' brain in biology. An image usually has a high correlation in some specific part areas. Therefore, in our EffectDet model, we use three different filters with the size of 1×1, 3×3 and 5×5 simultaneously, as shown in Fig. 2, to acquire the feature of different part areas rather than using a single filter with a larger size in the previous approach to improving efficiency. We also add 1×1 filters before the 3×3 and 5×5 filters, which can significantly reduce the number of weights inspired by NiN [14] architecture.

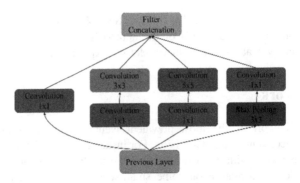

Fig. 2. Inception architecture

Based on the Inception architecture, we build our EffectDet model, as shown in Fig. 3. We use three Inception to acquire the feature with a Max Pooling layer added to the end of the second one to share weights and reduce the number of them.

3.2   EffectApp

As for our face recognition model, EffectApp, we realize that VGGFace uses relatively larger convolution kernels connected densely leading to waste on the resource of both computation and storage. Therefore, in the premise of ensuring accuracy rate of the model, we compress it properly.

We use pruning technology on EffectFace. First, we train the model in the traditional way and then prune the weights less than a fixed threshold value. Next, weights of the pruned model can be represented by sparse matrixes which can use CSR or CSC

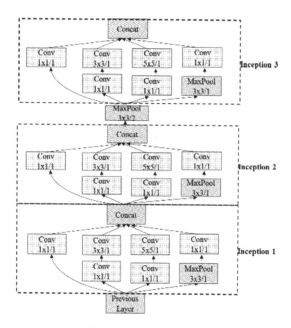

Fig. 3. EffectDet model.

to store. These sparse matrixes need 2a + n+1 storage units where a represents the number of non-zero value in the matrixes and n represents the number of columns or rows. Finally, we re-train the pruned model, which is sparsely connected.

To further reduce the number of weights of the model, we also use weights-sharing technology. All weights are clustered and weights in the same cluster use one shared value in codebook via an index matrix. In this way, the number of values of the weights to store is reduced. In addition, the gradients of weights are also clustered and shared in the same way while updating the weights see Fig. 4.

During this clustering and sharing process, we use K-means for clustering at the beginning. We cluster n weights $W = \{w_1, w_2, \ldots, w_n\}$ into K categories $C = \{c_1, c_2, \ldots, c_k\}, n \gg k$, with the goal of minimizing the class mean square see Eq. 1. Then we initialize the codebook to figure out the value that weights in the same cluster should share. There are three different initialization method [15] Forgy (random), Density-based and Linear. In DNN, weights of large value are more important [16], while the random approach ignores this. So we choose linear initialization for our EffectApp model to improve the accuracy.

$$\arg\min_c \sum_{i=0}^{k} \sum_{w \in c_i} |w - c_i|^2 \tag{1}$$

The compression rate of our approach shown as Eq. 2. We assume a network layer contains n weights and each weight is in size of b-bit. Through our approach, these n weights clustered into k categories sharing k values. The size of each codebook index is

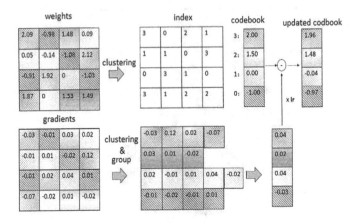

Fig. 4. clustering and sharing weights as well as gradients

log_2k-bit. The things we need to store are codebook of shared values k*b and the codebook index matrixes n * log_2k

$$\text{Compression Rate} = \frac{kb + nlog_2k}{nb} \qquad (2)$$

Besides the compression technology, we also change the loss function of the previous VGGFace for our EffectApp model for face recognition. Since Softmax classifier is indirect and not efficient, we use TripletLoss [13] as the loss function of our model. Instead of classifying the image at the end of the neural network, our model just acquires the feature vector of the image as the output of the net. In other words, our network model just aims to acquire the feature vector of the input face image and with these feature vectors we can make our application such as face recognition separately through a simple way and does not depend on the neural network. Therefore, the overhead of the DNN is reduced and the model is more efficient.

The main idea of the TripletLoss aim function is to ensure that the feature vector of a face image x_i^a is far closer to the ones of its positive samples x_i^p than the ones of its negative x_i^n samples see Fig. 5 and Eq. 3 where α is a margin that is enforced between positive and negative pairs and T is the set of all possible triplets in the training set and

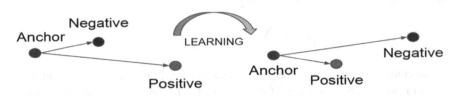

Fig. 5. Training based on TipletLoss

has cardinality N. The equation of the TripletLoss function see Eq. 4 where $f(x) \in \mathbb{R}^d$ embed an image $\times$ into a d-dimensional Euclidean space, here d = 128.

$$\left\| x_i^a - x_i^p \right\|_2^2 + \alpha < \left\| x_i^a - x_i^n \right\|_2^2, \forall \left(x_i^a, x_i^p, x_i^n \right) \in T \tag{3}$$

$$\sum_i^N \left[\left\| f(x_i^a) - f(x_i^p) \right\|^2 - \left\| f(x_i^a) - f(x_i^n) \right\|^2 + \alpha \right]_+ \tag{4}$$

Triplets selection is the key for training the network with TripletLoss function. Generating all possible triplets would result in many triplets that are easily satisfied (i.e. fulfill the constrains Eq. 3). These triplets would not contribute to the training and result in slower convergence, as they would still be passed through the network. To accelerate the convergence, we use the online triplets selection [13]. We choose the farthest positive exemplar and closest negative exemplars satisfying Eq. 5 from each mini-batch used for SGD.

$$\left\| f(x_i^a) - f(x_i^p) \right\|^2 < \left\| f(x_i^a) - f(x_i^n) \right\|^2 \tag{5}$$

Through TripletLoss, each output of the EffectApp is a fixed 128-bit feature vector of the input face image rather than an n-dimension vector where n equals to the number of categories classified which could be very large by using Softmax. By reducing the dimension of the output, the efficiency of our model is also improved.

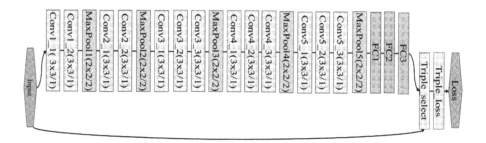

Fig. 6. EffectApp model

Finally based on VGG16 with weights compression and TripletLoss, our EffectApp model is built as Fig. 6.

4 Evaluation

Our hardware experiment platform consists of a 6-core Intel(R) Xeon(R) E5-2620v3, 2.40 GHz CPU and an Nvidia(R) Geforce(R) GTX970 GPU with CUDA. And we use Caffe as our deep learning framework.

Table 1. Settings of some hyperparameters

	base_lr	gamma	step_size	batch_size	max_iter
EffectDet	0.0001	0.1	1,000	10	100000
EffectApp	0.05	0.1	2,000	12	400000

We use QIM (Quantifying Hyperparameter Importance) to set the training hyper-parameters based on Plackett-Burman (PB) Design [27] for our models. We find that the importance of the base learning rate (base_lr) for both our EffectDet and EffectApp models are 43% and 46% respectively which are higher than any other parameters. Some of the hyperparameters are set as Table 1.

To deploy our models, we use python API to extend Layers in Caffe. Each layer needs to implement 3 methods: setup() for initialization, forward() for forward propagation and backward() for backward propagation and SGD. Specifically, we add three layers for our EffectApp model: TripleData Layer for data input and online triplets selection, TripleSelect Layer to add tags and TripleLoss Layer to implement the loss function. In addition, after we acquire feature vectors, a k-NN algorithm with k = 10 is used to classify the face image.

Our goal to design the EffectDet model is to maximize the efficiency and minimize the number of weights. So we compare it with Alexnet to test whether we achieve our goal. Out test is based on the ImageNet [17] dataset.

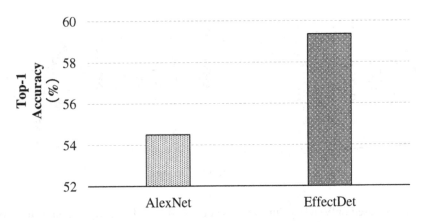

Fig. 7. Top-1 accuracy of Alexnet and EffectDet

We first test the Top-1 accuracy of both models see Fig. 7. Then we measure the size of both models' weights, where Alexnet is about 230 MBytes while our EffectDet is only 29 MBytes. We use the area of circles to represent the number of weights see Fig. 8.We can see that the top-1 accuracy of our EffectDet model is 5% better than Alexnet while the size of weights is approximately only a tenth of the latter, which presents the high efficiency of our model.

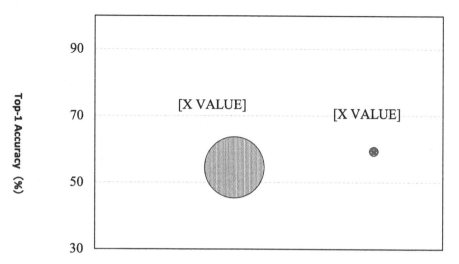

Fig. 8. Top-1 accuracy and weights size of Alexnet and EffectDet

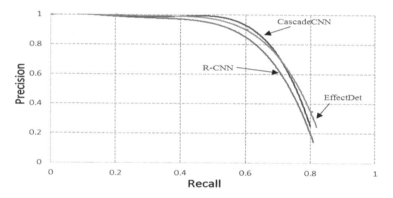

Fig. 9. PR of EffectDet with R-CNN and CascadeCNN

We also compare our EffectDet with R-CNN [18] and CascadeCNN [19] and plot PR diagram. Figure 9 shows that our EffectDet has similar performance with CascadeCNN while R-CNN is relatively inferior.

As for our face recognition model, EffectApp, we compare its efficiency and accuracy with those of VGG16 since our model is based on it. Figure 10 shows the compare of the number of weights of both models where EffectApp(p) represents the pruned model and EffectApp(p + s) represents pruned model with weights-sharing technology. We can see both pruning and weights-sharing technology can reduce the number of weights dramatically (by more than 50% of each layer) especial in fully-connected layers (by more than 95%). In general, the number of weights of EffectApp (p) is 8% of that of VGG16 and EffectApp(p + s) is only 5% of it.

In the aspect of accuracy, we implement k-NN algorithm through the feature vectors acquired by EffectApp. Figure 11 shows the compare of EffectApp, VGGFace

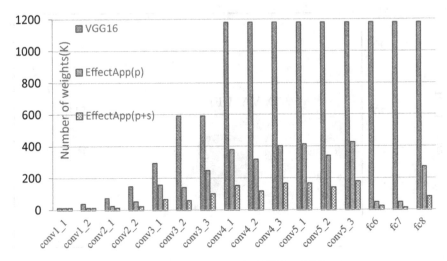

Fig. 10. Number of weights of VGG16 and EffectApp

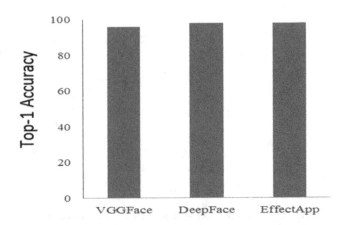

Fig. 11. Accuracy of VGGFace, DeepFace and EffectApp

and DeepFace and Fig. 12 represents the ROC of the three models. All the three models achieve more than 95% on top-1 accuracy and the ROC diagram presents that the performance of our EffectApp model is better than VGGFace but slightly weaker than DeepFace.

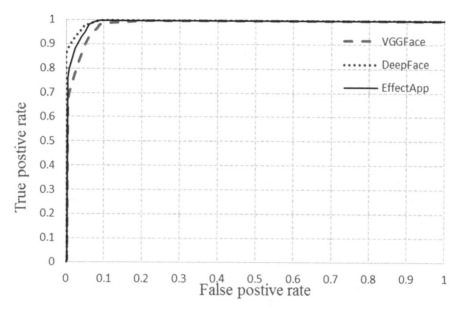

Fig. 12. ROC of VGGFace, DeepFace and EffectApp

5 Summary

In this paper, we present a fast and efficient deep neural network model EffectFace for face recognition based on the analysis of several previous models. It includes two sub-modules which are EffectDet for face detection and EffectApp for face recognition. We optimize the network architecture inspired by NiN for EffectDet to reduce the number of weights. In EffectApp model, based on VGGFace, we first use pruning and weights-sharing technology to reduce the number of weights. And then we change the traditional Softmax loss function to TripletLoss to acquire feature vectors of face images rather than classify images within the DNN, which reduces the dimension of the output of the network to fixed 128 dimensions. At last, with the feature vectors acquired, we implement a simple k-NN algorithm to finish the classification. The experiments show that without compromising the accuracy, our model significantly reduce the total number of weights (in EffectDet, the number of weights is 1/8 of that in previous model, and in EffectApp, it's only 5% of the original VGGFace) and therefore, its efficiency is improved.

References

1. Li, H., Lin, Z., Shen, X., et al.: A convolutional neural network cascade for face detection. In: Proceedings of the IEEE Conference on Computer Vision and Pattern Recognition, pp. 5325–5334 (2015)
2. Farfade, S.S., Saberian, M.J., Li, L.J.: Multi-view face detection using deep convolutional neural networks. In: Proceedings of the 5th ACM on International Conference on Multimedia Retrieval, pp. 643–650R. ACM (2015)
3. Szegedy, C., Liu, W., Jia, Y., et al.: Going deeper with convolutions. In: Proceedings of the IEEE Conference on Computer Vision and Pattern Recognition, pp. 1–9 (2015)
4. Simonyan, K., Zisserman, A.: Very deep convolutional networks for large-scale image recognition. arXiv preprint arXiv:1409.1556 (2014)
5. Mignon, A.: PCCA: a new approach for distance learning from sparse pairwise constraints. In: Computer Vision and Pattern Recognition, pp. 2666–2672. IEEE (2012)
6. Chopra, S., Hadsell, R., LeCun, Y.: Learning a similarity metric discriminatively, with application to face verification. In: Proceedings CVPR (2005)
7. Guillaumin, M., Verbeek, J., Schmid, C.: Is that you? Metric learning approaches for face identification. In: 2009 IEEE 12th International Conference on Computer Vision, pp. 498–505. IEEE (2009)
8. Hu, J., Lu, J., Tan, Y.P.: Discriminative deep metric learning for face verification in the wild. In: Proceedings of the IEEE Conference on Computer Vision and Pattern Recognition, pp. 1875–1882 (2014)
9. Huang, C., Zhu, S., Yu, K.: Large-scale strongly supervised ensemble metric learning: U.S. Patent 8,873,844[P], 28 October 2014
10. Schroff, F., Kalenichenko, D., Philbin, J.: Facenet: a unified embedding for face recognition and clustering. In: Proceedings of the IEEE Conference on Computer Vision and Pattern Recognition, pp. 815–823 (2015)
11. Sun, Y., Wang, X., Tang, X.: Deeply learned face representations are sparse, selective, and robust. In: Proceedings of the IEEE Conference on Computer Vision and Pattern Recognition, pp. 2892–2900 (2015)
12. Taigman, Y., Yang, M., Ranzato, M.A., et al.: DeepFace: closing the gap to human-level performance in face verification. In: Proceedings of the IEEE Conference on Computer Vision and Pattern Recognition, pp. 1701–1708 (2014)
13. Schroff, F., Kalenichenko, D., Philbin, J.: FaceNet: a unified embedding for face recognition and clustering, 815–823 (2015)
14. Lin, M., Chen, Q., Yan, S.: Network in network. arXiv preprint arXiv:1312.4400 (2013)
15. Han, S., Mao, H., Dally, W.J.: Deep compression: compressing deep neural networks with pruning, trained quantization and huffman coding. Fiber 56(4), 3–7 (2016)
16. Han, S., Pool, J., Tran, J., Dally, W.J.: Learning both weights and connections for efficient neural networks. In: Advances in Neural Information Processing Systems (2015)
17. Deng, J., Berg, A., Satheesh, S., et al.: Large scale visual recognition challenge (2012). 1. www.image-net.org/challenges/LSVRC/2012
18. Girshick, R., Donahue, J., Darrell, T., et al.: Rich feature hierarchies for accurate object detection and semantic segmentation. In: Computer Vision and Pattern Recognition, pp. 580–587. IEEE (2013)
19. Zhang, K., Zhang, Z., Li, Z., et al.: Joint face detection and alignment using multitask cascaded convolutional networks. IEEE Signal Process. Lett. 23(10), 1499–1503 (2016)
20. LeCun, Y., Boser, B., Denker, J.S., et al.: Backpropagation applied to handwritten zip code recognition. Neural Comput. 1(4), 541–551 (1989)

21. LeCun, Y., Denker, J.S., Solla, S.A., et al.: Optimal brain damage. NIPs **2**, 598–605 (1989)
22. Hassibi, B., Stork, D.G.: Second order derivatives for network pruning: optimal brain surgeon. In: Advances in Neural Information Processing Systems, p. 164 (1993)
23. Han, S., Pool, J., Tran, J., et al.: Learning both weights and connections for efficient neural network. In: Advances in Neural Information Processing Systems, pp. 1135–1143 (2015)
24. Weinberger, K., Dasgupta, A., Langford, J., et al.: Feature hashing for large scale multitask learning. In: Proceedings of the 26th Annual International Conference on Machine Learning, pp. 1113–1120. ACM (2009)
25. Shi, Q., Petterson, J., Dror, G., et al.: Hash kernels for structured data. J. Mach. Learn. Res. **10**(Nov), 2615–2637 (2009)
26. Ganchev, K., Dredze, M.: Small statistical models by random feature mixing. In: Proceedings of the ACL08 HLT Workshop on Mobile Language Processing, pp. 19–20 (2008)
27. Vaillant, R., Monrocq, C., Cun, Y.L.: Original approach for the localization of objects in images. IEE Proc. Vis. Image Sig. Process. **141**(4), 245–250 (1994)

A Power Efficient Hardware
Implementation of the IF Neuron Model

Shuquan Wang, Shasha Guo, Lei Wang$^{(\boxtimes)}$, Nan Li, Zikai Nie, Yu Deng,
Qiang Dou, and Weixia Xu

National University of Defense Technology, Changsha, Hunan, China
leiwang@nudt.edu.cn

Abstract. Because of the human brain's parallel computing structure
and its characteristics of the localized storage, the human brain has great
superiority of high throughput and low power consumption. Based on
the bionics of the brain, many researchers try to imitate the behavior of neurons with hardware platform so that we can obtain the same
or close computational acceleration performance like the brain. In this
paper, we proposed a hardware structure to implement single neuron
with Integration-and-Fire(IF) model on Virtex-7 XC7VX485T-ffg1157
FPGA. Through simulation and synthesis, we quantitatively analyzed
the device utilization and power consumption of our structure; meanwhile, the function of the proposed hardware implementation is verified
with the classic XOR benchmark with a 4-layer SNN and the scalability
of our hardware neuron is tested with a handwritten digits recognition
mission on MNIST database using a 6-layer SNN. Experimental results
show that the neuron hardware implementation proposed in this paper
can pass the XOR benchmark test and fulfill the need of handwritten
digits recognition mission. The total on-chip power of 4-layer SNN is
0.114 W, which is the lowest among the ANN and firing-rate based SNN
at the same scale.

Keywords: SNN · FPGA · Hardware neuron

1 Introduction

With the development of machine learning, especially the increasing rigid
demand for computing speeds of the deep learning, people are increasingly
expecting to improve the computational performance of computer systems. However, due to the well-known storage limits and power constrains, the computer
system of the classic Von Neumann structure is often subject to bandwidth constraints and can not provide sufficient data for computational components. In
fact, as early as 2004, some important manufacturers have turned their attention

Supported by Advanced General Chip, Project Name: The Design of Supercomputer
Chip, NO. 2017ZX01028-103.

© Springer Nature Singapore Pte Ltd. 2018
C. Li and J. Wu (Eds.): ACA 2018, CCIS 908, pp. 140–154, 2018.
https://doi.org/10.1007/978-981-13-2423-9_11

to improving performance through multi-core architecture. Unlike computers of Von Neumann structure, biological brain is highly parallel. Neurons store data in local units and have a low power consumption when they are in a inactive period. In order to obtain the same or close computational acceleration performance like the brain, many researchers have turned to the study of the brain [1,2,7,17,19]. However, the structure of the brain has its biological characteristics and it can not be simply reused in the area of hardware SNN implementation.

First, there is a contradiction between biological plausibility and scalability. If we adopt a very complex mathematical neuron model, the hardware resource cost of hardware neuron will be unacceptable and the scalability of the single hardware neuron will be very poor. On the contrary, if we use a very simple mathematical model, the biological behavior reproduction ability of the hardware neuron will be poor and it will have a little biological plausibility. So we should make a choice to balance the biological plausibility and scalability. Moreover, there is a contradiction between the calculation accuracy and limited storage space. For local storage strategy, the hardware neuron needs to store the parameters in local storage unit. In practical applications, the performance of neurons are influenced by the accuracy of the parameters involved in the calculation process. It means a great storage resource consumption when we store the parameters locally. However, the resource of storage is limited. The third problem is a contradiction between functional flexibility and power consumption. If most of the parameters are fixed in the hardware neuron, the design flexibility and adaptability of the hardware neuron will be very poor. However, if little parameters are fixed, it will significantly increase the hardware cost and additional power consumption of the hardware neuron.

Concerning these, Schrauwen et al. [2] proposed an FPGA hardware implementation scheme which is based on the LIF model and using a tree-like synapse structure to improve the operation speed of neurons. Moreno et al. [3] proposed a POE chip solution scheme and it can adapt itself to different problems just like the biological organisms. Hampton et al. [4] proposed a new developmental model structure in order to obtain the evolution of robust neural networks. Floreano et al. [5] used an evolutionary pulsed RNN scheme to obtain real-time machine control performance. However, few of them concern the factors of hardware consumption and scalability and these factors are very important concerning the large number of hardware neurons in SNN.

To make a balance between power consumption and function flexibility, we propose a hardware structure based on FPGA and it has more biological plausibility, scalability and better computing performance. The main contributions are as follows: 1. Various of neuron modes are compared and analyzed for the concerning of power reduction and functional flexibility. 2. A hardware neuron of IF model structure is implemented, which has a potential on the functional flexibility and network scalability. 3. The strategy of synaptic multiplexing and a trick of using addition instead of multiplication are adopted, which reduce the hardware device overhead and decrease the complexity of single neuron. Experimental results show the hardware neuron we proposed can satisfy the need of solving XOR problem and accomplish the mission of handwritten digits recognition on MNIST. It also has a good performance on power reduction and the total on-chip power of 4-layer SNN is 0.114 W.

2 Background

2.1 Biological Neuron

There are three components of single biological brain neuron: dendrites, soma, and axon (see Fig. 1). Dendrites receive action membrane potential from other connected neurons through synapses, and pass it to the soma later. The soma produces a corresponding membrane potential change based on the spikes it receives, which can essentially be analogous to a weighting process. When the membrane potential exceeds a threshold, the neuron generates a new spike. The transmission of this new spike mainly relies on axon. Notice that, when the previous spike is triggered, the neuron is in the refractory period and the spikes arriving in this period will have little influence.

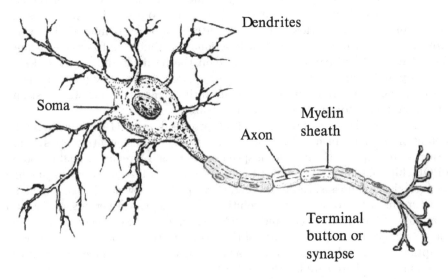

Fig. 1. The components of single biological brain neuron [6].

2.2 Mathematical Models

The mathematical models of neurons have been proposed and divided into five categories: Biological-Plausibility, Biological-Heuristics, Integration-and-Fire, McCulloch-Pitts, and other neuronal categories [7]. There are four typical models we care more: Hodgkin-Huxley model [8], Izhikevich model [9], Integrate-and-Fire model [10], and McCulloch-Pitts model [11]. Hodgkin-Huxley model can describe the biological neuron working process through four differential equations and it has a good biological plausibility. Izhikevich model is a simplification of Hodgkin-Huxley model. It can reproduce biological behaviors simply and accurately. McCulloch-Pitts model is an abstraction of neuronal behaviors and it transforms the spiking behavior into a mathematical procedure. Integrate-and-Fire model is characterized by implementation convenience and functional flexibility. With the basic IF model, we can add a leakage mechanism, introduce a nonlinear process, or add adaptive parameters to form a series of variants. We can imitate the behavior of biological neurons using different variants with different complexity.

3 Related Work

So far, most works are focusing on two directions: ASIC-based implementation and FPGA-based implementation. For the ASIC-based works, most of them are proposed to satisfy the desire of large-scale neural network developing. For FPGA-based works, they are mainly focusing on the functional verification procedure and the exploration of SNN practical application.

There are four famous ASIC based neuromorphic chips: TrueNorth [1], Neurogrid [12], BrainScaleS [10], and SpiNNaker [13]. IBM's TrueNorth [1] takes full account of the need to reduce power consumption, adopts digital circuits, with asynchronous event-driven simulation approach. It uses leaky-IF model and achieves interconnection of neuron core with $256 * 256$ cross arrays. The Neurogrid system [12] from Stanford focuses on the real-time performance of large-scale SNNs. The system uses digital-analog hybrid circuit, synaptic multiplexing mode, and integrates hardware and software system. Its parent node constitutes a network through routing, and can realize real-time processing of neural information, which makes it the best choice in the field of robotic control. The BrainScaleS system [10] from the University of Heidelberg aims at ultra-real-time performance. The system uses a digital-analog hybrid circuit to control the operating speed of the system. It can achieve up to 1,000 times the actual speed of neurons and is widely used in large-scale parameter space exploration due to its excellent computational speed. The SpiNNaker [13] of the University of Manchester focuses on the adaptability of the hardware implementation platform to different neuron models. The system uses a digital circuit to form the entire network through 500,000 simplified processing cores. The nodes communicate with each other through data packets. Its unique programmable module can support multiple neuron models, synapse models, and learning algorithms and it provides a excellent scalable and flexible hardware platform for researchers through the Internet.

For FPGA-based works, most of them focus on the exploration of designing space and performance gaining with different neuron models. Shayani et al. [14] proposed a spike neural network scheme using PLAQIF (Piecewise Linear Approximation of Quadratic Curve) integration and fire model. Maguire et al. [15] mainly reviewed the implementation details of an FPGA-based SNN network and proposed an IF model-based design using an event-driven approach and a time-multiplexing method. Coding the signal with the fire frequency method, the FPGA implementation of the SNN was finally performed and Optimized. Morgan et al. [16] proposed a reconfigurable and scalable network-on-chip solution based on the mixed-signal architecture (EMBRACE) FPGA scheme, using the SNN architecture to build a 2-layer network, effectively solving the XOR problem. Wang et al. [17] proposed a neural network architecture (NEF) for real-time pattern recognition SNN networks. They use an online pseudo-inverse update method (OPIUM) to update weights and simulates 64 neurons with a hardware neuron in a time multiplexing way.

4 Preliminary Idea

4.1 Coding Scheme Selection

Most of works use the information of spiking time with the firing rate scheme and spiking train method is less considered [9,17]. In addition, with the limitation of on-chip memory storage resources, many works use the 16-bit coding scheme to represent the membrane potential or membrane current without concerning longer bits scheme [14]. However, it is the spiking train based coding method which uses the information of spiking time more and the 16-bit coding scheme often leads to a accuracy distortion for the limited bits. What's more, since the spiking train scheme only cares one bit in every time period, we can significant reducing the power consumption with the trick of realizing multiplier with multiple selections and adders. Therefore, concerning the power consumption reduction and accuracy, we adopt a 32-bit spiking train based scheme as our coding scheme.

4.2 Neuron Model Selection

As we know, Hodgkin-Huxley model is relatively complex in terms of hardware implementation and it is not scalable in the realization of large-scale SNN. Though McCulloch-Pitts model is simple enough, it is not the best optimal concerning the biological plausibility. Izhikevich model is simple and it can accurately replicate the behavior of biological neurons. However, its model is fixed and it is not flexible enough to satisfy the need of different applications. Relatively speaking, Integration-and-Fire model is flexible and adaptable. We can conveniently increase or decrease the complexity with tricks to satisfy the needs of practical applications. The highest hardware complexity of the IF module variants is just comparable to Izhikevich model. The ability of biological neuron behavior reproduction is also in a reasonable range. Therefore, considering the complexity and the scalability of single hardware neuron, we choose to use the IF model structure as the base model of our hardware neuron.

4.3 Mathematical Method

As it showed, the IF model can be abstracted to a special circuit (see Fig. 2).

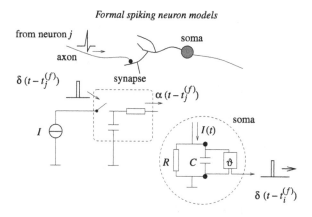

Fig. 2. The abstract circuit of IF model, where R is the biological neuron equivalent resistance, C is the biological neuron equivalent capacitance, v is the current neuron firing threshold, α and δ are input and output spike function regarding to time, t^f is the firing time [18].

With mathematical expression, the model follows (1), where τ_m is the time constant, its value is $\tau_m = RC$. V is the current membrane potential, I_e is the current action current, and E_L is the initial membrane potential. Then with integration method, Eq. (1) can be transformed to (2).

$$\tau_m \frac{dV}{dt} = E_L - V + RI_e \tag{1}$$

$$V(t) = E_L + RI_e + (V(t_0) - E_L + RI_e)\exp^{\frac{-(t-t_0)}{\tau_m}} \tag{2}$$

Concerning $dt = 1\,\text{ms}$, with the Euler integration method, Eq. (2) can be transformed to (3), where V(t + dt) is the membrane potential at the next moment, and V(t) is the current membrane potential. Concerning the accuracy of final realization, the equation we adopt in the hardware neuron is Eq. (3).

$$V(t + dt) = E_L + RI_e + (V(t) - E_L + RI_e)\exp^{\frac{-(t-t_0)}{\tau_m}} \tag{3}$$

5 Hardware Neuron

5.1 Architecture

A single hardware neuron mainly includes three parts: weight summation module, integration and fire module, and new signal generation module. These modules are respectively corresponding to dendrites, soma, and axon of biological

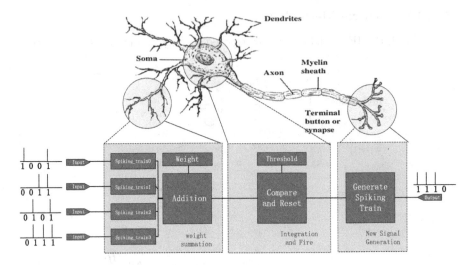

Fig. 3. The corresponding part of the biological neuron of each hardware implementation modules. Both the input and the output are encoded with spiking train method.

neurons (see Fig. 3). The weight summation module mainly weights the input signals from different neurons and then sums them. The integration and fire module is mainly responsible for converting the weighted sum from the weight addition module into the internal membrane current. Then the current participates in the corresponding differential equation operation to determine whether to fire or not, according to the situation of the accumulated membrane potential. The new signal generation module mainly determines the type of signal based on the incoming signal of the integrated and fire module.

5.2   Key Components

The weight summation module has 4 input signals corresponding to 4 synapses of neurons. The input signals are multiplied with the corresponding weights and added at the same time. During the actual training of the SNN network, the weights may be manually set or randomly generated by adding a weight generation module externally, which is specifically designed according to the application needs. Note that, since we use the spiking train based coding method, the weighting process can be simplified. If the spiking occurs, the corresponding weights are summed. If the spike does not occur, the corresponding weights are not added. Therefore, no multiplier is required in the actual hardware implementation scheme.

The integration and fire module mainly saves the accumulated value of neural membrane potential through an internal register. If the accumulated value of neural membrane potential exceeds the threshold, a spike occurs which means an excited behavior of biological neurons is reproduced. The module multiplies the weighted sum signal by a preset reference current value to generate the current neural action membrane current. Then, the membrane current of this neuron is introduced into Eq. 3 and the current membrane potential is calculated based on the cumulative value of the neural membrane potential at the previous moment. If the threshold is exceeded, an enable signal is passed to the new signal generation module. If the threshold is not exceeded, the neural action membrane current is cleared, and the next timing calculation is performed.

The new signal generation module determines the procedure of spike generation. In our scheme, the signal is encoded using the spiking train based method. If the spike occurs in the unit of time δt, the signal shows "1", and if the spike doesn't occur, it shows "0". Considering the error that the system hardware device delays by t_d, the time step is set to less than δt. Through repeated measurements, we take δt as 3 ms. With this spiking train method, we can not only avoid the error of the firing rate, but also meet the requirements of different application precisions by adjusting the coding mode of the spiking train without any changes on the actual hardware implementation.

5.3   Implementation of SNN

The SNN for solving XOR problem has four layers and the architecture is showed (see Fig. 4). It has one input layer, one output layer and two hidden layer. And the number of neurons is 9. Each of the node symbolizes a hardware neuron, which we proposed. And the weight of each neuron comes from the software SNN which has the same topology of this hardware SNN.

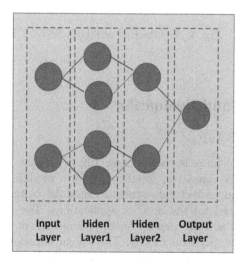

Fig. 4. Architecture of 4-layer SNN.

The SNN for handwritten digits recognition on MNIST database has 6 layers and it has 1594 neurons. The details is showed (see Fig. 5). The first layer is a input layer and it has 784 neurons. The second layer and the fourth layer are convolutional layers. Each has 144 and 16 neurons. The third and the fifth layer are max-pooling layers. The sixth layer is a full connection layer for final classification.

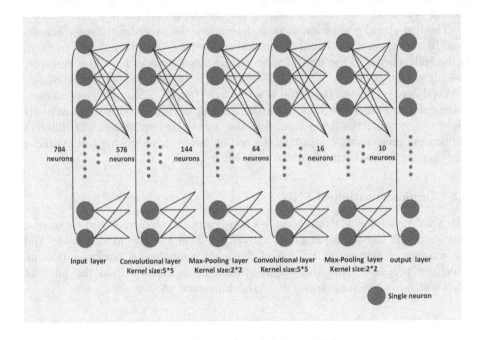

Fig. 5. Architecture of 6-layer SNN.

6   Experiment and Evaluation

6.1   Experiment Setup

The experimental platform is showed (see Fig. 6). It has five modules: SNN network module, SNN simulator, weight transform module, encoding module, decoding module, and correct rate statistics module. Note, the SNN network module can be replaced for the need of applications. The SNN simulator is a software SNN, which is implemented on the framework of Caffe, and it has a same topology like the SNN on FPGA. The weight transform module receives weights from SNN simulator and transforms them into the proper form to satisfy the need of SNN network module. The spiking train encoder module and decoder module are mainly responsible for spiking train encoding and decoding process. The correct rate statistics module, mainly in the stage of SNN network testing, performs quantitative statistics on the correct rate of the SNN network based on the input and output.

The experimental platform is based on the VC709 evaluation board of the Virtex-7 XC7VX485T-ffg1157 FPGA. The memory bandwidth of this board can easily reach 40 Gb/s, and it can develop connectivity functions and common evaluation. It can quickly provide powerful support for high-performance and high-bandwidth applications, hardware and software. Hardware designing and synthesizing is using Vivado. It has many functions and we can estimate power consumption, timing, and footprint for each stage of the design flow to achieve pre-analysis and optimize integrated functions. ANN modeling is implemented with MATLAB and SNN modeling is based on the Brian2 [20], which is a simulator for spiking neural networks and it is convenience in neuron model modeling.

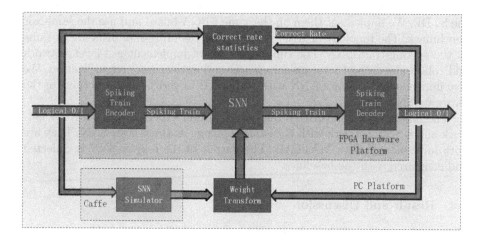

Fig. 6. Architecture of our experimental platform.

6.2   Benchmark

As we know, XOR benchmark is a basic benchmark for the neural network and it can verify the function of SNN on the area of data classification [21]. So we use XOR benchmark to verify the functionality of our scheme. Therefore, we implemented a 4-layer SNN on the FPGA platform using the proposed neurons and verified the XOR function and the corresponding relationship between number of correct input and fitness score assignment value are showed in Table 1.

The MNIST database of handwritten digits is a subset of a larger set available from NIST. It has a training set of 60,000 examples, and a test set of 10,000 examples. The 60,000 pattern training set contained examples from approximately 250 writers and the sets of writers of the training set and test set were disjoint. So we use this database to accomplish the mission of handwritten digits recognition, which is complex enough for us to evaluate the scalability and calculating performance of our hardware neuron.

Table 1. Fitness score value

Number of correct input	0	1	2	3	4
Fitness score assignment value	0	1	4	9	16

6.3   Baseline

The baselines of our experiment for solving XOR problem are a ANN network with the activation function of sigmoid and a firing-rate SNN network with signals coding in a firing rate way. The firing-rate SNN is implemented with the same hardware neuron as the spiking-train SNN. The weight updating strategy of ANN is based on the classic BP algorithm and the firing-rate SNN is based on the STDP. We implement them on the same FPGA board and use the same xor benchmark. The topology of ANN network and the firing-rate SNN are as same as the spiking-train SNN. For simplification, we implement a 4-layer network and collect the data of total on-chip power and devices resource utilization. We also implement a software ANN with MATLAB to verify the correctness of the hardware SNN results.

The baselines of handwritten digits recognition experiment are a ANN network and a SNN network with the same topology as the 6-layer SNN. They are both implemented with MATLAB. The output of the 6-layer SNN is collected and compared with the baselines.

6.4   Result and Discussion

The membrane potential of the hardware neuron is determined through a procedure of accumulation (see Fig. 7). Each of the spike represents 1 unit of measurement and the correspond weight is 1. At the beginning, spikes arrive and the accumulation membrane potential is lower than 5. When the total accumulation membrane potential is higher than 5, the hardware neuron spikes. As it shows, Our hardware neuron can perfectly reproduce the spiking behavior of biological neuron.

To satisfy the requirement of XOR function, which means that if inputs are all the same, the corresponding output is logical 1 and if inputs are not same, the corresponding output is logical 0. We designed our spiking train coding scheme as follows. At the input port, we use '0101' to symbolize logical '1' and '0001' to symbolize logical '0'. At the output port, we use '0100' to symbolize logical '1' and '0000' to symbolize logical '0'. In a word, it is a result of xor processing on every bits. The wave figure is watched on each cycle. Experimental results show that the neuron hardware implementation proposed in this paper can satisfy the requirement of XOR function and the wave figure shows that the 4-layer SNN using our hardware neurons can satisfy all the four results of xor benchmark. Thus, it can reach the fitness score assignment value of 16 (see Fig. 8).

The devices resource cost of each network with 4-layer structure is showed (see Fig. 9). We can find that the spiking-train based SNN costs the least devices

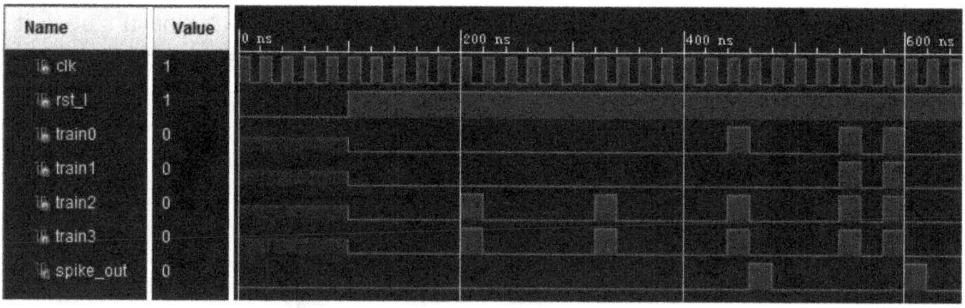

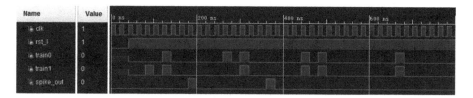

Fig. 7. The procedure of the hardware neuron spiking behavior. The threshold we set is 5. And it proves the membrane potential is iteratively introduced into the procedure of calculation.

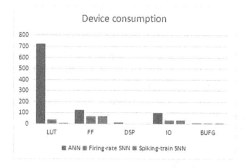

Fig. 8. Functional verify for XOR benchmark with wave figure.

and the ANN costs the most. Since the spiking-train based SNN transforms data in spiking train mode, it doesn't need to use a wide bandwidth, while the firing-rate based SNN needs.

Fig. 9. Device consumption.

With Table 2, We can also find that the hardware neuron we proposed is simple and needs less devices resource compared with the ANN with the same accuracy. And our scheme costs almost the same as firing rate based scheme except the IO resource and DSP resource. The IO utilization of spiking train based SNN is just 24% while firing rate based SNN is 64%. The DSP utilization of firing rate based SNN is 1.88% while spiking train based SNN doesn't need it. Concerning the large number of neurons in SNN, it is very meaningful for power reduction.

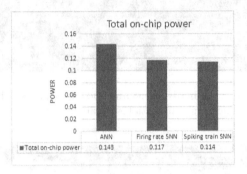

Fig. 10. Total on-chip power.

Table 2. The ratio of each device resource.

	LUT	FF	DSP	IO	BUFG
ANN	0.45%	0.14%	1.88%	64.67%	3.13%
Firing-rate based SNN	0.42%	0.12%	1.88%	64%	3.13%
Spiking-train based SNN	0.39%	0.11%	0%	24%	3.13%

Since ANN hardware implementation scheme needs to realize a complex sigmoid function, its power consumption is huge. At the same time, since the firing rate based SNN scheme needs to realize a multi-bites Multiplier while the spiking train based SNN needs only Multiple selectors and adders, the spiking train based SNN gets a lower power consumption. The total power consumption of the spiking rate based SNN is 0.114 W while ANN is 0.143 W and the firing rate based SNN is 0.117 W (see Fig. 10). We also find that the dynamic power consumption of the spiking train based SNN is 0.012 W while the ANN is 0.041 W and the firing rate based SNN is 0.014 W. That means comparing with the baseline, our scheme has a good performance at the aspects of device utilization, total on chip power consumption and dynamic power consumption.

We compared the output of 6-layer SNN with its baselines. The experimental result shows, the output is as same as the SNN implemented with MATLAB. Since the hardware implemented 6-layer SNN can process spikes in a parallel mode and need little middle transformation process, its calculating time is much shorter than the ANN. That means the hardware neuron we proposed can be used to handle a much complex mission and it has a good performance on the aspects of scalability. We also compare it with [14] and our hardware neuron has a simple soma unit, which means it needs less devices. What's more, since our scheme adopt a 32 bit spiking train scheme while [15] adopt a 18 bit spiking train scheme, the accuracy of our hardware neuron is higher than [15]. In a word, the function of our hardware neuron can satisfy the need of practical applications with high precision, while the consumption of FPGA resource is very low.

7 Conclusion

In this paper, we propose a hardware neuron based on FPGA and use the spiking train based coding method to encode the signal. The proposed IF model based neuron can reduce the hardware implementation complexity while ensuring the performance of computing, biological plausibility and scalability for the construction of large-scale SNN. In terms of signal representation, the spiking train coding method we have adopted can make better use of the information of spiking time and reduce the devices resource cost in a significant way. Finally, we compare the device utilization and power consumption of different schemes and the power reducing advantage of our hardware neuron is verified with experiments.

Although we strive to ensure that the implementation of a single neuron hardware consumes resources and enhances performance as much as possible, the actual solution of the spiking train coding scheme is still very simple. In the future, our work will focus on the supporting of more complex IF models, the using of FPGA off-chip storage resources, the exploration of a wider time-domain spiking train code design, the construction of a large-scale SNN hardware implementation platform.

References

1. Merolla, P.A., et al.: A million spiking-neuron integrated circuit with a scalable communication network and interface Science. Science **345**(6197), 668–673 (2014)
2. Schrauwen, B., van Campenhout, J.: Parallel hardware implementation of a broad class of spiking neurons using serial arithmetic. In: ESANN, pp. 623–628 (2006)
3. Moreno, J., Thoma, Y., Sanchez, E., Eriksson, J., Iglesias, J., Villa, A.: The POEtic electronic tissue and its role in the emulation of large-scale biologically inspired spiking neural networks models. Complexus **3**(1–3), 32–47 (2006). https://doi.org/10.1159/000094186
4. Hampton, A.N., Adami, C.: Evolution of robust developmental neural networks. In: Artificial Life IX. The Ninth International Conference on the Simulation and Synthesis of Living Systems (2004)
5. Floreano, D., Epars, Y., Zufferey, J., Mattiussi, C.: Evolution of spiking neural circuits in autonomous mobile robots. Int. J. Intell. Syst. **20**, 100 (2005)
6. Carlson, N.: Foundations of Physiological Psychology. Simon & Schuster, Needham Heights (1992)
7. Schuman, C.D., et al.: A Survey of Neuromorphic Computing and Neural Networks in Hardware (2017)

8. Bonabi, S.Y., Asgharian, H., Bakhtiari, R., Safari, S., Ahmadabadi, M.N.: FPGA implementation of a cortical network based on the Hodgkin-Huxley neuron model. Front. Neurosci. **8**, 379 (2014)
9. Rice, K.L., Bhuiyan, M.A., Taha, T.M., Vutsinas, C.N., Smith, M.C.: FPGA implementation of Izhikevich spiking neural networks for character recognition. In: International Conference on Reconfigurable Computing and FPGAs. Reconfig, pp. 451–456. IEEE (2009)
10. Millner, S., Grübl, A., Meier, K., Schemmel, J., Schwartz, M.O.: A VLSI implementation of the adaptive exponential integrate-and-fire neuron model. Adv. Neural Inf. Process. Syst. **23**, 1642–1650 (2010)
11. Izeboudjen, N., Farah, A., Titri, S., Boumeridja, H.: Digital implementation of artificial neural networks: From VHDL description to FPGA implementation. In: Mira, J., Sánchez-Andrés, J.V. (eds.) IWANN 1999. LNCS, vol. 1607, pp. 139–148. Springer, Heidelberg (1999). https://doi.org/10.1007/BFb0100480
12. Benjamin, B.V.: Neurogrid: a mixed-analog-digital multichip system for large-scale neural simulations. Proc. IEEE **102**, 699–716 (2014)
13. Furber, S.B., et al.: The SpiNNaker project. Proc. IEEE **102**, 652–665 (2014)
14. Shayani, H., et al.: Hardware implementation of a bio-plausible neuron model for evolution and growth of spiking neural networks on FPGA. In: NASA/ESA Conference on Adaptive Hardware and Systems, pp. 236–243 (2008)
15. Maguire, L.P.: Challenges for large-scale implementations of spiking neural networks on FPGAs. Neurocomputing **71**, 13–29 (2007)
16. Morgan, F., et al.: Exploring the evolution of NoC-based Spiking Neural Networks on FPGAs. In: International Conference on Field-Programmable Technology, pp. 300–303 (2009)
17. Wang, R.: Neuromorphic hardware architecture using the neural engineering framework for pattern recognition. IEEE Trans. Biomed. Circuits Syst. **11**, 574–584 (2017)
18. Kistler, W., Werner, M.: Spiking Neuron Models. Cambridge University Press, New York (2002)
19. Schemmel, J., et al.: A wafer-scale neuromorphic hardware system for large-scale neural modeling. IEEE International Symposium on Circuits and Systems (2010). https://doi.org/10.1109/ISCAS.2010.5536970
20. Stimberg, M., et al.: Equation-Oriented Specification of Neural Models for Simulations (2014). https://doi.org/10.3389/fninf.2014.00006
21. Maher, J., McGinley, B., Rocke, P., Morgan, F.: Intrinsic hardware evolution of neural networks in reconfigurable analogue and digital devices. In: 14th Annual IEEE Symposium on Field-Programmable Custom Computing Machines, FCCM, Seattle, pp. 321–322 (2006)

paraSNF: An Parallel Approach for Large-Scale Similarity Network Fusion

Xiaolong Shen[1,4], Song He[2], Minquan Fang[3], Yuqi Wen[2], Xiaochen Bo[2(✉)], and Yong Dou[1(✉)]

[1] College of Computer, Nationality University of Defense Technology, Changsha, China
{shenxiaolong11,yongdou}@nudt.edu.cn
[2] Department of Biotechnology, Beijing Institute of Radiation Medicine, Beijing 100850, China
wenyuqi7@163.com, boxiaoc@163.com, 809848790@qq.com
[3] Huawei Technologies Co., Ltd., Hangzhou, China
fmq@hpc6.com
[4] Science and Technology on Parallel and Distributed Laboratory, Nationality University of Defense Technology, Changsha, China

Abstract. With the rapid accumulation of multi-dimensional disease data, the integration of multiple similarity networks is essential for understanding the development of diseases and identifying subtypes of diseases. The recent computational efficient method named SNF is suitable for the integration of similarity networks and has been extensively applied to the bioinformatics analysis. However, the computational complexity and space complexity of the SNF method increases with the increase of the sample numbers. In this research, we develop a parallel SNF algorithm named paraSNF to improve the speed and scalability of the SNF. The experimental results on two large-scale simulation datasets reveal that the paraSNF algorithm is 30x–100x faster than the serial SNF. And the speedup of the paraSNF over the SNF which running on multi-cores with multi-threads is 8x–15x. Furthermore, more than 60% memory space are saved using paraSNF, which can greatly improve the scalability of the SNF.

Keywords: Similarity network fusion · Data integration
Parallel SNF · Multi-core CPU · Compressed storage

This work was mainly supported by the National Natural Science Foundation of China under Grant (No. U1435219), the National Key Research and Development Program of China under (No. 2016YFB0200401), grants from the Major Research Plan of the National Natural Science Foundation of China (No. U1435222), National Natural Science Foundation of China (No. 61572515) and the Major Research Plan of the National Key R&D Programof China (No. 2016YFC0901600).

X. Shen and S. He—These authors contributed equally to this work.

© Springer Nature Singapore Pte Ltd. 2018
C. Li and J. Wu (Eds.): ACA 2018, CCIS 908, pp. 155–167, 2018.
https://doi.org/10.1007/978-981-13-2423-9_12

1 Introduction

With the rapid development of high throughput biotechnology, the cost of acquisition multi-omics data of a disease becomes lower. The related biology knowledgebase and database is accumulating rapidly. For example, TCGA project [1] generates multi-omics data of more than 11,000 tumor patients, and provides rich data source for the integrated analysis of multi-omics data towards the assisted diagnosis and treatment of serious diseases. Integrated analysis [2,3] of multi-omics data can help us identify disease subtypes and provide individualized treatment. We can also explore the biological process of diseases by comparing the features of omics data between different patient groups. Curtis et al. [4] found new subtype of breast tumors by integrating the genomics data and transcriptomic data.

Similarity network fusion is an important part of multi-omics data integrated analysis strategy. Wang et al. proposed the SNF method [5] in *Nature Methods*, which fused multiple similarity networks constructed by multi-omics data of tumor patients to identify the subgroups of various tumors and to improve our understanding of diseases. The complexity and accuracy of the SNF is superior to other algorithms, such as iCluster [6] and PSDF [7]. Moreover, the online and offline tools [8] of the SNF offers researchers more convenient ways to use the SNF method to integrated analysis. However, the proposition of precision medicine initiative and the lower cost of multi-omics data generation necessarily bring the explosive growth in the multiple dimensional data of patients with various diseases. The complexity of the SNF method is $O(n^3)$, where n is the number of samples. The computation time will mushroom by the increase of samples. Hundreds of patients' similarity network fusion takes seconds in the case of Wang's research paper, but it will take hours or days to fuse when the number of patients reaches ten thousands, limiting our capacity of rapidly identification patient subtypes. Furthermore, the algorithm is thus so memory-intensive that it is unable to process larger-scale datasets.

Due to advances in parallelism, multi-core CPU has become the standard configuration of personal computer, work station and server. Although the multi-core processor is gaining popularity, there is no report on advances about the SNF algorithm based on multi-core processor to the best of our knowledge. How to benefit the performance and efficiency of the SNF algorithm by exploiting the advantages of the multi-core CPU is an issue that needs to be addressed. In this context, a parallel SNF algorithm based on multi-core CPU, named paraSNF, is proposed in this paper. The computing speed is much faster than the serial SNF algorithm. Moreover, the computational overhead is considerably reduced and the storage space is saved by making full use of the sparsity and symmetry of matrices.

The speedup and scalability of the SNF are investigated for this paper and the contributions are summarized as follows. (1) A parallel SNF algorithm named paraSNF is proposed to improve the scalability and speedup of the serial SNF algorithm. (2) The experimental result reveal that the paraSNF is 30x–100x faster than the serial SNF. (3) More than 60% memory space are saved using paraSNF through compressed storage.

The rest of this paper is organized as follows. Section 2 describes the serial SNF algorithm. Section 3 presents the paraSNF algorithm based on multi-core CPU, and analyzes the space utilization and computing efficiency of the algorithm. Section 4 provides the experimental results on real-word datasets, and analyzes the proposed algorithm's performance and accuracy. Section 5 concludes the research and discusses the future work.

2 Background

2.1 SNF Method

Suppose we have n samples for m data types. The main steps of the SNF method includes:

Step1: Compute the similarity networks.

Firstly, compute the distance matrices. m $n \times n$ distance matrices are computed for each data type, denoted as $\boldsymbol{D}^{(v)}$, where $v = 1, 2, \cdots, m$.

Secondly, compute the similarity matrices. m $n \times n$ similarity matrices are computed for each data type, denoted as $\boldsymbol{W}^{(v)}$, $v = 1, 2, \cdots, m$. $\boldsymbol{W}^{(v)}$ is the scaled exponential similarity kernel of the vth data type determined by the weight matrices $\boldsymbol{D}^{(v)}$.

Step2: Integrate the similarity networks. The m similarity networks are iteratively fused into a single similarity network.

Firstly, compute m normalized weight matrices $\boldsymbol{P}^{(v)}$ as follows:

$$P^{(v)}(i,j) = \begin{cases} \frac{W^{(v)}(i,j)}{2\sum_{k \neq i} W^{(v)}(i,k)}, & j \neq i \\ \frac{1}{2}, & j = i \end{cases} \tag{1}$$

Secondly, compute m matrices measuring the local affinity as follows:

$$S^{(v)}(i,j) = \begin{cases} \frac{W^{(v)}(i,j)}{\sum_{k \in N_i} W^{(v)}(i,k)}, & j \in N_i \\ 0, & otherwise \end{cases} \tag{2}$$

where N_i represents a set of the ith sample's neighbors in the corresponding similarity network.

Thirdly, iterate as follows:

$$P_t^{(v)} = S^{(v)} \times \frac{\sum_{k \neq v} P_{t-1}^{(k)}}{m-1} \times (S^{(v)})^T, \quad v = 1, 2, ..., m, \quad t = 1, 2, ..., T \tag{3}$$

where T is the maximum iterations. After t steps, the fusion matrix is computed as follows:

$$P_{\infty} = \frac{1}{2} \sum_{v=1}^{m} P_t^{(v)} \tag{4}$$

Step3: Cluster the fused similarity network using spectral clustering method [9].

The complete SNF algorithm is shown in Algorithm 1.

Algorithm 1. The serial SNF algorithm

Input:
  n: the number of samples. m: the number of data types.
  $nf^{(v)}$: features number of the vth data type, $v = 1, 2, \cdots, m$.
  $\boldsymbol{F}^{(v)}$: the feature matrices of samples in the vth data type, whose size is $n*nf^{(v)}$,
  $v = 1, 2, \cdots, m$.
Ouput:
  1) Initialize m features matrices $\boldsymbol{F}^{(v)}$.
  2) Compute similarity networks.
      Compute $\boldsymbol{D}^{(v)}$ and $\boldsymbol{W}^{(v)}$, v=1,2,..., m.
  3) Integrate the similarity networks.
      Compute $\boldsymbol{P}_0^{(v)}$ and $\boldsymbol{S}_0^{(v)}$
      for t =1:T
          Compute $\boldsymbol{P}_t^{(v)}$
      end
  4) Cluster the fused similarity network.

2.2   Time Distribution of the SNF Method

As illustrated in Algorithm 1, the SNF method consists of the following stages: Initialization, calculation of the similarity networks, similarity network integration, and clustering. Considering the S2-COAD model in Table 2 which contains 9292 samples with 3 types of data, Table 1 shows the time consumption of each step and its proportion to the total time.

Table 1. Time distribution of the serial SNF

Step	Time (s)	Percentage (%)
Initialization	184.39	4.2
Calculation of the similarity networks	126.08	2.9
Integration	4098.90	92.5
Clustering	20.93	0.5

Table 1 indicates that the time consumption of the SNF algorithm is concentrated in the integration the similarity networks. The time complexity of this steps is $O(n^3)$, where n is the number of samples. The paraSNF method is proposed in this paper to improve the computational and storage efficiency of the serial SNF method. We focus on the first 3 steps since these steps account for more than 99% of the total time.

3   Parallel SNF Algorithm (paraSNF)

3.1   Initialization

In the serial algorithm, the data is stored as the text file, and is read very inefficiently. In order to improve the initialization performance, we propose to store the input data as the binary file. Experimental results indicate that in addition to saving memory space, binary storage improves the initialization speed more than 100x.

3.2 Parallel Optimization of Vector-Vector, Matrix-Vector Matrix-Matrix and Operations

Analysis of the SNF algorithm shows that the algorithm entails many vector-vector, matrix-vector and matrix-matrix operations, including the pair-wise distance matrices $D^{(v)}$, the similarity matrices $W^{(v)}$, and the key step of iteratively updating $P^{(v)}$. Computing the products of very large matrices and vectors is very common in the SNF algorithm. Computing the multiplication of matrix-vector and matrix-matrix is a fundamental operation in linear algebra library and has been applied to many scientific areas to improving the computing efficiency, such as the popular DGEMM function in BLAS, MKL, OPENBLAS and so on. But the functions of these libraries are very limited. Some simple functions cannot be executed without calling several library functions. As we all know, Data prefetching has been proposed as a technique for hiding the access latency of data referencing patterns [10,11] Calling several library functions will greatly increases the data prefetching times and increases the cache miss rate. To facilitate discussion, we take the exponential function $c(i) = \alpha * \exp(-(\frac{a(i)}{b(i)})^2/u)$ as an example, where a, b and c denote the $n*1$ vectors, α and μ is scalar, exp denotes an exponential function. If the BLAS library is selected, the following five operations need to be executed in sequence to compute $c(i)$, as shown in code1. If n is large, each operation will entails prefetching all of the corresponding vectors into the cache. In code1, the vectors a and b need to be prefetching to cache once, and the matrix c needs to be prefetching to cache 5 times. In order to reduce the frequency of data prefetching, a segment-wise calculation algorithm is proposed in this paper, as shown in code2. In code2, vectors a, b and c are divided into n/N continuous sequences of size N.

As the simple exponential function is divided into n/N times, the vectors with a size N will be loaded into the cache at each time. After the five operations are executed sequentially, the pointer drifts so that the next vector of the size N can be loaded into the cache. In this way, the task can be accomplished by loading a, b and c only once, reducing the prefetching times and improving the algorithm's speed. Experimental results show that the performance is optimal when the vector of length N is 25% of the L3 cache.

For matrix-matrix operations $C = A * B$, we use the Block-Cyclic based algorithm. Matrices are subdivided into sets of blocks as the Connon method [12–16]. For the sake of simplicity, we assume that all the matrices are $n*n$ squares, and that both the number of the vertical blocks and the number of horizontal blocks are equal to q (i.e. the size of all blocks is equal to $k*k$, where $k = n/q$). Figure 1 shows the data assignment and data flow direction for the Cyclic-Block based algorithm, where $n = 12$, $k = 4$, $q = 3$. We define subtask $S(i,j)$ compute the blocks $C(i,j)$, where $C(i,j)$ is the ith row and j^{th} column matrix block of

Code1: Original algorithm without segment	Code2: Segment-wise calculation algorithm

vdDiv(n, a, b, c);
vdMul(n, c, c, c);
cblas_dscal(n, -1.0/u, c, 1);
vdExp(n, c, c);
cblas_dscal(n, alpha, c, 1);
	for (int i = 0; i <n / N; i++){
	    vdDiv(N, a + i*N, b + i*N, c2 + i*N);
	    vdMul(N, c2 + i*N, c2 + i*N, c2 + i*N);
	    cblas_dscal(N, -1.0 / u, c2 + i*N, 1);
	    vdExp(N, c2 + i*N, c2 + i*N);
	    cblas_dscal(N, alpha, c2 + i*N, 1);
	}

C, so the set of subtasks forms a square grid. In this case, the basic subtasks are responsible for computing the separate blocks. It is also required that each subtask hold only one block of the multiplied matrices at each iteration. In this way, some simple functions can be executed sequentially which can reduce the cache missing rate.

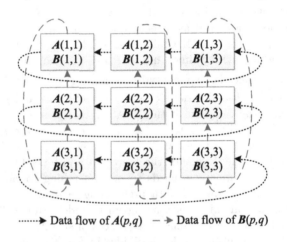

········▶ Data flow of $A(p,q)$ ─ ▶ Data flow of $B(p,q)$

Fig. 1. Data assignment and data flow.

Experimental results indicate that the matrix-matrix operation can be computed fastest when the space consumed by the correlation matrix in each subtask approximates to L3 cache.

3.3 Matrix Sparsity

Symmetry. Let $\rho(x_i, x_j)$ denote the Euclidean distance between patients xi and xj. We have $\rho(x_i, x_j) = \rho(x_j, x_i)$, and $\rho(x_i, x_i) = 0$, which means $D^{(v)}$ is a symmetric matrix with diagonal elements of 0. In this way, only the upper triangle of matrices $D^{(v)}$ need to be calculated and then the upper triangle is copied to the lower triangle. Suppose we have n samples (e.g., patients) and

m types of data (e.g., mRNA gene expression). Each sample has $nf^{(v)}$ dimensions. Benefiting from the sparsity of the symmetric matrices, the computational complexity of the distance matrix is more than halved from $n * n * nf^{(v)} * m$ multiplications and $2 * n * n * nf^{(v)} * m$ additions to $n * (n-1) * nf^{(v)} * m/2$ multiplications and $n * (n-1) * nf^{(v)} * m$ additions. Similarly, from analysis of the SNF algorithm, it is learned that the similarity graphs and the fused matrix are also symmetric. Matrix symmetry considerably alleviates the computational load of the paraSNF and improves its speed.

Sparsity. While updating the similarity matrices $P_t^{(v)}$, the kernel matrix $S^{(v)}$ only encodes the similarity of the K most similar neighbors for each sample, which means only K elements are used in each rows and the rest are 0. As K is usually between 10 and 30, the number of samples n is usually largely than 10,000. Therefore, the number of non-zero elements is less than 0.5% of the $S^{(v)}$, and the $S^{(v)}$ is very sparse. What's more, each row of $S^{(v)}$ has the same number of non-zero elements, making it easy to store $S^{(v)}$ using the Compressed Sparse Row (CSR) format. The key step of the SNF is to iteratively update similarity matrix with Eq. 3. Given $n = 10,000$ and $K = 20$, the computational complexity and time complexity of the sparse matrix are reduced to less than 1% of the dense matrix, thereby greatly enhancing the algorithm's performance.

3.4 Storage Optimization

According to the analysis of the previous section, the matrices $D^{(v)}$, $W^{(v)}$, $P^{(v)}$ and $S^{(v)}$ are all symmetric. By storing only the upper triangular half of these matrices, more than 60% of the storage space can be saved. To reduce the memory requirements of large sparse matrix $S^{(v)}$, the Compressed Sparse Row format was used to considerably save the storage space most of $S^{(v)}$.

Nonetheless, when solving the large-scale SNF problems, the memory space needed to store the matrices might be still excessive, even if sparse representations are employed for them. Further analysis of the algorithm reveals that matrix $F^{(v)}$ is not needed anymore after computing the distance matrices. Therefore, the paraSNF saves memory by making matrices $F^{(v)}$ and $W^{(v)}$ share the same storage space with matrix $W^{(v)}$.

4 Experimental Result

4.1 Experimental Environment

The SNF and paraSNF experiments were performed on a server with dual quad-core processor, 256 GB memory, 2 6-cores Intel® Xeon® CPU E5-2640 v3 @2.60 GHz and Ubuntu 14.04 OS.

4.2 Simulation Datasets

To simulate similarity network fusion for large-scale samples, we constructed two simulation datasets S1 and S2 (Table 2).

The dataset S1 is constructed by the following steps:

(i) Generate linearly separable samples which can be divided into three clusters, and denote these samples as *Virtual Data 1*.

(ii) Add $N(0,1)$ noise into *Virtual Data 1*, and denote these samples as *Virtual Data 2*.

(iii) Add noise into *Virtual Data 1* according to the Gamma distribution, of which shape is 1 and scale is 0.5. And denote these samples as *Virtual Data 3*.

Thus, dataset S1 is consisted of three views data including *Virtual Data 1*, *Virtual Data 2*, and *Virtual Data 3* (Fig. 2). For compare the calculative efficiency of the paraSNF, we set the scale of simulation dataset S1 as 9999, 19998, and 30000, denoted as S1-9999, S1-19998, and S1-30000 separately.

The dataset S2 is constructed by the following steps:

(i) Download five tumor datasets from the SNF paper [5,17], including colon adenocarcinoma (COAD), breast invasive carcinoma (BIC), lung squamous cell carcinoma (LSCC), kidney renal clear cell carcinoma (KRCCC) and glioblastoma multiforme (GBM),

(ii) Add $N(0,1)$ noise into these datasets and generate other simulation samples. Thus, dataset S2 is consisted of original samples from the SNF paper and generated samples, denoted as S2-COAD, S2-BIC, S2-LSCC, S2-KRCCC and S2-GBM.

Table 2. Samples in each simulation datasets

	S1-9999	S1-19998	S1-30000	S2-COAD	S2-BIC	S2-LSCC	S2-KRCCC	S2-GBM
n	9,999	19,998	30,000	9,292	10,605	10,706	12,322	21,715
$nf^{(1)}$	2	2	2	23,088	23,094	23,074	24,960	12,042
$nf^{(2)}$	2	2	2	17,814	17,814	12,042	17,899	1,305
$nf^{(3)}$	2	2	2	312	354	352	329	534

4.3 Analysis of Parallel Fusion

We used the paraSNF method to fuse the similarity networks in the datasets S1 and S2, and evaluated the precision of fusion result from two aspects.

Firstly, assess the accordance between true labels and integrated clustering labels by the paraSNF. Since that the samples in the dataset S1 is linearly separable with true labels but those in the dataset S2 has no true labels, we only uses the fusion result based on S1 to evaluate the precision in this paper. Normalized mutual information (*NMI*) is used to assess the accordance between true labels and integrated clustering labels. It's illustrated that *NMI* is always over 0.95 regardless of the sample scales (Table 3).

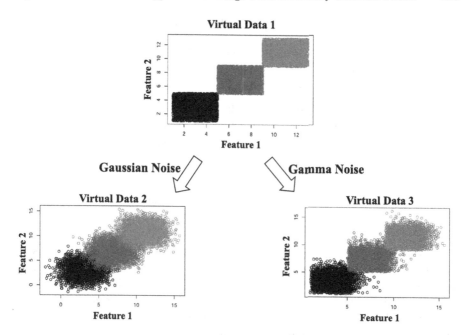

Fig. 2. Generate the simulation datasets S1.

Secondly, compare the fusion result using the SNF and the paraSNF method. We applied these methods to datasets S1 and S2 and found that the difference of fusion matrix is less than 10^{-13} and the cluster results are totally same.

Table 3. NMI between true labels and integrated clustering results

	S1-9999	S1-19998	S1-30000
NMI	0.9666	0.9603	0.9598

4.4 Memory Consumption and Performance

In this paper, SNFmatlab2.1zip from Bo Wang is used as the baseline, and its code is available at http://compbio.cs.toronto.edu/SNF/SNF/Software.html. By setting the singlecompThread parameter of MATLAB, the single-core single-thread performance and multi-core multi-thread performance of the SNF were tested. The speedup ratio of the paraSNF with respect to the two performances was compared.

Memory Consumption. As discussed in Sect. 3.4, the matrices are put into compressed storage using the attributes of symmetric and sparse matrices. Storage schemes of the paraSNF are optimized via space reused. Table 4 shows storage space consumption of the algorithm on dataset S2.

Table 4. Demand of the SNF and the paraSNF for memory space on different datasets

	SNF (GB)	paraSNF (GB)	Percentage (%)
S1-9999	1.676	0.652	38.9
S1-19998	6.704	2.608	38.9
S1-30000	15.088	5.869	38.9
S2-COAD	1.804	0.679	37.6
S2_BIC	2.293	0.827	36.1
S2-LSCC	2.275	0.781	34.3
S2-KRCCC	3.041	1.062	34.9
S2-GBM	8.186	3.075	37.6

As shown in Table 4, the first two columns present the demand of the SNF and the paraSNF for memory space. The last column describes the memory space ratio between the paraSNF and SNF. From the results in this table, it can be seen that memory consumption of the paraSNF is less than 40% of that of the SNF. Therefore, the storage strategy proposed in this paper considerably reduces the algorithm's demand for memory.

4.5   Speedup

Cache Access Optimization. For the sake of simplicity here, we only compare the performance of code1 and code2 in Sect. 3.2. The L3 cache of CPU used in the experiment is 20 MB (2,621,440 double). Figure 3 shows the influence of the continuous sequences size on time spent for code1 and code2. From the results in this figure, it can be seen that when the sequences size is 25% (N = 655,352) of L3 cache, code2 use the least time. Therefore cache access optimization increases the cache hit rate and improves the algorithm's performance.

Speedup of the paraSNF. We define Speedup1 refers to how much the paraSNF is faster than the SNF sequential algorithm (we called serial SNF), Speedup2 refers to how much the paraSNF is faster than the SNF on multi-cores and multi-threads (we called multiSNF). The definitions of Speedup1 and Speedup2 are as follows:

$$Speedup1 = \frac{Execution\ time\ of\ the\ serial\ SNF}{Execution\ time\ of\ the\ paraSNF} \tag{5}$$

$$Speedup2 = \frac{Execution\ time\ of\ the\ multiSNF}{Execution\ time\ of\ the\ paraSNF} \tag{6}$$

Figure 4 compares the speedup ratio of the paraSNF and SNF. Figure 4a and b shows Speedup1 and Speedup2 respectively on dataset S1 and S2.

It can be learned from Fig. 4a that by adopting the binary storage strategy, the initialization speedup of the paraSNF is improved by two orders of magnitude. The efficiency of the paraSNF in calculating the similarity network is

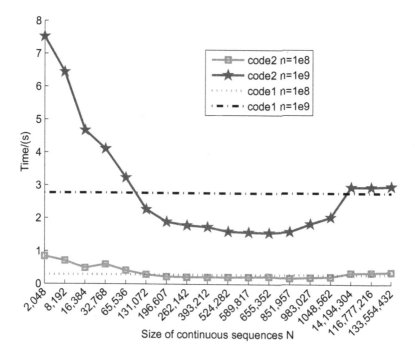

Fig. 3. The influence of continuous sequences size of code2.

4.5x–7.5x faster than the serial SNF while the speedup1 ratios are 40x–136x when integrate the similarity networks. The line of total time shows that the speedup1 in 8 different dataset are up to 30x–100x. As shown in Fig. 4b the speepup2 are up to 9x–20x when integrate the similarity networks even though the SNF running on multi-cores and multi-thread. It can also be learned that the larger the number of samples n is, the higher the speedup of the paraSNF is.

As the above experiments shows, the paraSNF algorithm is an efficient SNF algorithm. Firstly, the performance of paraSNF is improved through re-construct the SNF algorithm with BLAS library. Secondly, the segment-wise calculation algorithm improve the cache hit ratio, which made the performance of the paraSNF is further improved. Thirdly, because of the sparsity and symmetry of the matrices in the SNF algorithm, the Compressed Sparse Row and the memory reused strategy were used, which not only reduced the calculate amount but also save the memory space and improved the scalability of the paraSNF. Above all, the paraSNF algorithm achieved better performance compared with both *serialSNF* and *multiSNF*.

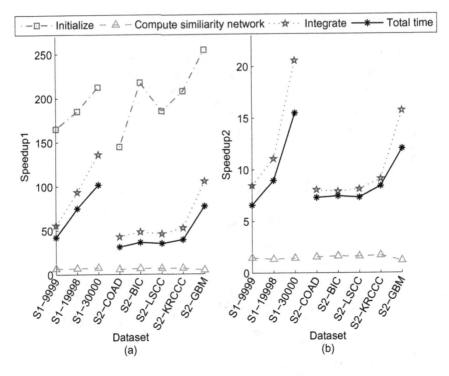

Fig. 4. Speedup of the paraSNF.

5   Conclusion

A parallel SNF algorithm based on multi-core CPU called paraSNF is proposed in this paper. Computational complexity is reduced by exploiting symmetry and sparsity of the correlation matrices in the SNF algorithm. Storage space is saved through compressed storage. Cache is also optimized to make full use of the potential of multi-core CPU. The speedups of the paraSNF to the serial SNF are up to 30x–100x, the speedups to multi-cores and multi-thread SNF is 8x–15x. Since the parallel acquisition of multiple data types of diseases will be lower-cost with the development of biotechnology, the data source will accumulate rapidly and massively. It needs more efficient algorithm to speed up the integrated clustering of multi-dimensional data. For involving many matrix and vector operations, the SNF method is very suitable for many-core GPU. How to speedup the SNF method using GPU and the CPU/GPU heterogeneous system is an issue that needs to be studied in the future.

References

1. Tomczak, K., Czerwińska, P., Wiznerowicz, M.: The Cancer Genome Atlas (TCGA): an immeasurable source of knowledge. Contemp. Oncol. **19**(1A), 68–77 (2015)
2. Levine, D.A.: Cancer Genome Atlas Research Network. Integrated genomic characterization of endometrial carcinoma. Nature **497**(7447), 67 (2013)
3. Verhaak, R.G.W., Hoadley, K.A., Purdom, E.: Integrated genomic analysis identifies clinically rele-vant subtypes of glioblastoma characterized by abnormalities in PDGFRA, IDH1, EGFR, and NF1. Cancer Cell **17**(1), 98–110 (2010)
4. Curtis, C., Shah, S.P., Chin, S.F.: The genomic and transcriptomic architecture of 2,000 breast tu-mours reveals novel subgroups. Nature **486**(7403), 346 (2012)
5. Wang, B., Mezlini, A.M., Demir, F.: Similarity network fusion for aggregating data types on a genomic scale. Nat. Methods **11**(3), 333 (2014)
6. Shen, R., Olshen, A.B., Ladanyi, M.: Integrative clustering of multiple genomic data types using a joint latent variable model with application to breast and lung cancer subtype analysis. Bioinformatics **25**(22), 2906–2912 (2009)
7. Yuan, Y., Savage, R.S., Markowetz, F.: Patient-specific data fusion defines prognostic cancer subtypes. PLoS Comput. Biol. **7**(10), e1002227 (2011)
8. He, S., He, H., Xu, W.: ICM: a web server for integrated clustering of multi-dimensional biomedical data. Nucl. Acids Res. **44**(W1), W154–W159 (2016)
9. Ng, A.Y., Jordan, M.I., Weiss, Y.: On spectral clustering: analysis and an algorithm. In: Advances in Neural Information Processing Systems, pp. 849–856 (2002)
10. Vanderwiel, S.P., Lilja, D.J.: Data prefetch mechanisms. ACM Comput. Surv. (CSUR) **32**(2), 174–199 (2000)
11. Liu, P., Yu, J., Huang, M.C.: Thread-aware adaptive prefetcher on multicore systems: improving the performance for multithreaded workloads. ACM Trans. Arch. Code Optim. (TACO) **13**(1), 13 (2016)
12. Krishnan, M., Nieplocha, J.: SRUMMA: a matrix multiplication algorithm suitable for clusters and scalable shared memory systems. In: 18th International Parallel and Distributed Processing Symposium. Proceedings. IEEE, p. 70 (2004)
13. Schatz, M.D., Van de Geijn, R.A., Poulson, J.: Parallel matrix multiplication: a systematic journey. SIAM J. Sci. Comput. **38**(6), C748–C781 (2016)
14. Li, D., Xu, C., Cheng, B.: Performance modeling and optimization of parallel LU-SGS on many-core processors for 3D high-order CFD simulations. J. Supercomput. **73**(6), 2506–2524 (2017)
15. Chen, C., Fang, J., Tang, T.: LU factorization on heterogeneous systems: an energy-efficient approach towards high performance. Computing **99**(8), 1–21 (2017)
16. Haixia, L.I.: Application of Cannon algorithm on parallel computers. J. Huangshi Inst. Technol. **3**, 006 (2010)
17. Supplementary Data. https://www.nature.com/articles/nmeth.2810#supplementary-information

An Experimental Perspective for Computation-Efficient Neural Networks Training

Lujia Yin, Xiaotao Chen, Zheng Qin, Zhaoning Zhang[✉], Jinghua Feng, and Dongsheng Li

Science and Technology on Parallel and Distributed Laboratory, National University of Defense Technology, Changsha, China
zzningxp@gmail.com

Abstract. Nowadays, as the tremendous requirements of computation-efficient neural networks to deploy deep learning models on inexpensive and broadly-used devices, many lightweight networks have been presented, such as MobileNet series, ShuffleNet, etc. The computation-efficient models are specifically designed for very limited computational budget, *e.g.*, 10–150 MFLOPs, and can run efficiently on ARM-based devices. These models have smaller CMR than the large networks, such as VGG, ResNet, Inception, etc.

However, it is quite efficient for inference on ARM, how about inference or training on GPU? Unfortunately, compact models usually cannot make full utilization of GPU, though it is fast for its small size. In this paper, we will present a series of extensive experiments on the training of compact models, including training on single host, with GPU and CPU, and distributed environment. Then we give some analysis and suggestions on the training.

Keywords: Neural networks training · Experiment · Distributed

1 Introduction

Neural networks are becoming increasingly effective and potential for major visual tasks such as recognition, detection and segmentation tasks [1,4,7–11]. Larger and Deeper neural networks require more computation at billions of FLOPs, with dozens or hundreds layers and channels [2–6]. However, inexpensive equipments with low power cost, such as embedded devices, mobile phones, cameras, robots, etc., can only afford several millions of FLOPs.

The inference time acceleration of deep neural networks on CPU/ARM architectures has attracted the attention of the deep learning community in recent years. Many architectures have been presented, such as MobileNet series [12,13], ShuffleNet [14], FD-mobilenet [15], etc. The computation-efficient models are designed for very limited computing power at the computational budget of hundreds of MFLOPs, and can run efficiently on ARM-based devices. For instance,

C. Li and J. Wu (Eds.): ACA 2018, CCIS 908, pp. 168–178, 2018.
https://doi.org/10.1007/978-981-13-2423-9_13

MobileNet v2 [13] runs at about 13 fps using only a single large CPU core of the Google Pixel 1 phone[1] and achieves an ILSVRC 2012 top-1 accuracy of 72.0%. These lightweight models have provided the possibility of highly-accurate mobile vision applications.

As shown above, computation-efficient models are quite efficient during inference time, however, the training efficiency for these models are quite different. The small models have different overall *computation v.s. memory access ratios (CMR)* compared with the large models, such as VGG, ResNet, Inception, etc., as illustrated in Table 1. In detail, most small models uses depthwise and pointwise convolutions instead of regular convolutions, which changes the CMR basically.

Because of different CMRs, different models fit different types of hardware platforms. From Table 1, it is shown that compact models have smaller ratios, which means that for the same amount of memory accesses, compact models can afford less computation, on the other hand, for the same computation, compact models need more memory accesses.

Thus, when the small models are trained in GPU, the speedup ratio is not the same as that in inference time. To further accelerate the models, distributed training is considered. Distributed training has also achieved great achievements. For instance, a ResNet-50 [4] model is trained on the ImageNet-1k dataset [16] in less than 1 h [17,18] using 256 GPUs. And the scalability on the training process achieves linear speedup ratio.

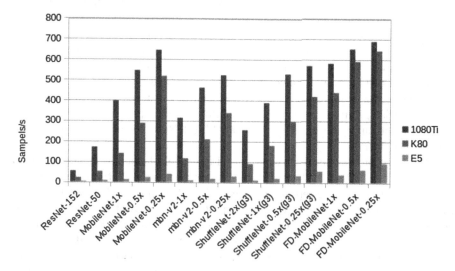

Fig. 1. Image processing speed (samples/s) on different networks and hardware platforms

---

[1] It is Chipset Qualcomm MSM8996 Snapdragon 821, CPU Quad-core (4 × 2.15/2.16 GHz Kryo).

In this paper, with extensive experimental results, we will show the training speed results for the compact neural networks, as shown in Fig. 1. The experiments are across different models and different hardware platforms. Further different scales of distributed hosts are set up to accelerate the training process, with up to 16 hosts and 128 GPUs.

In conclusion, we suggest that, first, computation-efficient neural networks face the memory bound and cannot make full utilization on GPU, and it is a model structure related problem; second, if you want to accelerate the GPU inference of the real time task, in which batch size is always one, *do not* use compact models; third, training on single host and on distributed cluster is a loosely coupling problem, and distributed training is beneficial for compact networks though it cannot overcome the low utilization rate of devices.

2   Related Work

Since AlexNet [8] won the ILSVRC-2012 [16] competition championship, Many successful deep neural network models have been proposed over the past few years. ResNet [4] has great recognition capabilities by adding residual connections between layers, which allows deeper layers and avoids model degeneration. ResNet-152 can achieve a top-1 accuracy of 78.6%. Another network Inception [1,2] enhances the expressiveness of the network by aggregating convolution kernels with different sizes and can also achieve a high accuracy.

Although these networks such as ResNet, Inception, etc. can achieve a high accuracy, the parameters of them are too huge. These computation-efficient models needs a mount of time to do both training and inference, which are not suitable for tasks on mobile devices. Some lightweight networks were proposed for these scenarios. MoibleNet series [12,13] uses depthwise seperable convolution [27] instead of traditional convolution, greatly reducing the amount of computation cost. For MobileNet v2, its top-1 accuracy reaches 72%. SuffleNet [14] uses pointwise group convolution and channel shuffle operation to reduce computation cost but accuracy doesn't decay. ShuffleNet-x2 achievess a great top-1 accuracy of 73.7%.

Optimisation in neural network for different platforms is another research direction. Gysel et al. [19] presented a framework named Ristretto that uses fixed point arithmetic to represent instead of floating point, which is an effective method to condense complex models on mobile devices. Mathew et al. [20] uses convolution sparsifying and fine tuning techniques to do full frame semantic segmentation on low power embedded devices and get a high speedup.

Another research direction is distributed training acceleration. However, reducing process in each iteration needs to wait for the slowest node, which causes communication latency. On the other hand, the mini-batch size will scale to a large number with the number of nodes increasing, which may leads to a significant drop in results. Facebook (Goyal et al.) [17] used 256 gpus to complete the imagenet training with ResNet-50 in one hour. Their strategy of linear learning rate scaling rule and warmup in initial learning stage effectively maintained the accuracy of the results within an acceptable range when the mini-batch size reached 8K. You et al. [18]. introduced LARS algorithm further increase the feasible mini-batch size limit to 32K and keep the accuracy from falling. They used 512 KNL chips and only took 31 min to complete the training with ResNet-50.

3 Computation, Memory Access and Devices

Due to the differences in hardware platforms, the computation capability of devices varies. Furthermore, the actual computation capability will also be limited by memory access wall as demonstrated in the roof-line model [26].

Computational complexity is commonly defined by the number of float-point multiplication-add operations in a single-image forward propagation. The computation complexity of one convolutional layer is calculated as $F^2 \cdot K^2 \cdot C_{in} \cdot C_{out}$ (FLOPs), in which F indicates the spatial width and height of the feature map, K is the kernel size and C_{in}, C_{out} indicates the input and output channel number.

Memory access is defined by the number of memory accesses during a single-image forward propagation. The number of memory accesses of one convolutional layer is calculated by weights memory access and output feature map memory access, excluding caching on chips. And the result is $(K^2 \cdot C_{in} \cdot C_{out} + F^2 \cdot C_{out} \cdot 2) \cdot 4$ (Bytes). Here the activation layers count double for the output feature map memory access.

Th roof-line model [26] gives a simple prediction for a theoretical computational efficiency upper bound of a specific models running on a specific device. The Roof-line model splits two bottleneck areas of memory-bound area and compute-bound area. The bottleneck inside memory-bound area is the memory bandwidth, while the bottleneck inside compute-bound area is the computational capability. And the prediction calculation is shown in Fig. 2 and described in the following paragraphs.

According to the roof-line model, we use the CMR to depict the *computation intensity*, which exhibits how many float-point operations can be performed by one byte of memory access. A higher CMR means the memory is better leveraged.

3.1 Model Differences

The computational complexity and the memory accesses[2] are shown in Table 1. From the table, it can be observed that (1) compact models have a smaller ratio, (2) within the same model, different width modifier significantly affects the ratio.

3.2 Device Differences

For instance, a NVIDIA Tesla P100 GPU has 3,584 CUDA cores and 16 GB memory, with 9.3 TFLOPs single-precision performance and 720 GB/s memory bandwidth, theoretically. While a NVIDIA GTX 1080Ti has 11.3 TFLOPs

---

[2] Unlike the original papers, the computational complexity and the memory accesses also include the pooling, lateral and activation layers.

Table 1. Computation to Memory Access Ratio of Inference (All data are divide by 1e6 from original quantity)

Models	Com. (MFLOPs)	Mem. Acc. (Mbytes)	Ratio (FLOPs/byte)
VGG-16	15470.26	661.76	23.37
ResNet-152	14696.84	518.22	28.36
ResNet-50	4999.61	220.69	22.65
MobileNet	568.74	57.18	9.946
MobileNet-0.5x	149.5	25.45	5.874
MobileNet-0.25x	41.03	11.94	3.436
mbn-v2	307.26	70.65	4.349
mbn-v2-0.5x	80.55	32.84	2.45
mbn-v2-0.25x	25.30	16.09	1.57
ShuffleNet-2x(g3)	514.97	49.31	10.44
ShuffleNet(g3)	135.93	24.66	5.512
ShuffleNet-0.5x(g3)	37.58	12.33	3.048
ShuffleNet-0.25x(g3)	11.19	6.16	1.817
FD-MobileNet-1x	144.49	23.88	6.050
FD-MobileNet-0.5x	40.13	10.11	3.969
FD-MobileNet-0.25x	12.04	4.6	2.617

single-precision performance and 484 GB/s memory bandwidth, and a NVIDIA Tesla K80 has 8.74 TFLOPs single-precision performance and 480 GB/s memory bandwidth . In comparison, a Raspberry Pi 3B with (SoC chip BCM2837, 1.2 GHz) has only about 10 GFLOPs computational capability, with 4 ARM Cortex-A53 1.2 GHz cores (without GPU), and about 3.6 GB/s DDR2 (1 GB) bandwidth.

Due to the complexity of the architecture of GPU/ARM/CPU and the memory access patterns cross layers of cache and memory, it is hard to compare two types of devices directly. In another way, we use a *computation v.s. bandwidth ratio (CBR)* to describe a device. The CBRs of P100, 1080Ti, K80 GPUs and Raspberry Pi 3B are 12.9FLOPs/Bps (9300 GFLOPs/720 GBps), 23.34 FLOPs/Bps, 18.2 FLOPs/Bps and 2.78 FLOPs/Bps, respectively.

As shown in Fig. 2, the red, blue and yellow lines indicate 1080Ti, P100, K80, respectively, and the slope of the slash indicates the memory access bandwidth. After the computation intensity reach the peak computational capability, the limitation turns into computation-bound from memory-bound. For instance, VGG-16 has an computation intensity of 23.37 FLOPs/byte, reaching the computation bound in most of the GPUs, and memory access bandwidth is not the bottleneck. On the other hand, MobileNet-like models with smaller computation intensity will reach the memory bound as illustrated in the figure, and can not make fully use of the GPUs. For example, MobileNet has an computation

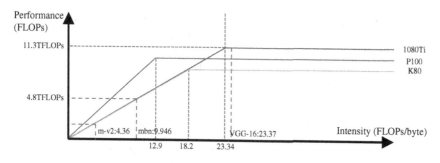

Fig. 2. Roof-Line Model for GPUs (Color figure online)

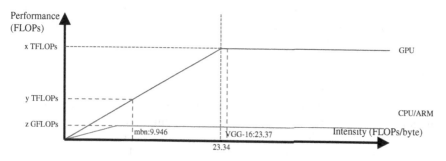

Fig. 3. Roof-Line Model for GPU and CPU/ARM

intensity of 9.9 FLOPs/byte, it only gets 9.9 FLOPs/byte · 484 GB = 4.8 TFLOPs peak computational capability when running on 1080Ti GPU. Also, as shown in Fig. 3, MobileNet is at the compute bound of the CPU. It is can make full use of CPU/ARM devices, though their peak speed is still much slower than GPUs.

4   Training and Distributed Training

4.1   Training

During inference, most intermediate results can be dropped after the layer has been computed. However, the training procedure is memory access intensive. During training, within each batch, all the intermediate results is reused in the back propagation. Unfortunately, back propagation is computed from the last layer back to the first layer, so it is a first-in-last-out (FILO) stack structure, and the outputs of each layer must be stored until back propagation. In consequence, the bus bandwidth is a main bottleneck of the training on CPU, which is smaller than bandwidth inside GPU (the bandwidth of single channel DDR4 2666 MHz is 21.3 GB/s).

The forward propagation of training is just the same as inference, so the computational complexity and the memory accesses are the same as inference.

The backward propagation needs an approximatively double memory access, one for input layer and another for the intermediate results produced in the forward propagation. The computational complexity is also doubled, for the same scale of gradient computation. Under this estimation, the intensive of training is the same as inference, for simplicity.

4.2 Distributed Training

We use multiple hosts to further accelerate the training process. We train the network with large mini-batch SGD and distributed parameter servers [21] in data parallel mode. A bulk synchronous SGD is used to updates the parameters, while KVstore holds the parameters as key-value pair form in DRAM to keep the synchronous communications.

We configure the learning rate according to the *linear scaling rule* [17]: when the mini-batch size is multiplied by k, multiply the learning rate by k. Gradual warm up [17] is also used. In order to reduce traffic between nodes, we only compute the batch normalization locally. Since the experiments is conducted on a shared storage system, splitting data on each nodes is not needed. Each epoch randomly selects part of the data of the entire training set. The engine maintains a queue of write dependencies and a queue of read dependencies. As long as an operation has no dependencies, it can be executed immediately without waiting. So the layer level calculation can be performed in a pipelined manner.

Each node in cluster runs both a server and a worker. For a cluster of n nodes, each node communicates with the other n-1 nodes. The workers pull data from the server and compute the gradient then send to the server. The servers receive the data sent by the workers and reduce the result then return to workers. However, since the total parameter amount are averaged over n nodes, this traffic does not increase significantly as the cluster size increases, it maintains $(n-1)/n$ ratio.

5 Experiment

We set up the experiments using MXNet (0.11.0) [22], with different model types, different hardware platforms and different scale of hosts. We use the ILSVRC 2012 dataset [16] to evaluate the acceleration and effectiveness. Within all the tests, we set batch size to 32 on per device (GPU/CPU), and set all the input of the images to 224×224.

The models used include ResNet-152/50, MobileNet v1 (1x, 0.5x, 0.25x), MobileNet v2 (1x, 0.5x, 0.25x), ShuffleNet (2x, 1x, 0.5x, 0.25x, with group 3), FD-MobileNet(1x, 0.5x, 0.25x), etc. Here the scale of MobileNet 1x is as the same level as ShuffleNet 2x, and MobileNet 0.5x, ShuffleNet 1x, FD-MobileNet 1x are at the same level.

The hardware platforms include NVIDIA Tesla K80 GPU (Kepler architecture), NVIDIA GeForce GTX 1080 Ti GPU (Pascal architecture), etc. Also, we choose Intel CPU to test different intensity. The CPU platform is Intel

E5-2690 v4@ 2.60 GHz CPU (28 cores) with MKL accelerated, and the main memory is 128 GB, is 8x 16 GB DDR4 and the total bandwidth is over 80 GB/s bandwidth.

The hosts scales include single host, and up to 32 hosts. The distributed scales are set up by hosts with 2x K80 (totally 4 GPUs in one host), however, for experiment requirement we only use one GPU inside. The interconnected network is InfiniBand [23]. Also, the storage use a distributed SAN [24] server.

5.1   Single Host Result and Analysis

From Table 2, it is shown that the GPU utilization rate is very low when training compact. And the result shows that the device utilization is also positive correlative to the computation intensity. Here we estimate the training computational complexity as triple as that of inference.

However, the roof-line model is a theoretical model to depict the up bound of the model run on a device. In practice, the speed of training is affected by many other factors as cache size, implementations of convolution operation, depth-wise operation, GEMM [25] operation.

Table 2. Computation Time on Single Host. M.MF.: Models Training MFLOPs, I.: Intensity, sam./s: Samples processed per second, GF/s: GFLOPs processed per second

Models	M.MF.	I.	1080 Ti		K80		E5	
			sam./s	GF/s	sam./s	GF/s	sam./s	GF/s
ResNet-152	44090.5	28.36	53.31	2350.5	20.77	915.8	3.07	135.4
ResNet-50	14998.8	22.65	169.85	2547.5	51.13	766.9	7.08	106.2
MobileNet-1x	1706.2	9.95	397.2	677.7	139.34	237.7	11.86	20.2
MobileNet-0.5x	448.5	5.87	545.94	244.9	287.6	129	22.3	10
MobileNet-0.25x	123.1	3.44	644.72	79.4	517.39	63.7	39.13	4.8
mbn-v2-1x	921.8	4.35	314.08	289.5	115.31	106.3	8.52	7.9
mbn-v2-0.5x	241.7	2.45	460.8	111.4	208.94	50.5	16.04	3.9
mbn-v2-0.25x	75.9	1.57	522.23	39.6	337.77	25.6	28.44	2.2
ShuffleNet-2x(g3)	1544.9	10.44	255.21	394.3	89.35	138	9.68	15
ShuffleNet-1x(g3)	407.8	5.51	387.82	158.2	178.88	72.9	18.53	7.6
ShuffleNet-0.5x(g3)	112.7	3.05	528.78	59.6	296.45	33.4	32.41	3.7
ShuffleNet-0.25x(g3)	33.6	1.82	569.2	19.1	418.23	14.1	54.01	1.8
FD-MobileNet-1x	433.5	6.05	581.39	252	438.21	190	36.02	15.6
FD-MobileNet-0.5x	120.4	3.97	651.59	78.5	590.96	71.2	60.71	7.3
FD-MobileNet-0.25x	36.1	2.62	688.88	24.9	642.98	23.2	91.77	3.3

5.2   Distributed Result and Analysis

In Table 3, the result is the computation speed on distributed cluster with synchronous method. The result is average samples processed per second of models on different scale of hosts, the data inside the brackets indicates the speed of each single host. The results show that each models achieve the linear speedup in the distributed acceleration. Full experiments validate the synchronous distributed method get the same performance on the ILSVRC accuracy.

Table 3. Computation Speed on Distributed Hosts (average samples processed per second on each host)

Models	1host	2hosts	4hosts	8hosts	16hosts
ResNet-152	20.77	38.9(19.4)	80.5 (20.1)	159.4(19.9)	249.9(15.6)
ResNet-50	51.13	97.8(48.9)	200.1 (50.0)	400.8(50.1)	776.4(48.5)
MobileNet-1x	139.3	274.8(137.4)	553.0 (138.2)	1113.3(139.1)	2212.2(138.2)
MobileNet-0.5x	287.6	569.1(284.5)	1146.9(286.7)	2281.8(285.2)	4543.0(283.9)
MobileNet-0.25x	517.3	1011(505.5)	2016.6(504.1)	4090.2(511.2)	8164.4(510.2)
mbn-v2-1x	115.3	227.5(113.7)	455.7 (113.9)	907.7(113.4)	1811.8(113.2)
mbn-v2-0.5x	208.9	420.1(210.0)	844.8 (211.2)	1689.0(211.1)	3363.7(210.2)
mbn-v2-0.25x	337.7	674.9(337.4)	1370.7(342.6)	2719.2(339.9)	5425.8(339.1)
ShuffleNet-2x-g3	89.35	177.8(88.9)	361.1 (90.2)	718.4(89.8)	1202.8(75.1)
ShuffleNet-1x-g3	178.8	357.8(178.9)	723.4 (180.8)	1441.6(180.2)	2134.0(133.3)
ShuffleNet-0.5x-g3	296.4	592.4(296.2)	1211.4(302.8)	2414.4(301.8)	4282.9(267.6)
ShuffleNet-0.25x-g3	418.2	833.8(416.9)	1687.2(421.8)	3326.0(415.7)	6633.4(414.5)
FD-MobileNet-1x	438.2	859.6(429.8)	1761.5(440.3)	3499.9(437.4)	6451.2(403.2)
FD-MobileNet-0.5x	590.9	1063.8(531.9)	2120.2(530.0)	4636.7(579.5)	8885.6(555.3)
FD-MobileNet-0.25x	642.9	1121.8(560.9)	2223.3(555.8)	5054.2(631.7)	9935.0(620.9)

6 Conclusion

In this paper, we suggest that, first, computation-efficient neural networks face the memory bound and cannot make full utilization on GPU, and it is a model structure related problem; second, if you want to accelerate the GPU inference of the real time task, in which batch size is always one, *do not* use compact models; third, training on single host and on distributed cluster is a loosely coupling problem, and distributed training is beneficial for compact networks though it cannot overcome the low utilization rate of devices.

References

1. Szegedy, C., Liu, W., Jia, Y., et al.: Going deeper with convolutions, pp. 1–9 (2014)
2. Szegedy, C., Ioffe, S., Vanhoucke, V., et al.: Inception-v4, inception-resnet and the impact of residual connections on learning. AAAI, vol. 4, p. 12 (2017)

3. Chollet, F.: Xception: deep learning with depth wise separable convolutions. arXiv preprint (2016)
4. He, K., Zhang, X., Ren, S., et al.: Deep residual learning for image recognition. In: Proceedings of the IEEE Conference on Computer Vision and Pattern Recognition, pp. 770–778 (2016)
5. Huang, G., Liu, Z., Weinberger, K.Q., et al.: Densely connected convolutional networks. In: Proceedings of the IEEE Conference on Computer Vision and Pattern Recognition, vol. 1, no. 2, p. 3 (2017)
6. Huang, J., Rathod, V., Sun, C., et al.: Speed/accuracy trade-offs for modern convolutional object detectors. In: IEEE CVPR (2017)
7. Simonyan, K., Zisserman, A.: Very deep convolutional networks for large-scale image recognition. Computer Science (2014)
8. Krizhevsky, A., Sutskever, I., Hinton, G.E.: ImageNet classification with deep convolutional neural networks. In: International Conference on Neural Information Processing Systems, pp. 1097–1105. Curran Associates Inc. (2012)
9. Girshick, R., Donahue, J., Darrell, T., et al.: Rich feature hierarchies for accurate object detection and semantic segmentation. In: IEEE Conference on Computer Vision and Pattern Recognition, pp. 580–587. IEEE Computer Society (2014)
10. Ren, S., He, K., Girshick, R.: Faster R-CNN: towards real-time object detection with region proposal networks. IEEE Trans. Pattern Anal. Mach. Intell. **39**(6), 1137–1149 (2017)
11. Long, J., Shelhamer, E., Darrell, T.: Fully convolutional networks for semantic segmentation. In: Computer Vision and Pattern Recognition, pp. 3431–3440. IEEE (2015)
12. Howard, A.G., Zhu, M., Chen, B., et al.: MobileNets: Efficient convolutional neural networks for mobile vision applications. arXiv preprint arXiv:1704.04861 (2017)
13. Sandler, M., Howard, A., Zhu, M., et al.: Inverted residuals and linear bottlenecks: mobile networks for classification, detection and segmentation. arXiv preprint arXiv:1801.04381 (2018)
14. Zhang, X., Zhou, X., Lin, M., et al.: ShuffleNet: an extremely efficient convolutional neural network for mobile devices. arXiv preprint arXiv:1707.01083 (2017)
15. Qin, Z., Zhang, Z., Chen, X., et al.: FD-MobileNet: improved MobileNet with a fast down sampling strategy. arXiv preprint arXiv:1802.03750 (2018)
16. Russakovsky, O., et al.: Imagenet large scale visual recognition challenge. Int. J. Comput. Vis. **115**(3), 211–252 (2015)
17. Goyal, P., Dollár, P., Girshick, R., et al.: Accurate, large minibatch SGD: training ImageNet in 1 hour. arXiv preprint arXiv:1706.02677 (2017)
18. You, Y., Zhang, Z., Hsieh, C.J., et al.: 100-epoch ImageNet training with AlexNet in 24 minutes. ArXiv e-prints (2017)
19. Gysel, P., Motamedi, M., Ghiasi, S.: Hardware-oriented approximation of convolutional neural networks (2016)
20. Mathew, M., Desappan, K., Swami, P.K., et al.: Sparse, quantized, full frame CNN for low power embedded devices. In: IEEE Conference on Computer Vision and Pattern Recognition Workshops, pp. 328–336. IEEE Computer Society (2017)
21. Li, M.: Scaling distributed machine learning with the parameter server, p. 1 (2014)
22. Chen, T., Li, M., Li, Y., et al.: MXNet: a flexible and efficient machine learning library for heterogeneous distributed systems. Statistics (2015)
23. InfiniBand Trade Association: InfiniBand Architecture Specification: Release 1.0 (2000)
24. Padovano, M.: System and method for accessing a storage area network as network attached storage: WO, US6606690[P] (2003)

25. Kågström, B., Ling, P., van Loan, C.: GEMM-based level 3 BLAS: high-performance model implementations and performance evaluation benchmark. ACM Trans. Math. Softw. (TOMS) **24**(3), 268–302 (1998)
26. Williams, S., Patterson, D., Oliker, L., et al.: The roofline model: a pedagogical tool for auto-tuning kernels on multicore architectures. In: Hot Chips, vol. 20, pp. 24–26 (2008)
27. Sifre, L.: Rigid-motion scattering for image classification. Ph.D. thesis (2014)

Parallel Computing System

Distributed Data Load Balancing
for Scalable Key-Value Cache Systems

Shanshan Chen[1,2]([✉]), Xudong Zhou[1], Guiping Zhou[1], and Richard O. Sinnott[3]

[1] School of Computer Science, Nanjing University of Posts and Telecommunications,
Nanjing, China
chenss@njupt.edu.cn
[2] Department of Computer Science and Engineering, Shanghai Jiao Tong University,
Shanghai, China
[3] School of Computing and Information Systems, University of Melbourne,
Melbourne, Australia
rsinnott@unimelb.edu.au

Abstract. In recent years, in-memory key-value cache systems have become increasingly popular in tackling real-time and interactive data processing tasks. Caching systems are often used to help with the temporary storage and processing of data. Due to skewed and dynamic workload patterns, e.g. data increase/decrease or request changes in read/write ratio, it can cause load imbalance and degrade performance of caching systems.

Migrating data is often essential for balancing load in distributed storage systems. However, it can be difficult to determine when to move data, where to move data, and how much data to move. This depends on the resources required, e.g. CPU, memory and bandwidth, as well as polices on data movement. Since frequent and global rebalance of systems may affect the QoS of applications utilizing caching systems, it is necessary to minimize system imbalances whilst considering the total migration cost. We propose a novel distributed load balancing method for the mainstream Cloud-based data framework (Redis Cluster). We show how distributed graph clustering through load balancing can be used to exploit varying rebalancing scenarios comprising local and global needs. During the rebalancing process, three phrases are adopted — random walk matching load balancing, local round-robin migration and data migration between the trigger node and new added servers. Our experiments show that the proposed approach can reduce migration time compared with other approach by 30s and load imbalance degree can be reduced by 4X when the locality degree reaches 50% whilst achieving high throughput.

Keywords: Key-value cache · Load balancing · Random locality

Jiangsu Overseas Research & Training Program for University Prominent Young & Middle-aged Teachers and Presidents, Nanjing University of Posts and Telecommunications Scientific Research Fund (NY215115).

C. Li and J. Wu (Eds.): ACA 2018, CCIS 908, pp. 181–194, 2018.
https://doi.org/10.1007/978-981-13-2423-9_14

1 Introduction

A high-performance in-memory key-value caching system is often very important to provide high throughput and low latency services. There is an ever-growing number of key-value data sets that need to be stored and served in in-memory systems, e.g. for real-time applications. The rapid growth in GET and PUT requests associated with these system models, demands a linearly scalable system with low overheads. The important problem is that the variability in workloads and associated cluster expansions can create unbalanced loads that degrade the latency and negatively impact on the overall throughput of the system. Prior research has demonstrated that load imbalances can result in more than 60% degradation in throughput and 300% degradation in latency [1,2].

There is thus a need for scaling a in-memory key-value stores, while tackling highly skewed and dynamic workloads. Skewed workloads can lead to severe load imbalances, which can result in significant performance degradation. Dynamic workloads can also cause more server node to be added which will waste the resources and cost more money. As an application executes, database workloads may change rapidly, e.g. from read-heavy to write-heavy workloads, zifp query distribution et al. A load balancer should be configurable to deal with diverse workloads and ideally optimize such configurations depending on the demand.

Consistent hashing [3] can help balance static resource utilization, however it is unsuitable for dynamic workload patterns. Several technologies have been proposed for handling data-driven load balancing including data replication and caching in the network layer, or data migration. Selective replication is used to replicate frequently used (hot) items to additional storage nodes. This will consume more hardware resources (storage) and require potentially complex mechanisms for data movement, data consistency, and query routing to deal with the load. Placing a front-end cache (or an array of frontend caches) is also a common way to cache such popular items whilst leveraging the additional hardware resources. Caching $O(NlogN)$ items is sufficient to ensure that the load on servers is uniform [4]. Data migration or hash space adjustment is a common technique to mitigate load imbalances for in-memory key-value caching system.

In this paper, we present a case study using the popular Cloud-based technology, Redis Cluster [5]. Redis Cluster is a very popular in-memory key-value, scalable storage system. Our goal is to demonstrate the system can remain in a balanced state, even when the amount of data grows, or when the access and usage patterns are changed. We demonstrate how it is possible to optimize (minimize) the addition or removal of servers that are required. In the distributed environment, it is hard to establish an efficient policy to rebalance the data-driven workloads, since the related information is constantly updated. Specifically, this paper offers the following novel contributions:

- We propose a lightweight, decentralized rebalancing mechanism to collect minimal statistical information needed for data migration. This is achieved through a non-aggressive and relatively fair load balancer, which reacts only if one node is severely overloaded after distributed graph clustering by load

balancing, it swaps and migrates load evenly to the under-loaded nodes in
the same locality.
- We trade off load balancing and necessary scalability required for performance. This means that adding new servers can be delayed as much as possible until all nodes are almost overloaded.
- We present experimental results show that performance can be improved
  when data migration occurs compared with baseline greedy balancer.

This paper is organized as follows. Section 2 gives an introduction to the
background and presents the motivation for the work in more detail. Section 3
describes our proposed methods and explains how we are able to improve system load balancing. Section 4 presents the experimental results of applying the
method. Section 5 introduces the related work and finally Sect. 6 concludes the
paper as a whole and identifies areas of potential future work.

2   Background

2.1   Load Rebalancing Process

Load rebalancing process should be done in two steps. The first step is to compute the current load distribution which can be done offline and periodically.
The second step is to make new assignments including replications or migrations based on the precomputed load of the first step. There is a challenge that
the second step could be finished in a short time such as several milliseconds
in order not to stop the cloud service. A near-perfect balance and process cost
minimization are needed for cloud services.

2.2   Load Rebalacing Method for Redis

Typical in-memory key-value caches use consistent hashing to map keys to cache
servers. Instead of directly mapping items to physical nodes, Redis Cluster calculates the result of CRC16 of key modulo 16384 and puts it into logical units called
slots depending on the hash value. The physical placement of slots on nodes are
undertaken in another separate procedure by Redis Cluster. This decoupling of
the logical and physical placement enables transparent data movement, which
avoids the need for immediate rehashing of data during cluster expansion and
thus is convenient for rebalancing.

Master-slave replication of Redis Cluster cannot be used for handling skew
workload and load rebalancing. Based on the popularity of slots, it is hard to use
multi-master replication for slots since one slot just belongs to one node. Hence
we need to migrate *hot slots* to under-loaded nodes.

2.3   Motivation of New Method

If sharding key distribution is not even or request rates vary greatly, then this
can give rise to load imbalances between nodes. When load imbalances occur,

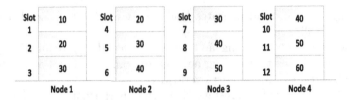

Fig. 1. Load imbalance scenarios from different loads for slots

the Redis Cluster can reshard partitioning through constant tuning over time manually. Ideally, a cache system should automatically learn and reassign the partitions based on their changing workloads.

Figure 1 shows an example of node load imbalance scenarios. The number in the rectangle represents the load of each slot. Redis Cluster itself can not provide load balancing for this case. Centralized algorithms for modifying Redis Cluster may result in lots of data migration to perform the rebalance. When workload patterns are changed or cluster expansion occurs, data has to be rebalanced across the cluster. The total cluster overheads can be significant since the node number can be up to 1000 in Redis Cluster. Hence a decentralized and low-cost migration method for Redis Cluster would also be highly beneficial.

For example, if there is a mechanism taken that Node 1 and Node 4 will average their loads through swapping between slot 1 and slot 11 based on the load shown in Fig. 1, on the other hand, Node 2 and Node 3 can average their loads, it will create a perfect load balancing. Even if Node 1 can not match Node 4 for the first time, we hope that the mechanism can enable all the nodes to undertake the approximate average load after multiple round iterations.

However, when workload change occurs every time, it will cost a lot of system overheads because of global iterations, and so localization can do a better job under the condition. The cluster manager can divide the cluster and keep all the local clusters balanced first. When the load changes a little, to rebalance the local cluster is just needed. This achieves better time efficiency and less exchanged messages than a whole cluster data migration.

3   Design and Implementation

Figure 2 gives an overview design of Redis Cluster load balancer system. In Redis Cluster, all the nodes are connected using a TCP bus and a binary protocol. They form a fully connected graph. The system is composed of three main components.

Client Component: the Client Component performs two main jobs include initiating client requests and caching key-to-slot mappings. Clients are able to perform operations similar to existing Redis, e.g. GET, PUT and DELETE.

New Mapping Component: when the rebalancing process finishes, it will receive a new mapping from the Redis Cluster and update the client-side mapping.

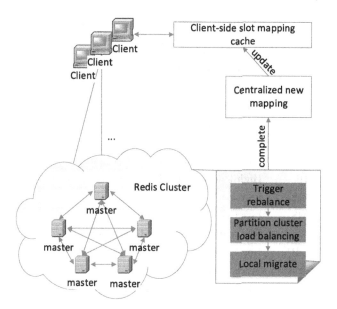

Fig. 2. Architecture for redis rebalancing

Redis Cluster Component: is the most important component in the system. This component generates the key-value replies to client queries and executes the load balancer. Every server in the cluster will initiate the migration when a local condition is met, i.e. the load migration process is not centralized. The load balancer is responsible for coordinating the load balancer process. It uses a *random walk matching* method for averaging the load and then divides the servers into multiple clusters while keeping the load balanced. Every node computes and gets the load information ranking of its neighbours, i.e. nodes in the same subgraph. When one server triggers the rebalance process, data migration will happen again between the server and its neighbours.

In this section, we present the details on how we tackled the problems mentioned in Sect. 2.3. Specifically, we propose a new approach called **global-local rebalance**. We present the details and implementation of this approach in the following sections. Ultimately, the system design and implementation has to meet three basic requirements: low movement between high bandwidth nodes, per-node storage efficiency, and minimize the request deviation.

3.1   Global-Local Rebalance

The following notation in Table 1 are used to describe the approach.

While Redis Cluster nodes form a full mesh, nodes also use a gossip protocol and a configuration update mechanism.

The global phrase (Phase 1) is used for early load balancing, which has been studied in the computation [6] and implementation for distributed graph

Table 1. Notations for rebalance

Symbol	Description
N	Number of nodes
S	Number of slots
K	Number of clusters
L_i	Load for node i
L^j	Load for slot j
AL	Average load for the total system
Ht	High load threshold
Lt	Low load threshold
MS_i^j	Least slot load generated by slot j in node i
λ	Resource usage ratio of read to write
RR_i^j	Read request rate for slot j in node i
WR_i^j	Write request rate for slot j in node i
U_i	CPU utilization for node i

clustering by load balancing finishes in a poly-logarithmic number of rounds. It establishes a partition of the graph close to an optimal partition based on a random matching model of load balancing. The approach sets the graph edges according to the available bandwidth. If the communication bandwidth is high, then the edge is set to 1 else 0. When two nodes match in a round, the averaging load procedure can finish by swapping some slots. Finally, each node is assigned by a cluster label. Through the algorithm, we get k-clusters with balanced size as shown in Fig. 3. Two nodes belong to the same cluster only if they have the same cluster label.

The local phrase (Phase 2) in the Algorithm 1 provides the local load balancing when one node becomes over-loaded over the time. When localities are formed, each server shares its load with other servers in its vicinity and migrates loads between the neighbours. Local data migration can occur using a round-robin approach. When the load on a node reaches a high threshold, it will try to swap and migrate enough of its load to make the load even across the local cluster. Swapping such slots can keep the memory usage balanced.

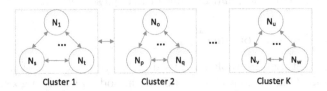

Fig. 3. Random localities

Server addition phrase (phase 3) is only carried out as a last resort in the algorithm. If the rebalancing can be done without additional servers, the efficiency of the existing cluster increases. If the load of the trigger node is still higher than the upper threshold, then new servers are added in the local vicinity and the migration continues (once these are provisioned).

Algorithm 1. Rebalancing Algorithm

//Phase 1: Decentralized Graph clustering, initialize load balancing
Require: N nodes, M overloaded nodes M<<N
Ensure: K clusters $C_1,...,C_k$, finishes in O(logN) rounds and implements early load balancing
//Phase 2: Local rebalance concurrently according to the dynamic workload
//Phase 2.1: For any cluster i, choose several slots from the largest to smallest and place them into a pool s from an overloaded node as a trigger node t
while $L_t >$ Ht **do**
    Choose several slots out of node to make the load L_t down to Lt
end while
//Phase 2.2: Swap and migrate the slots to low load neighbors in the same cluster
for node n in low load pool and slot s in migration pool **do**
    if $L_n + (L^s - MS_n^j)$ slot load difference $< AL_i$ **then**
        migrate(s, t, n)
        migrate(j, n, t)
    end if
end for
//Phase 3: Add one or more servers into one location if the migration pool is not empty
if $L_t >$ Ht **then**
    add new server i and migrate(s, t, i)
    if $L_i < AL_i$ **then**
        put node i into low load pool
    end if
end if

Since we consider items in the cache are all small sized key-value pairs that are evenly distributed based on the number of slots and total slot memory usage, the memory resource for each migration unit is considered to be similar, hence the CPU utilization becomes the most important metric. We calculate the utility load for node and slot as the following functions. As such, we can swap the slots to achieve the same memory utilization whilst reducing the CPU utilization.

$$L_i = RR_i * \lambda + WR_i * (1 - \lambda) + U_i \tag{1}$$

$$L^j = RR_i^j * \lambda + WR_i^j * (1 - \lambda) \tag{2}$$

$$for \quad \lambda < 0.5 \tag{3}$$

Distributing data for balancing requires spreading hot and cold data evenly across the cluster. In order to efficiently adjust the load, random localities are formed to divide cache servers into smaller groups. Each locality contains several servers and each server's neighbours given as a subgraph from the full connected graph. Figuring out a good threshold is crucial for the balancer. The parameter values Ht and Lt can be adjusted according to AL. Every node maintains statistical information for itself and its slots, including key-value read and write access (via sampling). These are collected periodically and at a high frequency.

During migration maintaining consistency is essential. While keys in one slot are being migrated, operations on keys will generate a TRYAGAIN error based on the Redis Cluster documentation. Once the rebalance process is completed, key-to-node mapping changes are stored temporarily to guarantee that all clients are able to see and cache the new mapping in an appropriate and short period of time.

Our method is useful especially if a large number of servers in different clusters are overloaded simultaneously, since the algorithm uses a partitioned graph as its core rebalancing structure and nodes in the graph can automatically inform their neighbours of updations and migrations that are taking place.

4   Experimental Results

4.1   Test Environment

In our experiments, we use Redis 3.2.0 as the implementation platform for the rebalancing performance evaluation. We use the benchmark YCSB (Yahoo! Cloud Serving Benchmark) [7] to test the performance of the original Redis performance and the performance after rebalancing. We explore the evaluation of the algorithm using a 6-node and a 10-node cluster.

Table 2. Hardware and software configurations

CPU	Intel(R) Xeon(R) E5645 CPU 2 X 6 @ 2.40 GHz
Memory	64 GB DDR3 @ 1333 MHz
Disk	3×1 TB SATA disk
Network	Intel(R) PRO/1000 Network Connection @ 1 Gbps
OS	CentOS 6.2

The hardware and software configurations for each service node are listed in Table 2. During the experiments, we predominately used QPS (number of operations per second) to evaluate the throughput performance together with the time to assess the effectiveness. In this paper we consider a node to be under-loaded when the memory usage is less than 50% of the max capacity and the request rate is less than the average rate. It is noted that all slots serve all operations such as PUT, GET and DELETE, so the capacity and the request rate would be changed when the slot size varies.

4.2 Global-Local Rebalancing Model Analysis

Degree of Load Imbalance. The maximum/average metric quantifies the degree of load imbalance. Our algorithm adopts a non-aggressive and efficient way to reduce the degree of load imbalance across the cluster by removing heavily-loaded slots from over-loaded servers.

Degree of Localisation. The average number of local servers is N/K. Servers in different locations can migrate slots in parallel without interference. All servers in a given localised partition are in geographical proximity to one another, so slot transferral to other servers in one locality is more efficient when considering the overheads of networking, bandwidth and the associated latency issues that can arise.

Baseline Greedy Balancer. When one node resource utilization reaches a given threshold, it initially adds a new server and migrates half of its load to the new one. Although the trigger node can migrate half of their load as soon as they are able, the total load on the cluster can be uneven because other server loads are not changed. This can result in a reduction of resource utilization.

Costs and Benefits. Costs can include message exchanges which will effect the network traffic. In our algorithm, message exchange cost complexity of global graph clustering is $O(T \cdot n \cdot k \log k)$ when the process finishes in T rounds with n nodes and k clusters. The global data migration time is also proportional to the number of rounds (T). Local message costs also include data transfer overheads to the specific locations selected for migration. And the benefits mainly refer to the performance improvement observed as a result of the reduction in the degree of imbalance.

4.3 Workload and Metric

In our experiment, we evaluate the migration performance and costs. A Zipfian (with parameter 0.99) workload of 100% read was used for the test generated by YCSB.

When the rebalancing process is complete, the system performance is improved. However, the process is time-consuming and influences the overall performance. It is important to rebalance loads quickly. Thus migration time and response time are important metrics to measure the overall performance.

Migration Time and Response Time. We quantify migration time as a form of resource consumption cost, which indicates the amount of time needed to execute a rebalancing process. We can also calculate the migration speed according to the amount of data transferred during the migration. The response time is the amount of time it takes from when a client request was submitted until the first response is produced.

In the experiment we observe how response time changes during the migration of slots from one node to another in Redis Cluster. To explore this, we loaded 90,000 keys into two nodes and 0 in all the other (four) nodes. After the

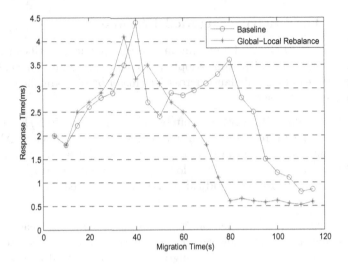

Fig. 4. Response time for migration slots

client queries commence and exceed a given threshold on one of the servers, the migration process is triggered until it finishes.

The cluster was divided into two localities. The migration was initiated at 10 s as presented in Fig. 4. We observe that in the beginning of the migration process there is a great increase in time taken, while at the end of process an obvious decrease appears. The trend is similar for the baseline half-migration and the approach using global-local rebalancing. However, our approach reduces migration time and peak response time compared with the half-migration baseline by 30s and 0.4ms. Our method can achieve shorter migration time and lower response time because one heavy node can migrate slots to the other two nodes evenly in the same locality which is different from the half-migration baseline.

Load Balancing and Resource Utility. Our method outperforms a baseline greedy balancer in term of load balancing (max/avg). We can roughly get load imbalance values of 1 and 1.5 respectively. In fact, the half-migration method tends to balance load at the cost of increasing the number of servers, however resource utility is actually inversely proportional to the number of servers.

Locality Degree. Here we use the percentage of the number of nodes in the trigger node at a given location compared to the number of nodes in the entire cluster. In this case, we extend the cluster to 10 nodes.

Figure 5 shows the load balance degree and the throughput with varying degrees of localisation. When the locality degree reaches 100%, we have full, global load balancing. Full global load balancing may produce the near-perfect balance, however the cost of the load information, data transferal and slot migrating is great. Therefore, it is unnecessary to perform global load balancing, and then tune a suitable locality degree parameter to subsequently minimize the inter-locality communication and migrate slots efficiently. In the experimental

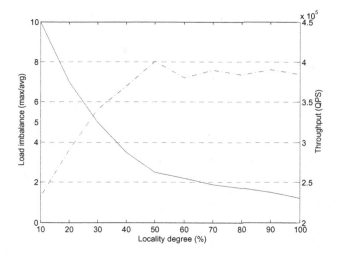

Fig. 5. Overall performance with varying degrees of locality

results, we observed that putting 50% of the nodes in the same locality offers the best performance, i.e. 5 out of 10 nodes should be co-located. Load imbalance degree can be reduced by 4X and high throughput is also achieved when the locality degree reaches 50%.

5   Related Work

Two load-balancing techniques offering consistent hashing and hot-content replication to mitigate load skew and improve cache performance were presented in [8]. Autoplacer [9] leverages self-tuning the data placement in replicated key-value stores to identify the right assignment of data replicas to nodes and to preserve fast data lookup, which is six times better than static placement based on consistent hashing. To reduce the skew workload, data has to be reliably replicated. Replication also can make the system more available in the presence of failures, however, it will also increase the storage costs and demand for replication consistency.

The caching layer can be used to balance the disk- and flash-based storage, however server-based caching is unsuitable for in-memory stores as there is little difference in performance between the caching and storage layers. Net-Cache [10] offers a new key-value store architecture that leverages the power and flexibility of new-generation programmable switches to cache data in the network. The disadvantage of the solution is that the architecture cannot handle write-intensive workloads. NetKV [11] has been designed and implemented as a scalable, self-managing, load balancer for memcached [12] clusters that exploit Network Function Virtualization (NFV) to provide efficient, software-based hot key packet processing. Splitting large items into independent chunks and handling each chunk independently is a common mitigation solution, however, it is not effective for many key-value cache systems, e.g. those with many small size items and a few large items [13].

Migrating data units is a useful method for balancing load, but it is difficult to implement in fully decentralized load balancers whilst low migration costs. Many works rely on a centralized proxy to dispatch the rebalancing process. MBal [2] offers a holistic solution whereby the load balancing model tracks hotspots and applies different strategies including key replication, server-local or cross-server coordinated data migration. However, it is not a distributed migration method. Mantle [14] decouples policy from mechanisms to let the designer inject custom load balancing logic. This offers a form of resource migration for file system metadata. In a novel way, Meezan [15] replicates popular objects to mitigate skewness and adjusts hash space boundaries in response to dynamic loads of memcached systems. Ambry [16] presents a scalable Geo-Distributed Object Store, which leverages techniques such as asynchronous replication, rebalancing mechanisms, and zero-cost failure detection. [17] presents a multi-resource load balancing algorithm for distributed cache systems by redistributing stored data. RackOut [18] uses a memory pooling technique that leverages one-sided remote read primitives of emerging rack-scale systems to mitigate load imbalances for scalable data serving. The Meta-Balancer framework [19] is proposed to automatically decide on the best load balancing strategy according to the application characteristics.

Load imbalances can increase as the number of shards increase [20] and when the number of keys is constant. This work also demonstrates how unnecessary distributions can hurt performance from theoretical analysis. Overbalancing is also not a good way to tackle load imbalances. Our work establishes a full and non-aggressive distributed way to perform data rebalancing.

6 Conclusions

To achieve optimal load balancing, a distributed and non-aggressive load balancing method was presented and explored with Redis Cluster. The method improves resource utilization and ensures higher scalability. Our analysis and experimental results show that a global-local rebalancing policy can gain better performance compared to baseline metrics due to the observed reduction in overheads demanded of many load balancing processes. We will study the system load balancing performance on a cloud cluster.

Acknowledgment. The authors would like to thank the anonymous reviewers for their valuable comments. This work is partially sponsored by the National Basic Research 973 Program of China (No. 2015CB352403), the National Natural Science Foundation of China (NSFC) (No. 61402014, No. 63100240, No. 61572263), the Natural Science Foundation of Jiangsu Province (BK20151511) and Nanjing University of Posts and Telecommunications Scientific Research Fund (NY215115).

References

1. Hong, Y., Thottethodi, M.: Understanding and mitigating the impact of load imbalance in the memory caching tier. In: Lohman, G.M. (ed.) ACM Symposium on Cloud Computing, SOCC 2013, Santa Clara, CA, USA, 1–3 October 2013, pp. 13:1–13:17. ACM (2013)
2. Cheng, Y., Gupta, A., Butt, A.R.: An in-memory object caching framework with adaptive load balancing. In: Réveillère, L., Harris, T., Herlihy, M. (eds.) Proceedings of the Tenth European Conference on Computer Systems, EuroSys 2015, Bordeaux, France, 21–24 April 2015, pp. 4:1–4:16. ACM (2015)
3. Karger, D.R., Lehman, E., Leighton, F.T., Panigrahy, R., Levine, M.S., Lewin, D.: Consistent hashing and random trees: distributed caching protocols for relieving hot spots on the world wide web. In: Leighton, F.T., Shor, P.W. (eds.) Proceedings of the Twenty-Ninth Annual ACM Symposium on the Theory of Computing, El Paso, Texas, USA, 4–6 May 1997, pp. 654–663. ACM (1997)
4. Fan, B., Lim, H., Andersen, D.G., Kaminsky, M.: Small cache, big effect: provable load balancing for randomly partitioned cluster services. In: Chase, J.S., Abbadi, A.E. (eds.) ACM Symposium on Cloud Computing in Conjunction with SOSP 2011, SOCC 2011, Cascais, Portugal, 26–28 October 2011, p. 23. ACM (2011)
5. https://redis.io/topics. "Redis cluster specification," Technical report (2018)
6. Sun, H., Zanetti, L.: Distributed graph clustering by load balancing. In: Scheideler, C., Hajiaghayi, M.T. (eds.) Proceedings of the 29th ACM Symposium on Parallelism in Algorithms and Architectures, SPAA 2017, Washington DC, USA, 24–26 July 2017, pp. 163–171. ACM (2017)
7. Cooper, B.F., Silberstein, A., Tam, E., Ramakrishnan, R., Sears, R.: Benchmarking cloud serving systems with YCSB. In: Hellerstein, J.M., Chaudhuri, S., Rosenblum, M. (eds.) Proceedings of the 1st ACM Symposium on Cloud Computing, SoCC 2010, Indianapolis, Indiana, USA, 10–11 June 2010, pp. 143–154. ACM (2010)
8. Huang, Q., Gudmundsdottir, H., Vigfusson, Y., Freedman, D.A., Birman, K., van Renesse, R.: Characterizing load imbalance in real-world networked caches. In: Katz-Bassett, E., Heidemann, J.S., Godfrey, B., Feldmann, A. (eds.) Proceedings of the 13th ACM Workshop on Hot Topics in Networks, HotNets-XIII, Los Angeles, CA, USA, 27–28 October 2014, pp. 8:1–8:7. ACM (2014)
9. Paiva, J., Ruivo, P., Romano, P., Rodrigues, L.E.T.: AUTOPLACER: scalable self-tuning data placement in distributed key-value stores. TAAS 9(4), 19:1–19:30 (2014)
10. Jin, X., et al.: NetCache: balancing key-value stores with fast in-network caching. In: SOSP (2017)
11. Zhang, W., Wood, T., Hwang, J.: NetKV: scalable, self-managing, load balancing as a network function. In: 2016 IEEE International Conference on Autonomic Computing (ICAC), pp. 5–14, July 2016
12. Fitzpatrick, B.: Distributed caching with memcached. Linux J. **2004**(124), 5 (2004)
13. Atikoglu, B., Xu, Y., Frachtenberg, E., Jiang, S., Paleczny, M.: Workload analysis of a large-scale key-value store. In: Proceedings of the 12th ACM SIGMETRICS/PERFORMANCE Joint International Conference on Measurement and Modeling of Computer Systems, ser. SIGMETRICS 2012, pp. 53–64. ACM, New York (2012)
14. Sevilla, M.A., et al.: Mantle: a programmable metadata load balancer for the ceph file system. In: Kern, J., Vetter, J.S. (eds.) Proceedings of the International Conference for High Performance Computing, Networking, Storage and Analysis, SC 2015, Austin, TX, USA, 15–20 November 2015, pp. 21:1–21:12. ACM (2015)

15. Huq, S., Shafiq, Z., Ghosh, S., Khakpour, A., Bedi, H.: Distributed load balancing in key-value networked caches. In: Proceedings of IEEE 37th International Conference on Distributed Computing Systems (ICDCS), pp. 583–593, June 2017

16. Noghabi, S.A., et al.: Ambry: Linkedin's scalable geo-distributed object store. In: Proceedings of the 2016 International Conference on Management of Data, ser. SIGMOD 2016, pp. 253–265. ACM, New York (2016). https://doi.org/10.1145/2882903.2903738

17. Jia, Y., Brondino, I., Jiménez-Peris, R., Patiño-Martínez, M., Ma, D.: A multi-resource load balancing algorithm for cloud cache systems. In: Shin, S.Y., Maldonado, J.C. (eds.) Proceedings of the 28th Annual ACM Symposium on Applied Computing, SAC 2013, Coimbra, Portugal, 18–22 March 2013, pp. 463–470. ACM (2013)

18. Novakovic, S., Daglis, A., Bugnion, E., Falsafi, B., Grot, B.: The case for RackOut: scalable data serving using rack-scale systems. In: Aguilera, M.K., Cooper, B., Diao, Y. (eds.) Proceedings of the Seventh ACM Symposium on Cloud Computing, Santa Clara, CA, USA, 5–7 October 2016, pp. 182–195. ACM (2016)

19. Menon, H., Chandrasekar, K., Kalé, L.V.: POSTER: automated load balancer selection based on application characteristics. In: Sarkar, V., Rauchwerger, L. (eds.) Proceedings of the 22nd ACM SIGPLAN Symposium on Principles and Practice of Parallel Programming, Austin, TX, USA, 4–8 February 2017, pp. 447–448. ACM (2017). http://dl.acm.org/citation.cfm?id=3019033

20. Saino, L., Psaras, I., Pavlou, G.: Understanding sharded caching systems. In: Proceedings of IEEE INFOCOM 2016 - the 35th Annual IEEE International Conference on Computer Communications, pp. 1–9, April 2016

Performance Analysis and Optimization of Cyro-EM Structure Determination in RELION-2

Xin You, Hailong Yang$^{(\boxtimes)}$, Zhongzhi Luan, and Depei Qian

School of Computer Science and Engineering,
Beihang University, Beijing 100191, China
{youxin2015,hailong.yang,zhongzhi.luan,depeiq}@buaa.edu.cn

Abstract. REgularised LIkelihood OptimisatioN (RELION) is one of the most popular softwares used in single particle cryo-EM structure determination. Although efforts have been made to optimize the workflow of RELION, the refinement step still remains as a bottleneck for our exploration of performance improvement. In this paper, we thoroughly analyze the cause of the performance bottleneck and propose corresponding optimization for performance speedup. The experiment results show that our approach achieves a speedup of 3.17× without degrading the resolution.

Keywords: Cyro-EM · Performance analysis and optimization
Relion

1 Introduction

Cryo-electron microscopy (cryo-EM) is a powerful technology for determining the 3D structure of individual proteins and macromolecular assemblies. The technology includes various steps from getting samples of proteins to get the final high resolution of partible 3D models. Although the technology can build a protein model with high resolution, the determination step is extremely computational-intensive. To fulfill the computation requirements, various cyro-EM software with different trade-offs are proposed, such as SPIDER (1981) [4], FREALIGN (2007) [5], EMAN2 (2007) [16], SIMPLE (2012) [2], RELION (2012) [14] and cryoSPARCRC (2017) [12]. Among all the software, RELION is most widely used for its objective and high-quality results in this field [6,10,18].

RELION (Regularized Likelihood OptimizatioN) implements a Bayesian approach for cryo-EM structure determination, which is one of the most popular methods for cryo-EM structure determination. It introduces pipelined workflow to automatically perform all the analysis work with high efficiency [3]. To leverage the emerging computation power from parallel architecture, Su et al. implements GPU-enhanced parallel version of RELION (GeRelion [15]), which can handle the massive computational loads and the growing demands for processing

© Springer Nature Singapore Pte Ltd. 2018
C. Li and J. Wu (Eds.): ACA 2018, CCIS 908, pp. 195–209, 2018.
https://doi.org/10.1007/978-981-13-2423-9_15

much larger cryo-EM datasets. Furthermore, Dari et al. [7] present an improvement of RELION, where GPUs are used to process the most computationally intensive steps to overcome the bottleneck of limited throughput. Moreover, a new software version over the origin RELION is proposed by the same research group (RELION-2 [7]) that dynamically allocates the memory requirement on GPUs to utilize the hardware better and improve the efficiency of the computation. Although the above works are proposed to optimize the performance of RELION for cryo-EM structure determination, there is still a large space left for performance optimization to meet the ever-increasing demands for processing even larger cryo-EM datasets. In this paper, we focus on the performance analysis and optimization of the cutting-edge RELION-2 software. Through comprehensive performance analysis, we identify several performance bottlenecks of RELION-2 and propose corresponding code and configuration optimizations, which significantly improves the performance of RELION-2.

Specifically, this paper makes the following contributions:

- We analyze the performance of RELION-2 and identify that the bottlenecks are *GetFourierTransforms* in expectation step and Pipe & Memon algorithm in maximization step.
- We propose several optimization strategies for improving the performance of RELION-2, including calculation redundancy optimization, GPU acceleration and CPU binding.
- We evaluate the performance of RELION-2 after applying the proposed optimizations, which achieves a speedup of 3.17× without degrading the resolution.

The remainder of this paper is organized as follows. In Sect. 2, we provide the bottleneck analysis of RELION-2. Section 3 presents the optimization strategies of our approach. Section 4 elaborates the experiment setup and analyzes the experimental results. Section 5 describes related work and Sect. 6 presents the conclusion from this paper.

2 Bottleneck Analysis

2.1 Execution Model Analysis

The design of RELION-2 is mainly composed of maximization (M-step) and expectation (E-step). Since the E-step is the most computation intensive step, we focus our study on E-step in this paper. The parallel E-step execution of RELION-2 adopts Master-Slave mode, which is described in Fig. 1. We can see that jobs are distributed for parallel processing through two steps. First, master process splits the input data as well as the computation across the slaves and sends the job as well as the data to the corresponding slave process. Then, each slave process spawns several threads on the CPU socket of each node. Each thread is able to launch GPU kernels for execution acceleration concurrently. To achieve load balance, the master process sends job and data whenever the slave process reports that it has no job remained to be done. This design of job assignment is also robust towards node anomaly. In case of node anomaly, other slave processes can dynamically pick up the jobs to mitigate the performance slowdown of abnormal nodes.

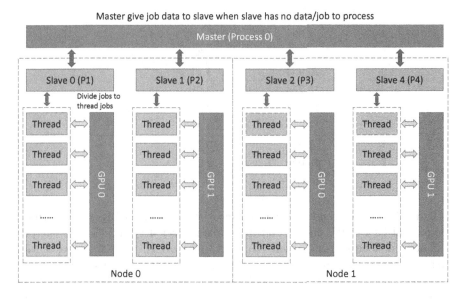

Fig. 1. The Master-Slave mode of RELION-2 (E-step).

2.2   Bottleneck Identification

To identify the performance bottlenecks of RELION-2, we first analyze the execution behavior across slaves to see if they achieve the load balance as expected. Specifically, we measure the waiting time of each slave process within E-step. The waiting time indicates the load imbalance among slaves indirectly. Ideally, the waiting time should equal to zero, which means each slave process progresses at the same pace and the load is perfectly balanced. However, as shown in Table 1, the waiting time across slaves is high skewed, with the longest waiting time more than 12× longer than the shortest waiting time. This means the slave processes still suffer from the load imbalance in RELION-2. The reason is that although the dynamic job distribution mechanism in RELION-2 is designed for load balance, it is still unable to handle the data skew that causes the imbalance across slaves. The data skew exists intrinsically because each image may have different valid orientations for E-step that leads to large variance of computation time. On the other hand, if we take the ratio of waiting time to the entire E-step execution time into account, the waiting time only takes up a small fraction of the execution (less than 3.2%) as shown in Table 1. Therefore, the load imbalance across slaves should not cause severe performance problem and thus is omitted in our optimization.

Table 1. Waiting time of slave processes within E-step.

Slave Rank	Total wait time (s)	Ratio within E-step (%)
1	1.692	0.26%
2	2.135	0.33%
3	20.953	3.20%
4	15.773	2.41%
5	15.123	2.31%
6	14.884	2.27%
7	1.927	0.29%
8	15.029	2.29%

To further understand the performance behavior of RELION-2, we run it on our local CPU-GPU cluster (setup details in Sect. 4.1) and analyze the performance bottleneck using Intel VTune [13]. Figure 2(a)–(c) shows execution hotspot results in three execution stages such as class2D, class3D and auto-refine. From Fig. 2(a)–(c) we can see that although E-step has been largely optimized in RELION-2, it is still a bottleneck across all three execution stages. As we further dig into the execution of E-step, we get the execution time break down shown in Fig. 2(d). In Fig. 2(d) we can see that *GetFourierTransforms* subroutine dominates the E-step across all three execution stages, taking up 45%, 50% and 40% of the E-step execution time respectively. Whereas *storeWeightedSums* and *getAllSquaredDifferences1* subroutines are the second and third largest performance bottlenecks across the execution stages.

In addition, we further investigate the M-step with hotspot analysis in class3D and refine3D stages, which takes 18% and 26% of the entire execution respectively. As shown in Fig. 3, *doGridding* subroutine takes up 65% and 90% of the M-step execution in class3D and refine3D respectively. This subroutine implements the Pipe & Menon algorithm [11] and thus the performance bottleneck of M-step. We notice that in class3D and refine3D, other step also takes up a notable portion of the entire execution time besides E-step and M-step as shown in Fig. 2. As we analyze the profiling results from VTune, we find that *applyPointSymmetry* subroutine and frequent math function calls dominate the execution time besides M-step and E-step in class3D and refine3D stage respectively.

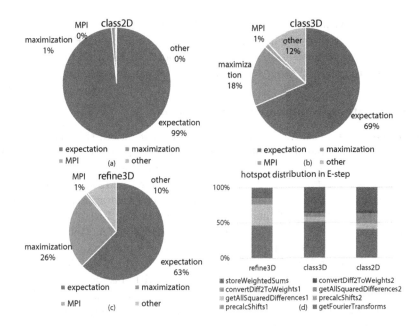

Fig. 2. Hotspot analysis of different execution stages in RELION-2.

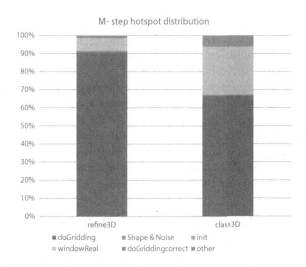

Fig. 3. Hotspot analysis of M-step in class3D and refine3D stage.

3   Optimization Strategies

Based on the bottleneck analysis results in Sect. 2, we propose several optimization strategies including calculation redundancy optimiztion, GPU acceleration and CPU binding to mitigate the performance bottlenecks in RELION-2, which are elaborated in the following sections.

3.1   Calculation Redundancy Optimization

As we discussed in Sect. 2.2 during bottleneck identification, the frequent math function calls consume a notable fraction of RELION-2 execution time. We investigate further of these math function calls and identify hotspot function *selectOrientationsWithNonZeroPriorProbability*, which searches for all possible orientations in previous iteration and defines which orientations to be further calculated. The algorithm of this function is listed in Fig. 4(a).

Within the hotspot function, *Euler_angles2direction* function contains sin and cos math operations and *gaussian1D* calculates square root of sigma value and exponents to get 1D Gaussian value for *diffang*, which are shown with the yellow lines in Fig. 4(a). The output part of the algorithm is highlighted in green, which produces *pointer_dir_nonzeroprior*, *directions_prior*, *superior* and *best_idir* for further calculation. After analyzing this algorithm, we identify the highlighted code dominates the computation.

We observe that the calculation of Fig. 4(a) is inefficient due to the frequent calls of expensive math functions in the loop without considering the loop invariant calculations. Specifically, we can see that line 3, 7 and 8 inside *gaussion1D* are loop invariant calculations, however calculated repeatedly inside the loop. These lines of code can be moved out of the loop to pre-calculate the corresponding values before entering the loop (shown in line 1, 3 and 4 in Fig. 4(b)). In addition, the condition statement in line 2 in Fig. 4(a) can also be moved out of the loop since the condition is invariant across iterations (shown in line 5 in Fig. 4(b)).

Moreover, we find an interesting behavior of the algorithm is that the possibility of executing line 9–12 in Fig. 4(a) is quite low. This means most of the *ACOSD* calculations are not used later in this algorithm. After analyzing the *ACOSD* function, we realize it is a monotonically decreasing function. Therefore, the condition comparison in line 8 in Fig. 4(a) that requires *ACOSD* calculation can be modified to line 10 in Fig. 4(b), which eliminates the need for *ACOSD* calculation and thus reduces the execution time.

3.2   GPU Acceleration of Pipe and Menon Iterative Algorithm

As shown in Fig. 3, *doGriddingIter* subroutine that implements Pipe & Menon iterative algorithm dominates the execution of M-Step. The execution flow of the original implementation of this algorithm is shown in the upper part of Fig. 5. In each iteration, the most time-consuming subroutines are forward and inverse Fast Fourier Transform (FFT), which are computed on CPUs. Fast Fourier Transform

	(a) Original Algorithm
1	for idir = 0, rot_angles.size() do
2	if sigma_rot > 0. and sigma_tilt > 0. Then
3	Euler_angles2direction(prior_rot, prior_tilt, prior_direction);
4	Euler_angles2direction(rot_angles[idir], tilt_angles[idir], my_direction);
5	...
6	diffang = ACOSD(dotProduct(best_direction, prior_direction))
7	biggest_sigma = XMIPP_MAX(sigma_rot, sigma_tilt)
8	if diffang < sigma_cutoff * biggest_sigma then
9	prior = gaussian1D(diffang, biggest_sigma, 0.)
10	pointer_dir_nonzeroprior.push_back(idir)
11	directions_prior.push_back(prior)
12	sumprior += prior
13	end if
14	if (diffang < best_ang)
15	best_ang = diffang
16	best_idir = idir
17	end if
18	end if
19	end for

	(b) Optimized Algorithm
1	biggest_sigma = XMIPP_MAX(sigma_rot, sigma_tilt)
2	cos_biggest_sigmaxcutoff = cos(biggest_sigma*sigma_cutoff)
3	Euler_angles2direction(prior_rot, prior_tilt, prior_direction);
4	sqrt_sigma = sqrt(2*PI*biggest_sigma*biggest_sigma)
5	if sigma_rot > 0. and sigma_tilt > 0. Then
6	for idir = 0, rot_angles.size() do
7	Euler_angles2direction(rot_angles[idir], tilt_angles[idir], my_direction);
8	....
9	diffang = dotProduct(best_direction, prior_direction)
10	if diffang > cos_biggest_sigmaxcutoff then
11	diffang = ACOSD(diffang)
12	prior = 1 / sqrt_sigma*exp(-0.5*((diffang / biggest_sigma)*(diffang / biggest_sigma)))
13	pointer_dir_nonzeroprior.push_back(idir)
14	directions_prior.push_back(prior)
15	sumprior += prior
16	end if
17	if (diffang > best_ang)
18	best_ang = diffang
19	best_idir = idir
20	end if
21	end for
22	end if

Fig. 4. Calculation redundancy optimization of algorithm *selectOrientationsWith-NonZeroPriorProbability*.

is a classical problem in scientific computing and there are a few highly optimized FFT libraries, such as Intel MKL on CPU [17] and Nvidia cuFFT on GPU [8]. In order to exploit the tremendous computation power of GPU on our server, we choose to replace the original *fftw* library with *cuFFT* library for accelerating the calculation on GPU.

One key to achieve higher performance on GPU is to improve the ratio of computation to data transfer. Therefore, we port the calculations between FFTs in each iteration to GPU kernels in order to eliminate data transfers between CPU and GPU across iterations. The execution flow of our GPU accelerated algorithm is shown in bottom part of Fig. 5. In our implementation, all calculations including FFTs are accelerated by GPU. In addition, we find that the FFT plans are the same in each iteration. Thus, we pre-calculate the plan before the iteration to eliminate unnecessary computation during the iteration. We put the plan computation as well as other initializations (e.g., memory allocation) in the GPU setup stage as shown in bottom part of Fig. 5.

3.3 CPU Binding Optimization

In addition to code optimizations, configuration tuning regarding the architecture features also benefits the performance significantly. RELION-2 automatically identifies GPU resources on the server and allocates MPI processes and threads to manage the computation between CPU and GPU. However, we notice that the run-to-run variance of RELION-2 is quite large even using the same configuration and input dataset. Figure 6(c) shows the variance of execution time across multiple runs. There is almost 300 seconds different between the shortest and longest runs.

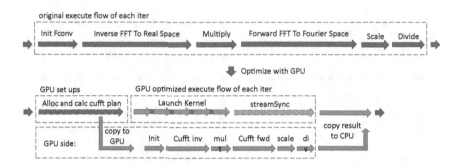

Fig. 5. Execution flow of original algorithm and GPU optimized algorithm.

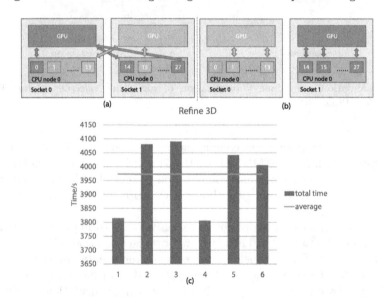

Fig. 6. CPU-GPU communication (a) before CPU Binding and (b) after CPU Binding (c) The variance of execution time across multiple runs.

As we further analyze the cause of the large variance, we find that the threads launched by the MPI process in RELION-2 are binding to processors randomly without considering the use of GPU. This leads to interleaved binding between CPU and GPU as shown in Fig. 6(a). Since there are lots of data communications between CPU and GPU to exchange calculated results, the interleaved binding makes the communication performance quite low. The NUMA architecture widely adopted on modern CPU exacerbates the performance penalty due to interleaved binding with high access latency to the remote memory node [9].

In order to solve this problem, we use *numactl* to manually bind threads launched by the MPI process to local CPU processor. Specifically, we bind the threads to the CPU processor local to the GPU represented by the MPI process. However, we do not bind the threads to specific cores but the NUMA memory

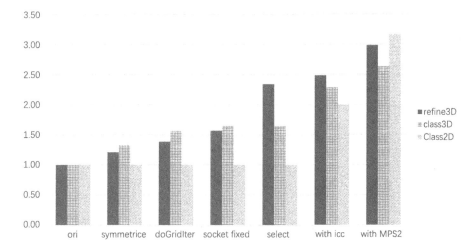

Fig. 7. The overall performance speedup of each processing stage.

node for preserving the scheduling flexibility as shown in Fig. 6(b). It is obvious that the aligned GPU-CPU binding enables higher communication performance of RELION-2.

4 Evaluation

4.1 Experimental Setup

All the experiments are conducted in our local 2-node cluster. Each node is equipped with 2× Intel 2680v4 CPUs and 2× Nvidia P100 GPUs. Each node has 128 GB memory and is connected to each other through FDR Infiniband network with maximum bandwidth of 25 Gb/s. The software environment is the same on each node, with CentOS 7 (kernel 3.10.0 x86_64), ICC v2017.6.064, GCC v4.8.5, MVAPICH2 v2.3, CUDA v9.0 and Intel VTune v2017.5.0 installed.

4.2 Overall Performance Improvement

First, we evaluate the overall performance improvement of RELION-2 after applying all the optimizations we proposed. Figure 7 shows the overall performance speedup of each stage. Each bar group represents the speedup achieved of the three stages with our optimization applied cumulatively from left to right. The *symmetrice* and *doGridIter* on the X axis represent the algorithm optimization (details in Sect. 4.3), and *socket fixed, select, with icc* and *with MPS2* on the X axis represent the configuration optimization (details in Sect. 4.4). It is clear that the overall performance improvement is quite significant across all stages, ranging from 2.63× to 3.17×. The detailed evaluation of each optimization is provided in the following sections.

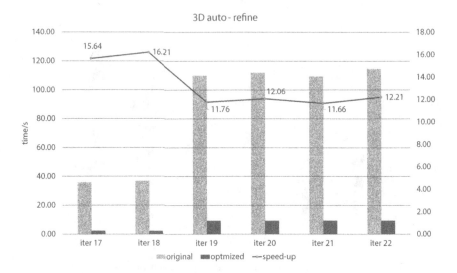

Fig. 8. Execution time and speedup with calculation redundancy optimization.

4.3 Algorithm Optimizations

Algorithm optimization includes the calculation redundancy optimization as well as the GPU acceleration proposed in Sects. 3.1 and 3.2. As shown in Fig. 8, after applying the calculation redundancy optimization, the performance of refine3D achieves significant improvement across representative iterations, with more than 16× speedup in the best case.

Figure 9(a)–(b) shows the performance improvement of class3D and refine3D stage within M-step across iterations. Both figures demonstrate that after applying the GPU acceleration, the execution time of the computation reduces significantly. Especially, in refine3D, the speedup achieved with our optimization is up to 93×. Whereas in class3D, the performance speedup is more than 18×. The total execution time of M-step after applying GPU acceleration to refine3D and class3D is shown in Fig. 9(c), which achieves more than 28× and 11× speedup respectively.

GPU acceleration of symmetries subroutine also achieves notable speedup as shown in Fig. 9(d). After optimization, the performance of symmetries subroutine improves by more than 12× and 9× in refine3D and class3D respectively. Our GPU acceleration of symmetries subroutine effectively mitigates the performance bottleneck besides M-step and E-step.

4.4 Configuration Optimizations

Configuration optimization presents the performance results using the CPU binding optimization proposed in Sect. 3.3 as well as other configuration optimizations such as compiler option (e.g., GCC and ICC) and MPS setup.

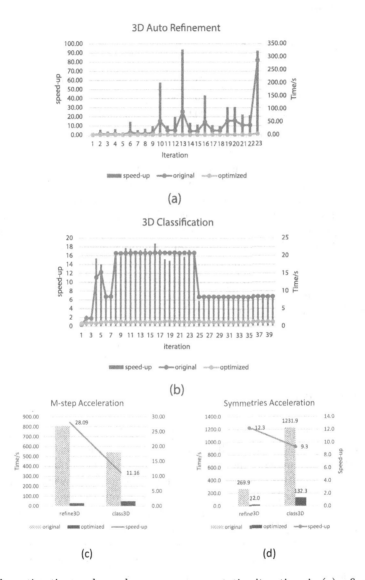

Fig. 9. Execution time and speedup across representative iterations in (a) refine3D (b) class3D, and total execution time and speedup of (c) M-step (d) Symmetries Function.

Table 2 shows the performance comparison of original random CPU binding and our aligned CPU binding with/without applying algorithm optimizations. The aligned CPU binding achieves extra 13% performance speedup with/without algorithm optimizations.

Table 2. Execute time of random CPU binding and aligned CPU binding.

	Random (s)	Aligned (s)	Speedup
Without algorithm opt.	4090.56	3622.09	1.13
With algorithm opt.	2934.7	2607.04	1.13

In addition to CPU binding, we also setup MPS with different configurations such as 2 slaves per GPU and 7 slaves per GPU. The results are shown in Fig. 10(a), which indicates that the configuration of 2 slaves per GPU is slightly better. The reason is due to the limited GPU computing resources. Although MPS can support the concurrent kernel executions, 7 slaves generate too many kernels for single GPU, which causes long queuing delay waiting for available GPU resources. Combining the optimal MPS setup and CPU binding, we can achieve a remarkable performance improvement, with 1.33× speedup compared to the original RELION-2.

Figure 10(b) present the total speedup of each stage after applying compiler optimization. It is obvious that all three stages work well with the combination of ICC compiler and MPS. For refine3D, class3D and class2D, it achieves a total speedup of 1.27×, 1.6× and 3.21× respectively using the ICC compiler and MPS.

5   Related Work

There are few existing works that attempt to optimize the performance of the RELION, which can be further divided into two categories based on their aspect to boost the performance. One aspect to improve the performance of RELION is to pipeline the entire workflow and perform the analysis work automatically, which is proposed by Fernandez-Leiro et al. [3]. From the user perspective, the performance of using the software is greatly improved with this pipelined app-roach. The second aspect is to optimize the particular steps within the workflow. Su et al. [15] implements a GPU-enhanced parallel version of single particle cryo-EM image processing (GeRelion). In their evaluation, GeRelion on 4 or 8 GPU cards is able to outperform RELION on 256 CPU cores, demonstrating improved performance and scalability of GeRelion. Furthermore, Dari et al. [7] presents an implementation of RELION (RELION-2) where GPUs are used to process the most computationally intensive steps within the workflow to overcome the bottleneck of limited bandwidth between CPU and GPU. Moreover, RELION-2 is able to dynamically allocate and reduce the memory requirement on GPUs, and thus make it feasible to even run on cost-effective personal workstations.

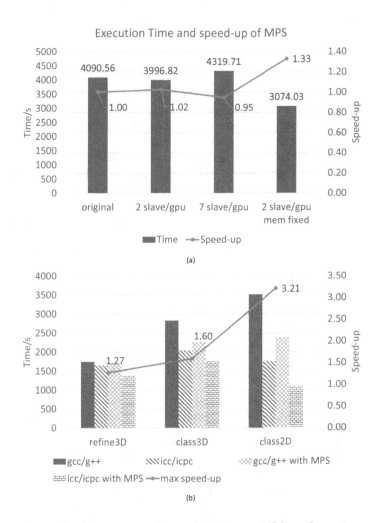

Fig. 10. Performance speedup under different MPS configurations.

cryoSPARC [12] optimized cyro-EM algorithm by introducing stochastic gradient descent(SGD) as the *ab initio* modeling algorithm. As SGD only uses subsets of large input dataset for estimation, this method can result in large computation reduction with notable performance speedup. In addition, as it estimates the *ab initio* from subsets of input images, it leads to different estimation of *ab initio* and final possible resolution of single-particle refinement. This method has already been merged into the latest version of RELION-2.1 [1].

6   Conclusion and Future Work

The ever increasing demand for cryo-EM structure determination with higher resolution is driving the performance optimization of RELION-2. This paper conducts comprehensive performance analysis of RELION-2 and identifies the bottlenecks for performance optimization. In addition, we propose several optimization strategies for improving the performance of RELION-2, including calculation redundancy optimization, GPU acceleration and CPU binding. Our experimental results demonstrate that our optimizations can improve the performance of RELION-2 by 3.17× without degrading the resolution. For future work, we would like to port the entire M-step to GPU in order to fully accelerate the computation of RELION-2. In addition, handling large data sets that can not fit into the GPU memory also poses challenge for further performance optimization.

Acknowledgments. This work is supported by the National Key R&D Program of China (Grant No. 2016YFB1000304) and National Natural Science Foundation of China (Grant No. 61502019).

References

1. Relion version 2.1 stable (2017). https://github.com/3dem/relion
2. Elmlund, D., Elmlund, H.: Simple: software for ab initio reconstruction of heterogeneous single-particles. J. Struct. Biol. **180**(3), 420–427 (2012)
3. Fernandez-Leiro, R., Scheres, S.H.: A pipeline approach to single-particle processing in relion. Acta Crystallogr. Sect. D: Struct. Biol. **73**(6), 496–502 (2017)
4. Frank, J., Shimkin, B., Dowse, H.: Spider-a modular software system for electron image processing. Ultramicroscopy **6**(4), 343–357 (1981)
5. Grigorieff, N.: Frealign: high-resolution refinement of single particle structures. J. Struct. Biol. **157**(1), 117–125 (2007)
6. Khoshouei, M., Radjainia, M., Baumeister, W., Danev, R.: Cryo-em structure of haemoglobin at 3.2 å determined with the volta phase plate. Nat. Commun. **8**, 16099 (2017)
7. Kimanius, D., Forsberg, B.O., Scheres, S.H., Lindahl, E.: Accelerated cryo-EM structure determination with parallelisation using GPUS in Relion-2. Elife 5 (2016)
8. Nvidia, C.: Cufft library (2010)
9. Ott, D.: Optimizing applications for NUMA. Intel® Developer Zone (2011). https://software.intel.com/en-us/articles/optimizing-applications-for-numa

10. Paulino, C., Kalienkova, V., Lam, A.K., Neldner, Y., Dutzler, R.: Activation mechanism of the calcium-activated chloride channel TMEM16A revealed by cryo-EM. Nature **552**(7685), 421 (2017)
11. Pipe, J.G., Menon, P.: Sampling density compensation in MRI: rationale and an iterative numerical solution. Magn. Reson. Med. **41**(1), 179–186 (1999)
12. Punjani, A., Rubinstein, J.L., Fleet, D.J., Brubaker, M.A.: cryoSPARC: algorithms for rapid unsupervised cryo-EM structure determination. Nat. Methods **14**(3), 290 (2017)
13. Reinders, J.: VTune (TM) Performance Analyzer Essentials: Measurement and Tuning Techniques for Software Developers. Intel Press (2004)
14. Scheres, S.H.: Relion: implementation of a bayesian approach to cryo-EM structure determination. J. Struct. Biol. **180**(3), 519–530 (2012)
15. Su, H., Wen, W., Du, X., Lu, X., Liao, M., Li, D.: GeRelion: GPU-enhanced parallel implementation of single particle cryo-EM image processing. bioRxiv p. 075887 (2016)
16. Tang, G., et al.: EMAN2: an extensible image processing suite for electron microscopy. J. Struct. Biol. **157**(1), 38–46 (2007)
17. Wang, E., et al.: Intel math kernel library. High-Performance Computing on the Intel® Xeon Phi^{TM}, pp. 167–188. Springer, Cham (2014). https://doi.org/10.1007/978-3-319-06486-4_7
18. Zhang, X., Yan, C., Hang, J., Finci, L.I., Lei, J., Shi, Y.: An atomic structure of the human spliceosome. Cell **169**(5), 918–929 (2017)

The Checkpoint-Timing for Backward Fault-Tolerant Schemes

Min Zhang[✉]

Lianyungang JARI Electronics Co., Ltd. of CSIC, Lianyungang, China
xingyuant@126.com

Abstract. To improve the performance of the backward fault tolerant scheme in the long-running parallel application, a general checkpoint-timing method was proposed to determine the unequal checkpointing interval according to an arbitrary failure rate, to reduce the total execution time. Firstly, a new model was introduced to evaluate the mean expected execution time. Secondly, the optimality condition was derived for the constant failure rate according to the calculation model, and the optimal equal checkpointing interval can be obtained easily. Subsequently, a general method was derived to determine the checkpointing timing for the other failure rate. The final results shown the proposal is practical to trade-off the re-processing overhead and the checkpointing overhead in the backward fault-tolerant scheme.

Keywords: Parallel computation · Fault tolerance · Checkpointing
Failure rate

1 Introduction

Checkpointing schemes are the famous backward fault tolerant techniques for the long-running parallel computations, such as scientific computing and telecommunication applications [1]. A saved state of the process is called a checkpoint, to reduce the number of logs to be replayed during the rollback recovery [2–4]. During failure-free execution, the time between two consecutive checkpoints is referred to as the checkpoint interval [5–8]. The checkpoint interval is one of the major factors influencing the performance of the fault tolerant scheme [9]. As the checkpoint interval decreases, in the presence of the failure event, the computation loss decreases. However, excessive checkpointing operations incur high overhead during the normal failure-free execution and may result in severe performance degradation. On the contrary, as the checkpoint interval increases, the overhead for the checkpointing operation during the failure-free execution decreases. However the computation loss caused by the failure event increases and deficient checkpointing may incur an expensive rollback recovery overhead. Therefore, a trade-off must be made to determine a proper checkpoint interval for high fault tolerant performance [10].

Young et al. introduced a first-order approximation to optimal time interval between checkpoints to reduce the total waste time [11]. Based on Young's work, Daly introduced a method for optimal checkpoint placement from a first order to a higher order approximation [12]. Ozaki et al. improved the checkpoint placement strategy

© Springer Nature Singapore Pte Ltd. 2018
C. Li and J. Wu (Eds.): ACA 2018, CCIS 908, pp. 210–218, 2018.
https://doi.org/10.1007/978-981-13-2423-9_16

based on min-max placement, the variation calculus approach and the classical Brender's fixed point algorithm respectively [13]. For the two-level recovery scheme, the expected total overhead of one unit from one hard checkpoint to another was obtained using Markov renewal processes and an optimal interval was computed [14]. To determine appropriate checkpoint sequence, Okamura et al. proposed an online adaptive checkpoint algorithm based on the reinforcement learning called Q-learning, and examined comprehensive evaluation of aperiodic time-based checkpointing and rejuvenation schemes to maximize the steady-state system availability by applying the dynamic programming [15].

2   The Execution Model

2.1   The Execution Model

Similar to the definitions in [9], checkpoint overhead is the expected overhead caused by a checkpointing operation and the mean checkpoint overhead is denoted as C. Checkpoint latency is the expected duration required to save the checkpoint, and the mean checkpoint latency is denoted as L. In practical implementations, checkpoint latency is larger than the checkpoint overhead. That means $L >= C > 0$. Rollback overhead is the time required to reload the last checkpoint during the rollback recovery phase and the mean rollback overhead is denoted as R. The failure rate is denoted as $f(t)$, and the cumulative distribution function (CDF) of the probability density function is denoted as $F(t)$. The inter-failure time is denoted as Mean Time To Failure ($MTTF$), and $MTTF = \int_0^\infty t dF(t) = \int_0^\infty f(t) t dt$. $H(.)$ is defined as the proportion of the effective execution time in the progress of the running application [16].

The interval between two consecutive failure events is referred to as a running unit. As shown in Fig. 1, the running unit begins with the failure event f at time t_0, and ends with the next failure event at t_0' ($t_n + L > t_0' > t_{n-1} + L$). During the running unit, the checkpoint C_i is started at time t_i ($i = 1, 2, 3 ..., n-1$), and the execution is divided into a set of intervals $\{I_1, I_2,...I_n\}$ separated by $\{C_1, C_2, C_3, ... C_{n-1}\}$. According to the symbols introduced above, each checkpointing operation incurs the checkpoint latency L while the checkpoint overhead is only C ($L >= C > 0$). For the sake of convenience, suppose that $t_0 = 0$.

According to the definition of the running unit mentioned above, each unit begins with the rollback recovery procedure (except the first unit), and finally ends with the next failure event (except the last unit at the end of the long-running execution). As illustrated in Fig. 1, the first running unit starts from reloading the latest checkpoint incurring the rollback overhead R, and then implements the subsequent failure recovery procedure. After the failure recovery procedure, the application can be recovered to the state just before the failure point and continues the following normal execution.

2.2   Effective Execution Time

For analysis, one running unit can be decomposed into two parts, including the essential part and the extra part. The useful computation execution which contributes to

212   M. Zhang

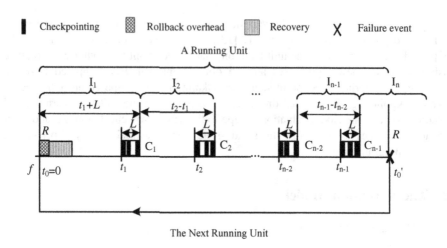

Fig. 1. The running model

the progress of the application eventually is referred to as the essential part. The additional execution which does not contribute to the progress of the application is referred to as the extra part. The essential and extra parts are both disjoint during the running unit. For the running unit in Fig. 1, the checkpointing and rollback operations belong to the extra part since they can't produce the useful computation execution which contributes to the progress of the application. During I_n, the computation prior to the failure event also belongs to the extra part since it would be wasted after the subsequent rollback operation.

As shown in Fig. 1, Let S be the total duration of all essential parts in a running unit, and X be the total duration of all extra parts in the unit. According to the theorem of the renewal process, the expected effective ratio of the long-running execution $H(\cdot)$ can be expressed as Eq. (1).

$$H(\cdot) = \frac{E(S)}{E(X+S)} \tag{1}$$

Specifically, $H(\cdot)$ reflects the average fraction of the time that the system performs the useful computation which advances the progress of the execution. In practice, maximizing $H(\cdot)$ is equivalent to the optimality of the fault tolerant performance. For this reason, $H(\cdot)$ is a convenient metric of the computation efficiency as it has a straightforward meaning.

2.3   Derivation

For the running unit shown in Fig. 1, all execution intervals are completed except the interval I_n. To derive $H(\cdot)$, let S_i be the duration of the essential part in the interval I_i. The duration of the essential part S_1 is $t_1 + L$-C-R, The duration of the essential part S_i

is $(t_i + L)$–$(t_{i-1} + L)$–C ($1 < i < n$). In the last interval S_n is zero as its computation is wasted due to the failure event.

If $n = 1$, no execution interval is successful and the total duration of the essential part in the running unit is zero. If $n > 1$, the total duration of the essential part S can be expressed as Eq. (2).

$$S = \sum_{i=1}^{n-1} S_i = t_{n-1} - (n - 1)C + L - R \tag{2}$$

If $n = 1$, that means the running unit ends prior to the completion of C_1. No execution interval is successful and the total duration of the essential part in the running unit is zero. As a result, the total duration of all essential parts in a running unit can be expressed as the following Eq. (3).

$$S = \begin{cases} 0 & n = 1 \\ t_{n-1} - (n - 1)C + L - R & n > 1 \end{cases} \tag{3}$$

Let $F(t)$ be cumulative distribution function of the inter-failure time with probability density function $f(t)$. Then we get $F(t_i + L) = P(t \le t_i + L) = \int_{0}^{t_i + L} dF(t) = \int_{0}^{t_i + L} f(t)dt$.

Let $P(I_{i+1})$ be the probability that the failure event f occurs in the interval I_{i+1} ($i = 1, 2, 3, \ldots$). In other words, $P(I_{i+1})$ denotes the probability that the system failure time t is strictly greater than $t_i + L$ on the cumulative operation time, and is equal to or less than $t_{i+1} + L$ ($i = 1, 2, \ldots$). Then we get $P(I_{i+1}) = P(t_i + L < t \le t_{i+1} + L) = \int_{t_i + L}^{t_{i+1} + L} f(t)dt$.

Due to $P(I_{i+1}) = F(t_{i+1} + L) - F(t_i + L)$, the expectation $E(S)$, can be derived from Eq. (3).

$$E(S) = P(I_1) \cdot 0 + \sum_{i=2}^{\infty} (P(I_i) \cdot (t_{i-1} - (i - 1)C + L - R))$$
$$= \sum_{i=1}^{\infty} (P(I_{i+1}) \cdot (t_i - iC + L - R)) \tag{4}$$

Through the variable substitution of $P(I_{i+1})$, the following Eq. (5) can be derived.

$$E(S) = \sum_{i=1}^{\infty} ((F(t_{i+1} + L) - F(t_i + L)) \cdot (t_i - iC + L - R)) \tag{5}$$

In practice, the expectation, $E(X + S)$ is equivalent to $MTTF$ as $E(X + S) = \int_{0}^{\infty} tdF(t)$. With given checkpoint sequence $\{t_1, t_2, t_3, \ldots t_n\}$, $H(\{t_1, t_2, t_3, \ldots\}|F(t))$, the expected effective ratio of the execution, can be expressed as Eq. (6) by combining Eq. (1) with Eq. (5).

$$H(\{t_1,t_2,t_3,\ldots\}|F(t)) = \frac{\sum_{i=1}^{\infty}((1-F(t_i+L))\cdot(t_i-t_{i-1}-C))+(L-R)(1-F(t_1+L))}{\int_0^{\infty} t\, dF(t)} \tag{6}$$

To optimize the fault tolerant performance with given failure distribution $F(t)$, the final objective is to choose the proper checkpoint sequence $\{t_1, t_2, t_3,\ldots\}$ so as to maximize the value of $H(\{t_1, t_2, t_3,\ldots\}|F(t))$.

3   Checkpoint-Timing

3.1   For the Constant Failure Rate

With the constant failure rate $r(t) = f(t)/(1-F(t))$, the inter-failure time is independently and identically distributed as standard exponential with $F(t) = 1-e^{-\lambda t}$ $(MTTF = 1/\lambda)$ and the optimal checkpoint interval is constant. The running unit can be simplified as in Fig. 2. Specifically, the duration of each execution interval I_i is $T + L$ constantly during the running unit, as $t_2-t_1 = \ldots t_n-t_{n-1} = T + L$ and $t_1 - t_0 = T$.

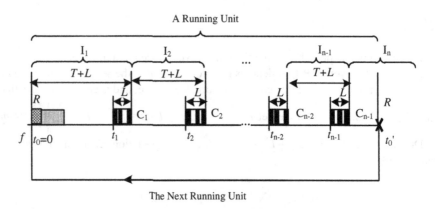

Fig. 2. The running unit with the constant failure rate

For the application following the exponential $F(t)$, let T be the constant checkpoint period and $H(T|F(t))$ denote the expected effective ratio of the execution. As a result, $H(T|F(t))$ can be derived as Eq. (7) from Eq. (6). The explicit derivation process of $H(T|F(t))$ is ignored here.

$$H(T|F(t)) = \lambda \cdot E(B) = \lambda e^{-\lambda(T+L)}\left(\frac{(T+L-C)}{1-e^{-\lambda(T+L)}} - R\right) \tag{7}$$

For the exponential $F(t)$, with the constant checkpoint period T_{opt}, the conditional probability of each interval I_i determined by $\{t_{i-1}, t_i\}$ is constant. This property is called the constant conditional probability of the interval as

$$\frac{F(t_i+L)-F(t_{i-1}+L)}{1-F(t_{i-1}+L)} = \frac{F(T_{opt}+L+t_{i-1}+L)-F(t_{i-1}+L)}{1-F(t_{i-1}+L)}$$
$$= F(T_{opt}+L) = 1 - e^{-\lambda(T_{opt}+L)}, \quad (i = 1, 2, 3 \ldots) \tag{8}$$

3.2 For the Other Failure Rate

With the varying failure rate $r(t) = f(t)/(1-F(t))$, the fixed equidistant checkpoint period is not optimal. In order to determine the maximum of $H(\{t_1, t_2, t_3, \ldots\} | F(t))$ in Eq. (6), the following Eq. (9) can be derived by $\frac{\partial H(\{t_1, t_2, t_3, \ldots\} | F(t))}{\partial t_i} = 0$.

$$F(t_{i+1}+L) - F(t_i+L) = \begin{cases} (t_i - t_{i-1} - C)f(t_i+L) & i > 1 \\ (t_1 + L - R - C)f(t_1+L) & i = 1 \end{cases} \tag{9}$$

With $F(t)$ and the first checkpoint timing t_1, the checkpoint timing sequence $\{t_2, t_3, \ldots\}$ can be obtained successively according to Eq. (9). Therefore, the appropriate t_1 can be obtained by maximizing $H(\{t_1, t_2, t_3, \ldots\} | F(t))$, and the corresponding $\{t_1, t_2, t_3, \ldots\}$ can be obtained according to Eq. (9).

For simplification, an appropriate checkpoint sequence $\{t_1, t_2, t_3, \ldots\}$ during a running unit can be determined one after another according to Eq. (10) below.

$$t_{i+1} = \begin{cases} F^{-1}\left(1 - e^{-\lambda(T_{opt}+L)}\right) - L & i = 0 \\ F^{-1}\left((1 - F(t_i+L))\left(1 - e^{-\lambda(T_{opt}+L)}\right) + F(t_i+L)\right) - L & i > = 1 \end{cases} \tag{10}$$

4 Discussions

With the constant failure rate $r(t) = f(t)/(1-F(t))$, the optimal checkpoint period T_{opt} is corresponding to the unique maximal $H(T_{opt} | F(t))$ in Eq. (7). Figure 3 is $H(\{t_1, t_2, t_3, \ldots\} | F(t))$ when $C = 2$ s and $R = 2$ s. Specifically, the z-axis is $H(\{t_1, t_2, t_3, \ldots\} | F(t))$ corresponding to the running unit, and the y-axis is the constant γ and the x-axis is the constant T.

With the varying failure rate $r(t) = f(t)/(1-F(t))$, the appropriate checkpoint timing sequence $\{t_1, t_2, t_3, \ldots\}$ can be obtained according to CDF, MTTF, T_{opt} and Eq. (10). According to the condition of optimality Eq. (10), The general checkpoint-timing algorithm for backward fault-tolerant schemes can be designed easily.

To validate our checkpoint-timing method, $F(t) = 1 - e^{-\left(\frac{t}{s}\right)^{\beta}}$ without constant $r(t)$ is introduced here ($\alpha > 0$, $\beta >= 1$). Figure 4 illustrates the appropriate checkpoint timing sequence generated according to CDF, MTTF, T_{opt} and Eq. (10) with given parameters $C = 6$s, $R = 6$s, $s = 30$, $L = 10$s, and $\varepsilon = 10^{-6}$. As shown in Fig. 4, the failure rate $r(t)$ of $F(t)$ is increasing when $\beta > 1$. The appropriate checkpoint interval is

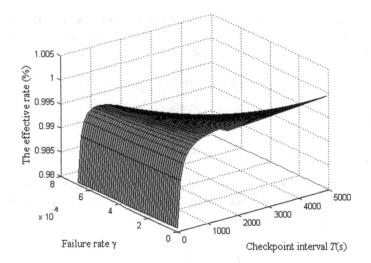

Fig. 3. Fault tolerant overhead ratio

non-increasing monotonically. The failure rate $r(t)$ is constant when $\beta = 1$, the appropriate checkpoint interval except the first one is equal.

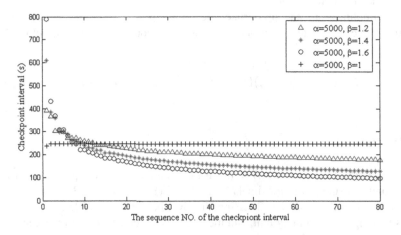

Fig. 4. The checkpoint timing sequence with $\beta \geq 1$

For $F(t) = 1 - e^{-\left(\frac{t}{\alpha}\right)^{\beta}}$ with $0 < \beta \leq 1$, Fig. 5 illustrates the appropriate checkpoint timing sequence generated according to CDF, $MTTF$, T_{opt} and Eq. (10) with given parameters $C = 6s$, $R = 6s$, $s = 30$, $L = 10s$, and $\varepsilon = 10^{-6}$. As shown in Fig. 5, different from $\beta \geq 1$, the value of the checkpoint interval increases monotonically while $0 < \beta \leq 1$.

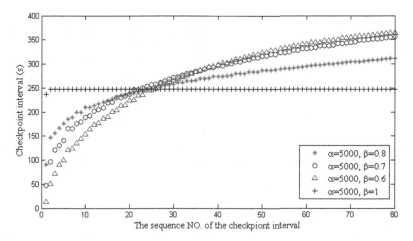

Fig. 5. The checkpoint sequence when $0 < \beta <= 1$

5   Conclusion

The checkpoint interval is one of the major factors influencing the performance of the backward fault tolerant scheme in the long-running parallel application. To trade-off the checkpointing overhead and the re-processing overhead in the presence of the possible failure event, a general checkpoint-timing method was proposed to determine the unequal checkpointing interval according to an arbitrary failure rate, to reduce the expected execution time. Firstly, a calculation model was introduced to evaluate the mean expected execution time. Secondly, the optimality condition was derived for the constant failure rate according to the calculation model, and the optimal equal checkpointing interval can be obtained easily. Subsequently, a general checkpoint-timing method was derived to determine the checkpointing timing for the other failure rate. The final results shown the proposed method is practical to determine an equal or unequal checkpoint timing sequence for the backward fault-tolerant scheme.

References

1. Li, T., Shafique, M., Ambrose, J.A., et al.: Fine-grained checkpoint recovery for application-specific instruction-set processors. IEEE Trans. Comput. **66**(4), 647–660 (2017)
2. Meroufel, B., Belalem, G.: Lightweight coordinated checkpointing in cloud computing. J. High Speed Netw. **20**(3), 131–143 (2014)
3. Salehi, M., Tavana, M.K., Rehman, S., et al.: Two-state checkpointing for energy-efficient fault tolerance in hard real-time systems. IEEE Trans. Very Large Scale Integr. Syst. **24**(7), 2426–2437 (2016)
4. Islam, T.Z., Bagchi, S., Eigenmann, R.: Reliable and efficient distributed checkpointing system for grid environments. J. Grid Comput. **12**(4), 593–613 (2014)

5. Fu, H., Yu, C., Sun, J., Du, J., Wang, M.: A multilevel fault-tolerance technique for the DAG data driven model. In: 2015 15th IEEE/ACM International Symposium on Cluster, Cloud and Grid Computing (CCGrid), Shenzhen, China, pp. 1127–1130 (2015)

6. Mendizabal, O.M., Jalili Marandi, P., Dotti, F.L., Pedone, F.: Checkpointing in parallel state-machine replication. In: Aguilera, M.K., Querzoni, L., Shapiro, M. (eds.) OPODIS 2014. LNCS, vol. 8878, pp. 123–138. Springer, Cham (2014). https://doi.org/10.1007/978-3-319-14472-6_9

7. Sweiti, S., Dweik, A.A.: Integrated replication-checkpoint fault tolerance approach of mobile agents "IRCFT". Int. Arab J. Inf. Technol. 13(1A), 190–195 (2016)

8. Awasthi, L.K., Misra, M., Joshi, R.C., et al.: Minimum mutable checkpoint-based coordinated checkpointing protocol for mobile distributed systems. Int. J. Commun. Netw. Distrib. Syst. 12(4), 356–380 (2014)

9. Elnozahy, E.N., Alvisi, L., Wang, Y.M., Johnson, D.B.: A survey of rollback-recovery protocols in message-passing systems. ACM Comput. Surv. 34(3), 375–408 (2002)

10. Treaster, M.: A survey of fault-tolerance and fault-recovery techniques in parallel systems. Technical report cs.DC/0501002, ACM Computing Research Repository, January 2005

11. Young, J.W.: A first order approximation to the optimum checkpoint interval. Commun. ACM 17(9), 530–531 (1974)

12. Daly, J.T.: A higher order estimate of the optimum checkpoint interval for restart dumps. Future Gener. Comput. Syst. 22, 303–312 (2006)

13. Ozaki, T., Dohi, T., Kaio, N.: Numerical computation algorithms for sequential checkpoint placement. Perform. Eval. 66, 311–326 (2009)

14. Naruse, K., Umemura, S., Nakagawa, S.: Optimal checkpointing interval for two-level recovery schemes. Comput. Math Appl. 51, 371–376 (2006)

15. Okamura, H., Dohi, T.: Comprehensive evaluation of aperiodic checkpointing and rejuvenation schemes in operational software system. J. Syst. Softw. 83(9), 1591–1604 (2010)

16. Endo, P.T., Rodrigues, M., et al.: High availability in clouds: systematic review and research challenges. J. Cloud Comput. Adv. Syst. Appl. 5, 16 (2016)

Quota-constrained Job Submission Behavior at Commercial Supercomputer

Jinghua Feng[1,2], Guangming Liu[1,2(✉)], Zhiwei Zhang[2], Tao Li[3],
Yuqi Li[2], and Fuxing Sun[2]

[1] College of Computer, National University of Defense Technology,
Changsha, China
[2] National Supercomputer Center in Tianjin, Tianjin, China
{fengjh,liugm,zhangzw,Liyq,Sunfx}@nscc-tj.gov.cn
[3] College of Computer and Control Engineering,
Nankai University, Tianjin, China
litao@nankai.edu.cn

Abstract. Understanding user behavior is great helpful for assessing HPC system job scheduling, promoting allocation efficiency and improving user satisfaction. Current research on user behavior is mainly focused on think time (i.e. time between two consecutive jobs) of non-commercial supercomputer systems. In this paper, we present a methodology to characterize workloads of the commercial supercomputer. We use it to analyze the 2.7 million jobs of different users in various fields of Tianhe-1A from 2016.01 to 2017.12 and 0.89 million jobs of Sugon 5000A from 2015.09 to 2017.03.

In order to identify the main factors affecting the user's job submission behavior on commercial supercomputers, this paper analyzed the correlation between user's job submission behavior and various factors such as job characteristics and quota constraint. The result shows that, on the commercial supercomputer, user s job submission behavior is not obviously affected by the previous job's runtime and waiting time. It is affected by the number of processors the job uses, the previous job's status and the size of the total resources that users can submit jobs. We also find that, there are three job submission peaks on each day. In the time window of 8 h, 86% jobs of a same user have the same number of processors and nearly 40% of them have little difference in runtime.

Keywords: Interval time · Think time · Quota constraint · User behavior

1 Introduction

High Performance Computing (HPC) is a mainstream for performing large-scale scientific computing [1, 2]. How to schedule and allocate resources faster, improve the resource utilization rate and reduce the average waiting time of a job have always been the objectives of the researchers. Understanding user behavior is great helpful for assessing HPC system job scheduling, promoting allocation efficiency and improving user satisfaction. Current research on user behavior is mainly focused on think time of

© Springer Nature Singapore Pte Ltd. 2018
C. Li and J. Wu (Eds.): ACA 2018, CCIS 908, pp. 219–231, 2018.
https://doi.org/10.1007/978-981-13-2423-9_17

non-commercial supercomputer systems. [3] presented the concept of Think Time, [4, 5] and other paper analyzed the correlation between Think Time and other factors such as response time, waiting time, job size, etc.

Supercomputers can be divided into non-commercial and commercial ones depending on the service model. The current related research focuses on non-commercial supercomputer systems, and there are also many commercial supercomputer systems. For example, there are six national supercomputing centers in China, including Tianjin, Shenzhen, Jinan, Changsha, Wuxi and Guangzhou. The six supercomputing centers own TaihuLight, Tianhe-2, Tianhe-1A and other world-class supercomputers. Users need to pay for the computing, and they usually use resources in accordance with the contract. The contract mainly limits the size of the total resources that users can submit jobs, which is the quota constraint. At the same time, there are more challenges to improve user satisfaction on the commercial supercomputers because of the commercial service model. It is important to understand the user's behavior of job submission in order to optimize job scheduling strategy and improve user satisfaction.

In this paper, we presented a methodology to characterize workloads on the commercial supercomputer, and the details for characterizing think time and interval time. We used it to analyze the 2.7 million jobs of different users in various fields of Tianhe-1A from 2016.01 to 2017.12 and 0.89 million jobs of Sugon 5000A from 2015.09 to 2017.03.

The main contributions of this paper include (1) presenting a methodology to characterize workloads on the commercial supercomputer; (2) using it to analyze the data based on 2.7 million jobs of Tianhe-1A and 0.89 million jobs of Sugon 5000A; (3) analyzing the correlation between interval time (IT), think time (TT) and alloc cpus (the number of processers the job uses), core time (total CPU time of the job), job status and group cpus (the user's quota constraint) to identify the main factors affecting the user's job submission behavior on commercial supercomputers; (4) analyzing the weekly pattern of the user's job submission behavior and the similarities of the successively submitted jobs.

2   Background and Related Work

Currently, there are some research focuses on workload characterizations, [6] presented the history of HPC system development and applications in China, HPC centers and facilities, and major research institutions, but it's before 2010. [7, 8] analyzed the system features of three supercomputers (Hopper, Edison, and Carver). [9] analyzed the I/O features of 6 years of applications on three supercomputers, Intrepid, Mira, and Edison. These papers present a detailed analysis of system performance, but none of them have focused on the user behavior.

[11] suggested that sessions of think time be identified based on proven user activity, namely the submittal of new jobs, regardless of how long they run. [10] presented the Questionnaire for User Habits of Computer Clusters (QUHCC) and gave them to a group of 23 distinct users of two different computer clusters hosted at TU Dortmund University. They analyzed the results to find factors that affect the user's behavior of using supercomputers. In fact, the sample of that paper is relatively small.

[4] analyzed the correlation between think time and runtime, waiting time. [5] further analyzed the relationship between think time and runtime, waiting time, slowdown and job size based on the data of the Mira supercomputer for one year was analyzed. It was considered that the user behavior was greatly affected by the waiting time. [12] extended the calculation of the think time to the HTC type application.

But the current research on user behavior is mainly focused on think time of non-commercial supercomputer systems,and they all think that think time is a key factor that reflects the user's job submission behavior.

3   Methodology

In this section, we present the system and workloads in focus for our investigation and elaborate on the key parameters studied.

3.1   Data Source

The analyses presented here are based on the 2.7 million jobs of different users in various fields from Tianhe-1A (TH-1A) supercomputer at the National Supercomputer Center in Tianjin since 2016 to 2017 and 0.89 million jobs from Sugon 5000A (Sugon-5000A) at the Shanghai Supercomputer Center [13]. The information of jobs in Tianhe-1A is from the SLURM [14] workload manager logs. And the information of jobs in Sugon 5000A is from Chinese Supercomputers Workloads Archive (CSWA) [15]. Currently, the Standard Workloads Format (SWF), which is defined by Parallel Workloads Archive [16].

Table 1 shows the summary of the main characteristics of the dataset. The jobs in Tianhe-1A, which consist of 1362091 jobs submitted by 733 users (2016) and 1329123 jobs submitted by 714 users (2017) from 5 science fields such as Basic Science, Biological, Material Science, Meteorological Science, Aerospace, and Other fields. In total, these jobs consumed over 892.98 million CPU hours. The jobs data in Sugon 5000A includes 869160 jobs submitted by 271 users and consumed over 100.31 million CPU hours, and the Standard Workloads Format does not have information about application areas.

Table 1. Jobs in the Tianhe-1A (2016.01-2017.12) and Sugon 5000A (2015.9-2017.3)

Science Field	#Users		#Jobs		CPU hours (millions)		#TT Jobs		#IT Jobs	
	2017	2016	2017	2016	2017	2016	2017	2016	2017	2016
Basic Science	251	176	300228	250831	148.87	112.87	64078	50926	229677	196350
Biological	20	30	70487	153769	32.33	55.58	5807	5583	22590	39025
Material Science	230	256	692110	633059	152.68	146.59	120838	90629	531529	447085
Meteorological Science	97	97	172960	182065	41.1	57.33	53149	76064	139944	164573
Aerospace	21	22	27567	22030	33.22	26.07	8657	7086	24599	18935
Other	95	152	65771	120337	32.02	54.32	20299	29472	53887	95376
TH-1A	714	733	1329123	1362091	440.22	452.76	272828	259760	1002226	961344
Sugon 5000A	271		869160		100.31		99887		515013	

*number of subsequent jobs with positive think time: $0 < TT < 8$ h, and Interval time: $0 < IT < 8$ h.

Although the number of users and jobs are different, Fig. 1 shows that the five science fields have a basic monthly job submission from 2016 to 2017 and the change of jobs submission percentage is small, and it is able to reflect the overall situation of actual users submitting jobs on commercial supercomputer systems.

3.2   Systems Description

Tianhe-1A is the world's top 1 supercomputer in 2010 at the National Supercomputer Center in Tianjin. It has been in service since 2011 and has been in operation for more than seven years. It is a typical representative of commercial supercomputer. Tianhe-1A supercomputer consists of 7168 computing nodes (12 cores, 24 GB memory per node) with a peak performance 4.7 PFlops.

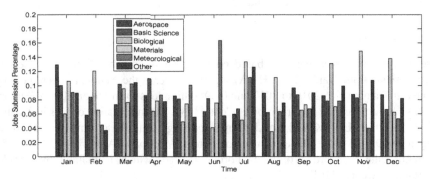

(a)   The jobs submission percentage in Tianhe-1A from Jan. to Dec 2016

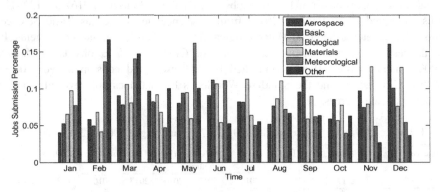

(b)   The jobs submission percentage from Jan. to Dec 2017

Fig. 1. The Monthly characteristics of job submission in Tianhe-1A from 2016 to 2017

Sugon 5000A supercomputer consists of 416 computing nodes (24 cores, 128 GB memory per node) with a peak performance 0.4 PFlops.

3.3   Characterizing the Think Time and Interval Time

When using the commercial supercomputer, users need to pay for the computing, and they usually use resources in accordance with the contract. The contract mainly limits the size of the total resources that users can submit jobs, which is the **quota constraint.**

For example, if the user can submit k jobs, each job occupies the resource N_j, and the user's quota constraint is M, thus $\sum_{j=1}^{k} N_j \leq M$. In the SLURM system, it is named **Group cpus** of the user.

Figure 2 describes the process of submitting a job under the quota constraint environment. After the user submits the job, the workload manager first performs quota check. If the sum of user's resource has not exceeded the quota, it proceeds to the next step for resource check. Otherwise, the job needs to wait.

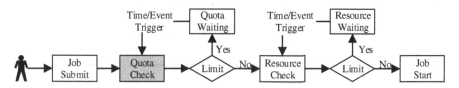

Fig. 2.   The step from job submit to job start on a quota-constrained supercomputer

The job has **Submit time** (t_{sub}), **Start time** (t_{str}) and **End time** (t_{end}). The **runtime** of job$_j$ is the timespan between End time and Start time (t_{end} - t_{str}); the **waiting time** of job$_j$ (W_j) is the timespan between Start time and Submit time (t_{str} - t_{sub}); the **response time** of job$_j$ (R_j) is the timespan between End time and Submit time (t_{end} - t_{sub}); And the **core time** is defined as the total CPU time of the job.

Alloc cpus is the number of processors the job uses. **Job Status** is the job end status with in {failed, completed, cancelled}.

If a user has a **quota constraint** (size of cpus), the waiting time consists of two parts: waiting time caused by quota-constrained and resource-constrained

$$W_j = Wq_j + Wr_j. \tag{1}$$

Think Time (TT): the termination of this job and the submittal of the next job by the same user.

Interval Time (IT): the timespan between the submission time of two sequential jobs by the same user.

If the submit time of job$_{j+1}$ early than the end time of job$_j$, TT(j, j + 1) < 0. It means the two subsequent jobs are overlapped. In this paper we only consider subsequent job submissions of positive think time, and less than eight hours, which is intended to represent subsequent job submissions belonging to the same working day like [5]. At the same time, in the data of this paper, jobs with 0 < TT < 8 h exceed 85% of all jobs with TT > 0 (90% on the Tianhe-1A, 85% on the Sugon 5000A). Table 1 shows the number of subsequent jobs with positive think times. We can see that there are a large number of jobs with negative think time, and the number of jobs that satisfy the requirement (TT > 0) accounted for only about 22% on TH-1A and 13% on Sugon 5000A. **About 80% of the user's jobs did not wait for the previous job to be submitted, so that think time may not be the best representative of all users' job submission behavior.**

Table 1 also shows the number of subsequent jobs (0 < IT < 8 h). In the Tianhe-1A system, the number of qualifying jobs exceeds 70%, and also more than 59% in the Sugon 5000A. Interval time is also helpful for understanding user's job submission behavior.

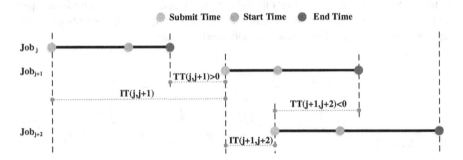

Fig. 3. Schematic of Think Time and Interval Time

From Fig. 3 we can see that if the submit time of job_{j+1} is later than the end time of job_j, the TT is contained by the IT. If the submit time of job_{j+2} is earlier than the end time of job_{j+1}, TT will be negative.

4   Analyze the Characteristics of User's Job Submission Behavior

4.1   Analysis of Job Characteristics in Terms of Runtime and Waiting Time

The analysis of think time behavior is often limited to the study of the impact of response time on user behavior. [5] pointed out that, at the non-commercial super-computer Mira, the think time of jobs follow linear trend with response time, runtime and waiting time. And jobs in different fields show similar characteristics.

Figure 4 shows how these components correlate with users' think times. From this we can see that the correlation between think time and response time, runtime, waiting time is not obvious on commercial supercomputers. Figure 4(a) shows that when the response time is small (<2100 s), TT will increase with the increase of response time. Subsequently, with the increase of response time, there is no obvious upward trend in TT. Figure 4(b) shows a phenomenon similar to (a).

Figure 4(c) shows that on a commercial supercomputer system, the TT does not change significantly as the waiting time changes, which is quite different from the phenomenon on a non-commercial supercomputer.

In order to better understand the user's job submission behavior, we also analyzed the correlation of IT and response time, runtime, and waiting time. The results show that the trend of IT with three parameters is similar to that of TT.

This phenomenon may be due to the fact that on commercial supercomputers, users clearly know that they have quota restrictions and tend to submit jobs more frequently. Therefore, the runtime of the previous job has no obvious effect on the user submitting the next job. IT and TT are basically irrelevant to the waiting time because on the commercial supercomputer system, the waiting time consists of two parts, waiting time caused by quota-constrained and resource-constrained. With the increase of waiting time, quota-constrained waiting time increases rapidly and nearly linearly, and takes up the main proportion of waiting time. The user is aware of this, so the waiting time does not significantly affect the behavior of the user submitting the job.

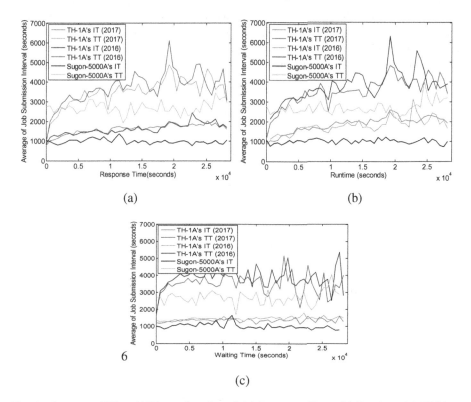

Fig. 4. Average of IT and TT as a function of (a) Response Time, (b) Runtime, (c) Waiting Time

4.2   Analyze the Correlation Between IT, TT and Alloc Cpus, Core Time, Job Status, and Group Cpus

This paper analyzes the correlation between IT, TT and alloc cpus (the number of using the job uses), core time (total CPU time of the job), job status and group cpus (the User's quota constraint) to identify the main factors affecting the user's job submission behavior on commercial supercomputers

Figure 5(a) shows that, user behavior seems to be impacted by the alloc cpus. The median IT is 69 s for small jobs and 338 s for large in 2017, and 89 s for small jobs and 352 s for large in 2016. Figure 5(b) shows that, the correlation between TT and alloc cpus is different from 2016 to 2017. The median TT is 156 s for small jobs and 263 s for large in 2017, and 133 s for small jobs and 130 s for large jobs 2016. This shows that the alloc cpus has no clear effect on TT, but it does significantly affect IT. With larger jobs, users need to spend more time preparing for the next job.

Figure 6(a) and (b) shows that, user behavior seems to be impacted by the Job Status. If the previous job failed, the user needs to spend more time adjusting and prepare to submit the next job. The median IT is 119 s for failed jobs, and for completed jobs 54 s in 2017. And the median TT is 295 s for failed jobs, and for completed jobs 162 s in 2016.

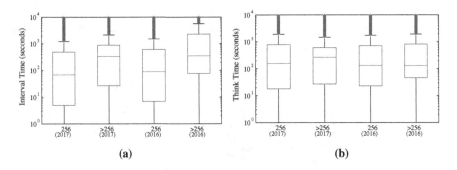

(a)   (b)

Fig. 5. The correlation between IT, TT and alloc cpus in Tianhe-1A

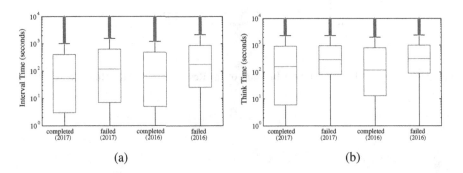

(a)   (b)

Fig. 6. The correlation between IT, TT and job status in Tianhe-1A

Figure 7(a) and (b) shows that, user behavior seems to be impacted by the core time. We divided the jobs into two categories according to the size of the core time. For the jobs (core time $> 10^5$) the IT and TT will increase significantly.

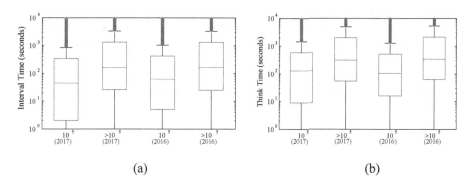

Fig. 7. The correlation between IT, TT and core time in Tianhe-1A

Figure 8(a) and (b) shows that, the correlation between IT, TT and group cpus is inconsistent. IT and groups cpus are negatively correlated. That is, the more resources a user can use, the more jobs he can submit, resulting in a smaller IT value. And this is easier to understand. But from Fig. 8(b) we can see a paradoxical phenomenon. The results of the 2016 and 2017 data show an opposite correlation. The median TT is 105 s for small Group cpus, and for large 190 s in 2017.

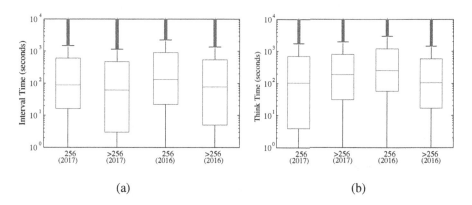

Fig. 8. The correlation between IT, TT and Group cpus in Tianhe-1A

Users with more resources have to spend more time preparing for jobs, which seems do not make sense. So we think that on commercial supercomputers, think time may not fully characterize user's job submission behavior.

4.3   Other Pattern of User's Job Submission Behavior on Commercial Supercomputer

Based on the data on Tianhe-1A, this paper further analyzes the weekly pattern of the user's job submission behavior and the similarities of the successively submitted jobs, which are helpful for job prediction and scheduling optimization.

Figure 9 shows that from Monday to Sunday, there are three peaks for the number of jobs submitted daily, which are 10–12 AM, 15–17 pm, and 21–23 pm. Moreover, users on Tianhe-1A have the habit of submitting jobs at night so that the results can be seen in the next working day. Since Saturday and Sunday are non-working days, the number of jobs submitted is less than that of the working day. There was a peak in the early morning of Wednesday, 2016, because a batch of jobs was submitted at 1–3 a.m.

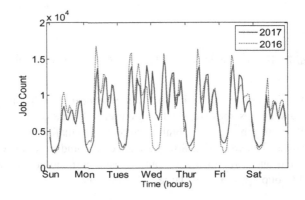

Fig. 9. User's job submission behavior weekly in Tianhe-1A

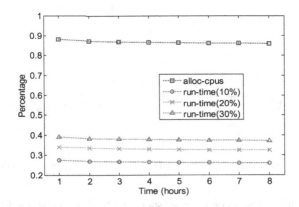

Fig. 10. The similarities of the successively submitted jobs in Tianhe-1A.

Figure 10 shows the similarity of successively submitted jobs, including alloc cpus and runtime. We can see that if the user's successively submitted jobs interval don't not exceed 8 h, over 86% of job's alloc cpus are the same. Therefore, we can research and predict the overall follow-up resource requirements based on the current resource usage and the pattern of the user's Job submission behavior. Figure 10 also shows that nearly 40% of the user's successively submitted jobs whose interval don't exceed 8 h had little difference of runtime ($\pm 30\%$), and more than 26% of jobs had very close runtime ($\pm 10\%$). These data can be combined with the job characteristics to further improve the accuracy of job execution time forecasting and thus optimize the scheduling system.

5 Summary and Discussion

Understand the user's job submission behavior, is helpful for job prediction, resource scheduling. The researchers used the think time as a key parameter reflecting the user's job submission behavior, and the research focused on non-commercial supercomputers.

In this paper, we first give the details about the methodology for characterizing think time and interval time, including the process for submitting jobs on the commercial supercomputer, data source, system description, definition and calculation of various variables, especially the quota-constrained waiting time. And use it to analyze 2.7 million jobs of different users in various fields in the Tianhe-1A from 2016.01 to 2017.12 and 0.89 million jobs in the Sugon 5000A for 2015.09 to 2017.03.

From the analysis results, the users' job submission behavior is different on the commercial supercomputer and non-commercial supercomputing. On commercial supercomputers such as Tianhe-1A and Sugon 5000A, the interval time of job submission is not obvious affected by the previous job's runtime and waiting time. because on the commercial supercomputer system, the waiting time consists of two parts: waiting time caused by quota-constrained and resource-constrained, with the increase of waiting time, quota-constrained waiting time in-creases rapidly and nearly linearly, and takes up the main proportion of waiting time. The user is aware of this, so the waiting time does not significantly affect the behavior of the user submitting the job.

This paper analyzes the correlation between IT, TT and alloc cpus (the number of using the job uses), core time (total CPU time of the job), Job Status and Group cpus (the User's quota constraint) to identify the main factors affecting the user's job submission behavior on commercial supercomputers. If the jobs need more resources, or the previous jobs run failed, users need more time to prepare for subsequent jobs. The larger the users' quota constraints, the shorter the time interval for users to submit jobs. However, it is necessary to emphasize that the conclusions drawn from the correlation between TT, IT and group cpus are inconsistent, we thinks that on commercial supercomputers, think time may not fully characterize user's job submission behavior.

We also analyze the weekly pattern of the user's job submission behavior and the similarities of the successively submitted jobs. The result shows that there are three peaks for the number of jobs submitted daily and if the user's successively submitted jobs interval don't not exceed 8 h, over 86% of job's alloc cpus is the same and nearly 40% have little difference of runtime.

Of course, the analysis of this article has some limitations, such as this study is mainly focused on HPC applications, and in fact TH-1A system also has a large number of HTC users, their user behavior and the results of those analysises may be different; the 8-hours limit may be a bit simple, the actual job submission is also subject to time and space constraints, for example, some users are accustomed to submit jobs at 21–23 pm, in order to see the results at next day and modify the job plan, the time interval may exceed 8 h. And in fact one system user may be shared by multiple people in a laboratory which is difficult to distinguish through the system data. Therefore, this paper treats one system ID as one user. Future research can be further combined with application characteristics to provide more optimization recommendations for job scheduling, this will make the research of this article more meaningful.

6   Conclusion

In this paper, we first give the details about the methodology for characterizing think time and interval time and use it to analyze the 2.7 million jobs of different users in various fields of Tianhe-1A from 2016.01 to 2017.12 and 0.89 million jobs of Sugon 5000A from 2015.09 to 2017.03.

(1) The users' job submission behavior of commercial supercomputers is different from non-commercial supercomputers. The interval of job submission is not obviously affected by the previous job's runtime and waiting time.

(2) This paper analyzes the correlation between interval time, think time and alloc cpus, core time, job status and group cpus. If the jobs need more resources, or its previous job failed, users need more time to prepare for subsequent jobs. The larger the users' quota constraints, the shorter the time interval for users to submit jobs. However, it is necessary to emphasize that the conclusions drawn from the correlation between think time, interval time and group cpus are inconsistent, we thinks that on commercial supercomputers, think time may not fully characterize user's job submission behavior.

(3) We also analyze the weekly pattern of the user's job submission behavior and the similarities of the successively submitted jobs. The result shows that there are three peaks for the number of jobs submitted daily and if the user's successively submitted jobs interval don't not exceed 8 h, over 86% of job's alloc cpus is the same and nearly 40% have little difference of runtime.

Acknowledgments. This research was supported by the National Key R&D Program of China (NO.2016YFB0201404) and Tianjin Binhai Industrial Cloud Public Service Platform and Application Promotion Project.

References

1. Geist, A., et al.: A survey of high-performance computing scaling challenges. Int. J. High Perform. Comput. Appl. **33**(1), 104–113 (2017)
2. Reed, D.A., Dongarra, J.: Exascale computing and big data. Commun. ACM **58**(7), 56–68 (2015)
3. Shmueli, E., Feitelson, D.G.: Uncovering the effect of system performance on user behavior from traces of parallel systems. In: International Symposium on Modeling, Analysis, and Simulation of Computer and Telecommunication Systems (MASCOTS), pp. 274–280 (2007)
4. Feitelson, D.G.: Looking at data. In: IEEE International Symposium on Parallel and Distributed Processing (IPDPS), pp. 1–9 (2008)
5. Schlagkamp, S. et al.: Consecutive job submission behavior at mira supercomputer. In: International Symposium on High-Performance Parallel and Distributed Computing (HPDC), pp. 93–96 (2016)
6. Sun, N., et al.: High-performance computing in China: research and applications. Int. J. High Perform. Comput. Appl. **24**(4), 363–409 (2010)
7. Rodrigo, G.P., et al.: Towards understanding job heterogeneity in HPC: a NERSC case study. In: IEEE/ACM International Symposium on Cluster, Cloud and Grid Computing (CCGrid), pp. 521–526 (2016)
8. Rodrigo, G.P., et al.: Towards understanding HPC users and systems: a NERSC case study. J. Parallel Distrib. Comput. **111**, 206–221 (2017)
9. Luu, H., et al.: A multiplatform study of I/O behavior on petascale supercomputers. In: International Symposium on High-Performance Parallel and Distributed Computing (HPDC), pp. 33–44 (2015)
10. Schlagkamp, S., et al.: Analyzing users in parallel computing: a user-oriented study. In: International Conference on High Performance Computing and Simulation, pp. 395–402 (2016)
11. Zakay, N., Feitelson, Dror G.: On identifying user session boundaries in parallel workload logs. In: Cirne, W., Desai, N., Frachtenberg, E., Schwiegelshohn, U. (eds.) JSSPP 2012. LNCS, vol. 7698, pp. 216–234. Springer, Heidelberg (2013). https://doi.org/10.1007/978-3-642-35867-8_12
12. Schlagkamp, S., et al.: Understanding user behavior: from HPC to HTC. Procedia Comput. Sci. **80**, 2241–2245 (2016)
13. http://www.ssc.net.cn/resources_1.aspx, 2018/04/28
14. Yoo, Andy B., Jette, Morris A., Grondona, M.: SLURM: Simple Linux Utility for Resource Management. In: Feitelson, D., Rudolph, L., Schwiegelshohn, U. (eds.) JSSPP 2003. LNCS, vol. 2862, pp. 44–60. Springer, Heidelberg (2003). https://doi.org/10.1007/10968987_3
15. https://git.ustclug.org/yshen/CSWA/tree/master/ssc. Accessed 28 Apr 2018
16. http://www.cs.huji.ac.il/labs/parallel/workload/. Accessed 26 Apr 2018

Author Index

.

Printed in the United States
By Bookmasters